THE ECONOMY OF IRAN

To my father

The Economy of Iran

Dilemmas of an Islamic State

Edited by
Parvin Alizadeh

I.B.Tauris *Publishers*
LONDON · NEW YORK

Published in 2000 by I.B.Tauris & Co Ltd
6 Salem Road, London W2 4BU
175 Fifth Avenue, New York NY 10010
www.ibtauris.com

In the United States of America and in Canada distributed by
St Martins Press, 175 Fifth Avenue, New York NY 10010

ISBN 1 86064 464 3

A full CIP record for this book is available from the British Library
A full CIP record for this book is available from the Library of
Congress

Library of Congress catalog card: available

Typeset in Sabon by Oxford Publishing Services
Printed and bound in Great Britain by MPG Books Ltd, Bodmin

Contents

Contents

Acknowledgements

I wish to thank Massoud Karshenas for his valuable comments on certain parts of the manuscript. I am also most grateful to Sohrab Behdad and Hassan Hakimian who provided me with invaluable advice on the preparation of the book. The shortcomings are, of course, my sole responsibility.

In particular I would like to thank my editor Anna Enayat who also indexed the book for I.B.Tauris. Susie MacAleese proofread and deserves special thanks, as does Jason Cohen who typeset the complicated graphs and tables.

I would also like to express gratitude to Nahid Alizadeh, Novin Berthoud Aghili, Parvin Paidar, Vida Sheik, Parisa Bahmanyar and, of course, Sima Motamen for intellectual stimulation and moral support.

Last but not least I owe thanks to Huri Khalilian, Nazy Sedaghat, Mahnaz Al-Sharif, Maryam Tavakol and Reza Tavakol for their inspiration and encouragement throughout this time.

Parvin Alizadeh

Notes on the Contributors

Seyed Morteza Afghah is an Assistant Professor of Economics at the University of Shahid Chamran, Ahvaz, Iran.

Parvin Alizadeh is an Associate Professor of Economics at Denison University, USA.

Sohrab Behdad is Professor of Economics at Denison University, USA.

Hassan Hakimian is a Senior Lecturer in Economics at the School of Oriental and African Studies (SOAS), University of London.

Massoud Karshenas is Reader of Economics at the School of Oriental and African Studies (SOAS), University of London.

Suzanne Maloney has a post-doctoral fellowship at the Brookings Institution, Washington DC.

Valentine M. Moghadam is Director of the Women's Studies Program and Associate Professor of Sociology at Illinois State University, USA.

M. Hashem Pesaran is Professor of Economics at Cambridge University and a Professorial Fellow of Trinity College, Cambridge.

Introduction

Parvin Alizadeh

The performance of the Iranian economy in the 1980s and 1990s has witnessed a marked deterioration, in absolute terms as well as relative to other countries in the region. The growth of the economy has slackened drastically. The economy, with a rapidly expanding population, has experienced a marked decline in investment, low labour productivity, a widening trade gap, a fast accumulation of debt and, above all, a sharp decline in the standard of living.

What are the determinants of economic performance? There is broad agreement among economists that macroeconomic stability – characterized by moderate and predictable inflation, a small budget deficit, and the relative stability of the real exchange rate – is essential for long-term economic growth.[1] Several empirical studies suggest that stable prices, a sensible exchange rate that does not discourage exports and good fiscal and monetary discipline are necessary, though not sufficient, conditions for a sustainable improvement in living standards. For instance, a large cross-country study by Fischer has shown that macro-economic stability is correlated with higher long-term rates of economic growth.[2] Similarly, an unmitigated commitment to exports appears to be indispensable for a sustainable rise in per capita income.

Viewed from this perspective, the deterioration in the perform-ance of the Iranian economy in the 1980s and 1990s can be largely explained by the macroeconomic instability that has characterized the period. Inflationary pressure not only prevailed throughout the 1980s, but has been further exacerbated in the 1990s. The last 20 years have also witnessed a sharp rise in unemployment, uncer-tainty over monetary and exchange rate policies, and sudden switches between fixed and floating exchange rate systems. Furthermore, macroeconomic instability has coincided with a

1

rapid growth in population, particularly during the 1980s. This factor has also accentuated the decline in living standards.

The deterioration of economic performance in the post-revolutionary period was in part induced by a number of negative external shocks. The economy not only endured the effects of the disruption of the revolution itself, but also the protracted and costly war with Iraq, a continuing economic embargo by the United States (which has entailed a freezing of Iranian assets) and erratic oil prices. However, the inability of the economy to adjust to external shocks not only highlights the rigidity of the economic structure inherited from the Pahlavi era but also the institutional set up and policy response by the state in the post-revolutionary period.

On the social side there has been a significant shift towards 'Islamization' and the 'sex segregation' of society. The most striking aspect of social transformation in the post-revolutionary period has been the changing social position of women, including a dramatic de-feminization of employment and increased sex segregation in employment and education.

What links these two seemingly unrelated issues is the pivotal role of the Iranian state in the economic sphere as well as in 'gender relations': that is, the socially constructed power relationship between men and women. Macroeconomic performance is inherently linked with government response to internal and external shocks as well as the socio-political determinants of policy response. The Islamic Republic has also played a decisive role in shaping the form and the extent of women's social participation. I borrow the view of Yuval-Davis and Anthias, and of Kandiyoti, that control of women's social position is central to processes of nation-building.[3] The state is essentially implicated in gender relations and each state embodies a specific gender regime. Women, on the one hand, bear the burden of being 'mothers of the nation', a duty that is ideologically defined, reflecting the ideological orientation of the state. On the other hand, women as mothers and educators transmit culture and tradition and subsequently reproduce the boundaries of ethnic/national groupings. The role and social position of women, therefore, has specific importance during the process of either nation-building or redefinition of nationhood.

The theme of this book is centred on the role of the state in the process of economic and social development in the post-revolutionary period. The emphasis, however, is on economic performance.

1. The Expanded Role of the State since the Revolution and Economic Performance

The active role of the Iranian State in the economic sphere has historical and structural foundations. The centrality of the Iranian State in determining the reproduction of the economic system has its roots in the medieval economy of Iran.[4] The centralized and bureaucratic aspects of the medieval state, and the lack of a stable landed aristocracy, arguably differentiate Iran from medieval Europe. In the latter, a far more decentralized state structure prevailed alongside relatively stable relationships of private property. Regardless of the socio-economic environment that fostered the historical specificity of the Iranian state there is general consensus amongst close observers of the Iranian economy about the 'decisive' historical role of the state.

Furthermore, a distinctive feature of the current Iranian state is that a sizeable oil revenue accrues to the government because of its monopoly right over oil.[5] The rentier nature of the state provides it with economic power and financial independence, although the state plays a central role in distributing this wealth to the population through direct subsidies and the creation of economic activities.

The populist Islamic revolution of 1979, however, heralded an expanded role for the state to safeguard the redistributive nature of the revolution.[6] This was manifested in a number of ways, including a reorientation of sectoral priorities towards agriculture in sharp contrast to the 'urban bias' of the pre-revolutionary period; the large-scale expropriation and reallocation of property; large scale nationalization of the modern manufacturing and banking sectors, and the rise of revolutionary organizations to safeguard and promote improved living standards for the low-income and rural population.

The enlarged role of the state in the post-revolutionary period is emphasized in articles by Hakimian and Karshenas, Pesaran, and Behdad in part one. Hakimian and Karshenas have pointed out that the expanded government role in the first decade after the revolution was, in certain instances, a response to revolutionary upheaval. For example, the flight of the owners and managers of a number of companies left the state with little option but to

Parvin Alizadeh

nationalize their firms. Furthermore, the rampant government control of production, distribution, foreign trade and exchange rate systems was fostered by 'the exigencies of running a war economy' in the 1980s. Throughout the years of the Iran–Iraq war, the period 1980–88, the government introduced a complex system of rationing and direct subsidies for a large number of commodities. Foreign exchange shortages from the mid-1980s, following the decline in the price of oil, were concurrent with the introduction of strict foreign exchange control and rationing. Furthermore, the shortfall in oil revenue from the mid-1980s led to a substantial budget deficit that in turn accentuated inflationary pressure in the economy.

It is also worth recalling that the policy environment in the 1980s was informed not only by an expanded government role and the mobilization of resources for the war effort, but also by the international isolation of the country. From the inception of the Islamic Republic the new regime, or more precisely the dominant forces within the regime, de-emphasized the importance of 'external constraints', including the mobilization of foreign resources. 'Political and economic independence', which were among the main aims of the revolution, were interpreted to mean a de-linking from the international capital market. But it was the American hostage crisis of the early 1980s which, above all, led to the political isolation of Iran and the imposition of American economic sanctions.

During the 1980s the Iranian economy thus faced a number of shocks, including the re-orientation of resources towards the war effort, substantial capital and managerial flight in the aftermath of the revolution and war, dwindling oil prices after the mid 1980s, international isolation, and above all dominance of distributive policies with little regard for 'profiteering' and large scale private capital accumulation.[7] Within this context, Iran not surprisingly experienced a marked deterioration in economic performance.

The article by Hakimian and Karshenas in addition provides a comparative analysis contrasting the growth performance of Iran with Turkey and Korea over the past four decades. The dramatic retrogression of the Iranian economy during the 1980s stands out both relative to its past performance and compared to the international economy at large:

During the two decades before 1975 per capita income in Iran grew faster than in Turkey and kept pace with Korea.

4

Introduction

> By 1975 the level of per capita GDP in Iran was more than double those attained in Korea and Turkey. However, since the late 1970s income per head in Iran has witnessed a rapid decline ... By 1990, GDP per capita in Iran had declined by half, almost down to the levels prevalent in the early 1960s and falling behind Turkey and Korea.
>
> (Hakimian and Karshenas, this volume)

Pesaran and Behdad also address the decline of the economy during the 1980s. Hashem Pesaran's empirical study indicates that the relationship between money supply growth, inflation and output has been adversely affected in the post-revolutionary period. This has 'consequences both for the efficacy of monetary policy in relation to the control of inflation, and for the economy's future financial development.' His study shows that the flexibility of real money balance has been severely affected over this period. Above all, the process of financial deepening that is positively linked to economic growth has been reversed in the post-revolutionary period. In sharp contrast to 'the strong trends in financial deepening during the period before the revolution ... the opposite trend is in evidence when the period after the revolution is concerned.'

Sohrab Behdad argues (in this volume) that the state's inability to promote private capital accumulation has had degenerative effects on the production process:

> The inability of the state in facilitating the production process, and the antagonism expressed towards capital and property cause a general retrenchment of capital and the capitalist relations of production. The other side of the coin is an expansion of petty commodity production in the economy. This is a degenerative process, creating tangles within the existing economic structure, obstructing the accumulation process and aggravating the economic crisis. This gives rise to what I have called 'structural involution'. Structural involution is manifested in sectoral shifts in production and employment, and in the increased peasantization of agriculture, de-proletarianization of the labour force and a huge expansion of service activities in a myriad of occupations such as those held by small retailers, street vendors and moonlighting cabbies.

It is against a background of declining income per capita and macroeconomic imbalances (including inflationary pressure, government budget deficit and foreign exchange shortages) that the government was forced to launch a comprehensive package of economic reforms within the context of the First Five-Year Development Plan covering the period 1989/90–1993/94 (Hakimian and Karshenas). The plan, as Pesaran has pointed out, 'represented the regime manifesto' for reconstruction of the economy following the end of the Iran–Iraq war in August 1988. Its main objectives were to regenerate the economy, to reconstruct the war-damaged regions, to encourage private investment and above all to liberalize trade and foreign exchange.

Although a high rate of growth was achieved during the first half of the plan, the reform programme was terminated in the mid-1990s. Consequently the government reverted to 'populist economic policies', that de-emphasize the risk of inflation and deficit finance, miscalculate the impact of external constraints, and underestimate the effects of uncertainty on private investors.[8] These populist policies, with their well known, dire consequences, are reminiscent of those pursued in several Latin American countries in the 1960s and 1970s.

1.1 The State and the Dilemma of Economic Reform

Why did the government's attempt at trade and foreign exchange liberalization, the key aspects of its reform programme, fail? In addressing this question, four types of issues, though overlapping, have been raised: (i) external constraints; (ii) the populist state; (iii) constitutional and legal constraints; (iv) pressure groups.

Hashem Pesaran's article highlights the decisive prominence of access to international capital markets, most notably international financial organizations such as the World Bank and the IMF, that provide long term loans at a reasonable rate of interest. Pesaran argues that the increased foreign exchange requirement that trade and exchange rate liberalization entails could not be met by long-term loans from the World Bank and IMF. Consequently, Iran's short-term external debt grew very rapidly in the early 1990s, increasing the vulnerability of the country to foreign exchange crisis in a hostile international environment:

> Ordinarily this amount of foreign indebtedness for a major
> oil producing country such as Iran would not have been a

real problem. But in view of US economic embargo and the inability of international organizations such as the IMF and the World Bank to help (again due to the threat of US veto) and the fact that as much as 76.1 of the $23.2 billion were in the form of short term debts, it appears that the Iranian authorities were left with no choice but to make a U-turn; reverting back to the 'closed door' policies of trade restrictions and foreign exchange controls. (Pesaran, this volume)

The importance of access to the international market has also been emphasized by Hakimian and Karshenas. They argue that debt-GDP ratio for Iran was considerably below those of several other developing countries such as Egypt and Venezuela. However, the cost of international isolation and the inability of the government to raise long-term credit in the international market was a rapid accumulation of short-term debt that led to Iran's abortive attempt at liberalization and structural reform in the mid-1990s.

Sohrab Behdad is concerned with the populist facade of the state which has disabled the government's capacity to implement economic reforms effectively. Government liberalization policies, which were accompanied by cutting subsidies and an increase in the price of products of mass consumption, escalated the level of public discontent and led to demonstrations in opposition to government policy in several cities. Behdad maintains that the effective implementation of liberalization policies necessitates formal abandonment of the remaining popular base of the Islamic Republic and is not politically feasible. Liberalization policies also entail safeguarding private property and facilitating capital accumulation by private investors, both domestic and foreign. However, there are constitutional limitations that restrain the sphere of activity of the private sector.

Article 44 of the constitution declares that the 'state sector is to include all large-scale industries, foreign trade, major mineral resources, banking, insurance, energy, dams and large-scale irrigation networks, radio and television, post, telegraphic and telephone services, aviation, shipping, roads, rail road and the like'[9] (Behdad, this volume). Another legal impediment to large-scale private investment, as Behdad points out, is the restrictive Labour Law of 1990.

Both Pesaran and Behdad assert that powerful internal groups have also hampered economic reforms. In addition to large state subsidies on food items, fuel and public services, the main causes of the excessive monetary expansion and inflation can be found, Pesaran argues, in the government's unwillingness to oppose the credit demands of politically powerful groups, including semi-public enterprises (owned and controlled by revolutionary organizations or *bonyads*). Behdad warns against the immense economic and political power of the revolutionary organizations and questions the economic rationale of their activities. *Bonyads*, which are new para-statal institutions, have been able to exercise a profound influence over the economy because of their immense economic power. They are the beneficiaries of the assets seized from the former royal family and other exiled members of the former elite, or nationalized after the revolution. *Bonyads* have also had privileged access to cheap sources of credit and foreign exchange during the 1980s and 1990s. Behdad maintains that the b*onyads* disperse their profit by payments to the families of martyrs, veterans of the Iran–Iraq war, and engage in activities that are ideologically oriented, both inside and outside the country.

1.2 *Revolutionary Organizations,* Bonyads

The article by Maloney in Part Two of this volume provides an insight into the evolution and influence of *bonyads*. She analyses their emergence in the context of the process of institution building to consolidate and strengthen the authority of the Islamic Republic after the revolution. They were further strengthened during the course of the Iran–Iraq war which consolidated the power of clerical authority. The mission of the *bonyads* further expanded after the ending of the war to include responsibility for those wounded in the war with Iraq. These organizations have institutionalized the ideological objectives of revolution. 'Their strategic mission as agents of economic development and income redistribution bestow these foundations with a mantle of social justice.' Yet the *bonyads*, which operate in the name of the 'deprived segments' of the population, have, in practice, developed into conglomerates, with immense economic and political power. Their operations are divided into charitable and productive activities. The latter includes a large number of enterprises in manufacturing, agriculture and services that were nationalized or left with no owner or manager after the revolution. Hence, the *bonyads* control a very substantial section of productive activities and employment. The main concern about their operations is the fact that these organizations are largely unaccountable to the government. Their profits are exempted from taxation and hence they are not legally bound to disclose their activities. It is a well-known fact that *bonyads* have effectively exercised pressure on the government for access to credit and subsidized sources of foreign-exchange. For instance, in the context of the multiple exchange rates that have prevailed for most of this period, the *bonyads* have privileged access to foreign exchange at the official exchange rate. By contrast, private importers have to pay the market rate, with a black market premium of 200 to 2000 per cent. Maloney argues that the growing power of these institutions, notably the largest and the most influential of them, the Bonyad-e Mostazafin, has undermined the ability of the state to impose its own will on the economy, although the same institution has contributed to the durability of Islamic state.

1.3 Population Growth

Economic performance cannot be understood without a context of demographic change.[10] The case of post-revolutionary Iran highlights the adverse effects of rapid population increase. The economic danger of a dramatic rise in population lies in the fact that most developing countries are unable to both increase the stock of capital and to enhance the rate of technical innovation to prevent a fall in labour productivity.[11] The population explosion, in addition to its adverse effects on capital per head, also reduces the country's saving ratio by leading to a higher dependency ratio of children who consume but do not produce. Of course, population growth presents a paradox since it can also act as a stimulus to economic growth through a variety of channels, including the stimulation of technical change. Nevertheless, the broad view as far as developing countries are concerned is that population growth represents a barrier to capital accumulation, human capital formation and capital deepening, and retards the rate of productivity growth.

Hassan Hakimian is concerned with the erratic pattern of population growth in the post-revolutionary period. The average population growth increased very sharply in the 1980s, and total population increased by 50 per cent from 1976–86. An equally dramatic drop followed in the 1990s. Nevertheless, Iran's total population has nearly doubled since the revolution. Hakimian scrutinizes the quality and reliability of population census data in

Parvin Alizadeh

the 1980s and 1990s. Furthermore, his study indicates that the upswing in population growth in the 1980s was concurrent with the pro-natalist stance that the Islamic Republic adopted towards family planning and population control. The downswing in population growth in the 1990s was also paralleled by a radical shift in government population policy. However, 'Iran stands out for a higher crude birth rate trend line by Middle Eastern standards since 1970.'

1.4 The Post-Revolutionary State

A very noticeable transformation in the structure of the Iranian state since the popular revolution of 1979 is its evolution from a monolithic and highly centralized entity to a decentralized and participatory one.[12] Despite the exclusion of secular political forces, and even some Islamic political tendencies from the political arena, the political process has nevertheless become, in comparison to the Pahlavi era, more inclusive of diverse political tendencies. The Islamic Revolution entailed a massive collective action by diverse social groups against the Pahlavi state. The parliament has become an entity of some consequence through which redistributionist and populist policies are advocated. Simultaneously para-statal organizations such as *bonyads* are capable of exercising immense pressure on the government's resources and policies. Meanwhile, the conservative factions of the political elite have been encouraging free enterprise and market forces.[13]

The ongoing power struggle within the regime has handicapped the state's ability to create an institutional framework conducive to capitalist development. The state as the organization that specifies and reinforces property rights has been unable to set up appropriate rules, compliance procedures and effective enforcement mechanisms to protect and promote private investment.[14]

Afghah's article in Part Two of this volume indicates that 'frequent changes in law and regulations' are the most important single factor to hinder the expansion of investment and production by the firm. 'A general manager stated that "changes in law and policies are so fast that one can call them weekly or even daily changes."' Afghah examines the effects of non-economic factors on firms' decisions to invest and produce. His questionnaire-based study covers the period 1988–94, which corresponds to the introduction and implementation of economic reforms and

10

liberalization policies in the post-war period. It indicates that the second most important factor to hinder production expansion by firms is the presence of a post-revolutionary culture unsympathetic to private investment and accumulation. Ordinary people, as well as government officials share anti-capitalist sentiments. Other factors that impeded investment decisions, such as the shortage of capital, the restrictive labour law and the shortage of foreign exchange, are of far less significance than these two.

Ample empirical studies from several developing countries indicate that 'government credibility' is of crucial importance for the effective implementation of economic reforms.[15] However, the instability of government policies in Iran has undermined the government's credibility in the sphere of economic policy with adverse implications for long-term investment. Policy changes are no longer effective signalling devices and are frequently met with scepticism on the part of a private sector already disillusioned by economic policies which, despite government promises to implement them, have been aborted. The precarious nature of policies has not only adversely affected the expansion of investment and production by firms but will have long-term consequences for government credibility.

2. The State and Development

The implicit theory of the state that the relevant contributions in Part One and Part Two of this volume adopt is that the state in the post-revolutionary era is 'incapacitated and captured' and has little autonomy from pressure groups. Behdad focuses on the political economy of liberalization policies and the role of the state. He explicitly maintains that the inability of the post-revolutionary state to facilitate private capital accumulation originates from its populist or pseudo-populist nature. The state, for instance, cannot remove constitutional and legal restrictions, including Article 44 of the constitution and particularly the labour law, that are the most visible onerous obstacles to the processes of capital accumulation by the private sector. The lack of state autonomy from pressure groups is implicit in articles by Pesaran, Hakimian and Karshenas, Maloney and Afghah. As previously mentioned, the state has been paralysed as far as the mobilization of external resources is concerned. The growth of the economy in the post-revolutionary period is adversely affected by financial constraints arising from the inability of the state to obtain long-term loans at a reasonable rate of interest. As the articles by Pesaran and by Hakimian and Karshenas show, the scale and the magnitude of required external resources is quite small by international standards. The radical anti-American faction within the regime as well as American reluctance to normalize relationships with Iran – although the relationship between the two governments has been improving recently – has hampered Iran's access to international capital markets.

A far more fundamental obstacle to economic development and productive investment, acknowledged by several authors in this volume, lies in the inability of the state to impose 'hard budget' discipline on state enterprises as well as on *bonyads*. The state has been also handicapped in its attempts to redirect the activities of *bonyads* and state enterprises towards economic efficiency and improved productivity. Virtually all large-scale enterprises in agricultural, industrial and service activities in Iran are either state owned or controlled by *bonyads*. These enterprises have not been subjected to the market discipline of financial viability, including the possibility of bankruptcy, which applies to private enterprises. Instead they have benefited from privileged access to cheap sources of credit and foreign exchange. *Bonyads*, for instance, have been able to pressurize the government to pursue a lax monetary policy to accommodate their credit requirements.

3. The Role of the State in Economic Development: A Comparative Perspective

The active role of the state in the economy, including the subsidization of industries, is by no means exclusive to Iran. Pervasive state intervention has historical precedents in technologically less advanced countries. However, there is substantial diversity in the role and nature of the state. The state can play a developmental role in the process of economic development, although the experience of a large number of developing countries, including post-revolutionary Iran, is indicative of 'government failure'.

Nascent industries during their transition from 'infancy' to 'maturity' have been protected and subsidized in almost all developed and developing countries. Developed countries, with the exception of Great Britain, which had the monopoly of industrialization at the time of the industrial revolution, protected and

promoted their infant industries at the time of their industrialization. The tradition of 'infant industry protection' dates back to
Freidrich List's advocacy of protection for less developed Germany
to facilitate the catching up process in the nineteenth century.[16]

Developing countries – except for Hong Kong which developed
through a free trade policy and whose small 'city state' status
distinguishes it from other developing countries – have heavily
protected and subsidized their industries. A deliberate policy of
industrialization, known as import substitution, which aimed at
the domestic production of previously imported goods, has been
implemented in virtually all developing countries of Latin America,
Asia and Africa since the 1950s and 1960s. The state in all
instances, through a variety of measures ranging from the imposition of tariffs and quotas to the provision of cheap credit to
domestic investors, has protected and promoted the domestic
production of industrial products. The magnitude and the duration of protection granted to 'infant' domestic industries in
developing countries has by far exceeded those in developed countries
at the time of their industrialization.[17] Nevertheless, the failure of
import substitution policies that fostered the proliferation of high
cost inefficient industries in a large number of developing
countries of Africa, Latin America and Asia, is part and parcel of
the recent history of economic development. A large number of
cross-country and country-wide studies have revealed the high
costs of 'government failure' caused by the implementation of
import substitution policies.[18]

Although the record of state intervention in developing
countries does not on the whole indicate a satisfactory result,
pervasive state intervention in several instances, in both developed
and developing countries, has been highly conducive to economic
development.

The historical experience of Germany, Russia and Japan indicates that state can implement a 'catching up' strategy in countries
that are latecomers in relation to technologically more advanced
economies. From a Gerschenkronian perspective, deliberate policies represent the substitution of the state action for the missing
entrepreneur. The cases of nineteenth-century Germany, Tsarist
Russia or Meiji Japan are clear indications of pervasive and
effective state intervention in the process of industrialization. In
Gerschenkron's thesis of 'economic backwardness' the important
innovation in the Germany of the nineteenth century was private

industrial banking willing to take equity position and provide long-term loans to private investors. In 'backward' Russia, government portfolios and equity financing were the main substitution for the missing entrepreneur. In Japan the state provided a major impetus to the modernization drive throughout the late nineteenth and early twentieth centuries.

The state has also played a developmental role in a number of developing countries. The impressive success of the first tier of East Asian NICs (South Korea, Taiwan, Singapore and Hong Kong), manifested in their stupendous growth rates prior to their recent financial crisis (which far from negating capitalist development is innate to such a process) highlights the positive role of the state in promoting capitalist development. It is a well-known fact, for example, that the subsidization of targeted enterprises of strategic importance to the economy was one of the major policy tools in South Korean development from 1960 to 1980.[19] Amsden has provided a detailed account of the Korean government's use of trade protection, selective credit subsidies, export targets for individual firms and public ownership of the banking sector. All these policies were employed in the service of acquiring and creating technological capabilities and of erecting industries that could eventually compete in the world market. The subsidization of domestic enterprises was aimed to offset the disadvantage of 'late industrialization' in the context of the industrialized world market.[20] The Korean state's relationships with its giant diversified business groups, the Chaebol, that were shaped and influenced by the state, has been well documented by Amsden and does not need elaboration.[21]

It is now widely acknowledged that Korea's development, as well as that of Taiwan and Singapore and previously that of Japan, has been state-centric.[22] The state shaped and determined the pattern of industrial accumulation in both the public and the private sector. The sharp contrast between the state-centric development of the first tier of East Asian NICs and 'government failure' in several other developing countries points to the diversity in the role and nature of the state in developing countries.[23]

The subsidization of para-statal enterprises in Iran is reminiscent of the public sector enterprise system in Africa in the 1960s and 1970s and in the centrally planned economies of East European countries rather than the state-led growth of Korean enterprises.[24] While the Chaebol in Korea benefited from government subsidies, they were given strict export targets by the government to demonstrate their international competitiveness. In contrast, para-statal enterprises in Iran, like those in the Soviet-style economies of Eastern Europe (prior to their transition to a market economy), operate under soft budgetary constraints. The lack of market and financial discipline in Iran has allowed a proliferation of inefficient enterprises that are not only incapable of international competition but are operating at 30–40 per cent of their capacity.

3.1 The Developmental State

The diversity in the role and the nature of the state in developing countries has posed a serious issue in economic policy. What type of state is capable of implementing policy reforms or of formulating appropriate policies?

There is broad recognition that the presence of a 'developmental state' in South Korea, Taiwan and Singapore has been the most important factor in generating economic development.[25] The term 'developmental state' made its formal debut in the work of Johnson on East Asian developmental states and particularly Japan, although the term is now widely used to describe any 'strong' or 'hard' state capable of accomplishing nationalist goals.[26] Johnson conceptualized the developmental state as a 'plan rational' state in contrast to the 'plan ideological' state, which dominated the centrally planned economies of socialist countries. In the latter case development policies were of an ideological nature, placing emphasis on self-sufficiency and autarchy and with little regard for financial discipline and international competitiveness. The developmental state is also differentiated from the regulatory state of typical liberal-democratic or social-democratic regimes. A very important characteristic of the Japanese state according to Johnson was to set substantive social and economic targets for the private sector.[27] In this respect the developmental state is distinguished from the regulatory state which simply provides a context for the activity of the private sector.

Moreover, the idea of the developmental state does not fall into the Marxist tradition of state theory. The state is not the agent or representative of the dominant class or group (extracting income from the rest of the population in the interests of this class or group), nor is it the product of class balance.[28]

The developmental state, as the concept has been articulated by Johnson and others, including Evans, White and Wade and

Leftwich, is distinguished by a high degree of autonomy.[29] This allows the state to define national goals and accomplish them without having to compromise with various pressure groups. Hence an important feature of the developmental state is its independence from social classes. This is what has distinguished developmental states in South Korea, Taiwan, and Singapore from bureaucratic-authoritarian states in Latin America. As White and Wade have pointed out, dedicated political elites in some Latin American regimes may have wanted to pursue developmental policies similar to those of South Korea and Taiwan, but they could not.[30] They came to power in circumstances in which many existing groups, including agricultural oligarchies, already had considerable power and capacity to exercise influence against the state.

Developmental states are not, of course, static but evolve. Charlton and Donald have pointed out that Korea and Taiwan, having moved up the ladder of industrial and product-cycle, are now evolving from the hard and dictatorial developmental state of the 1960s and 1970s into 'soft authoritarian, consultative, and increasingly compromising development managers'.[31] Furthermore, not all relatively autonomous states are developmental. Several states in Sub-Saharan Africa with substantial autonomy and a lack of domestic constraints have shown no commitment to development.[32]

However, the developmental state is characterized by a commitment to economic development by the political and bureaucratic elite. Such elites, as White and Wade have noted, are capable of 'minimizing commitments to existing groups, and preventing counter-elites from defining their opposition in politically relevant terms.'[33]

In other words, developmental states have been capable of implementing policies without being pressurized by various social groups. Consequently, their economic policies are not shaped by the interests of dominant groups. Instead the elite has substantial autonomy to formulate and implement policies in accordance with 'national interest'. The political factors that shape the drive and pace of developmental strategy through the structure of the state include nationalism, external threat, regional competition and the wish to 'catch up' with the West.[34] In countries like Korea and Taiwan, the 'threat of communism' played an important role in creating a drive for national development.

16

4. The Iranian State

Two factors distinguish the post-revolutionary Iranian state from the developmental state. The state in Iran is an 'ideological' as distinct from a 'rational' developmental state. Furthermore the post-revolutionary state has little autonomy from pressure groups.

From the time the Islamic Republic was established until now there has been tension between the 'ideologues' and the 'modernists' within the regime. Despite the apparent victory of the modernists in the May 1997 presidential election, the conflict between the two camps has not been settled. Furthermore, in the last two decades virtually all the technocratic elite in Iran have been chosen from the ranks of 'good Moslems' with 'reliable revolutionary credentials' rather than on the basis of merit. Even the 'modernist' political elite, who are careful not to be identified as 'infidel', have followed the same criteria in their selection of top bureaucrats.

The post-revolutionary state is also incapacitated by its lack of autonomy from social groups. This is clearly manifested in continuing friction between different factions of the Islamic Republic, despite shifts in alliances and re-alliances between different groups, which has characterized the structure of the state since its inception.

This is in sharp contrast to the autonomy of the pre-revolutionary Iranian state. The autonomy of the shah's state was similar, if not greater, than the states of East Asian NICs, although Iran provided 'a laboratory of import substitution' in contrast to the export orientation of industrialization in East Asian NICs. In the latter countries, industrial policies were aimed at improved efficiency and international competitiveness, while in Iran industrialization was primarily oriented to the domestic market with little concern for competitiveness and efficiency.[35]

Nevertheless, the state in the pre-revolutionary period was capable of articulating and accomplishing 'national goals' without being hindered by opposition or being forced into coalition and compromise with social groups. Of course, increasing oil revenues provided the Iranian state with an abundant supply of foreign exchange to finance imports of capital goods and necessary raw materials for industrial accumulation. The state, however, was capable of providing an institutional set up favourable to private investment. Government not only directly invested in certain industries but also provided a stable macroeconomic environment and substantial incentive to the private sector. In this 'investor-friendly' climate, private investment expanded at an unprecedented rate. The remarkable expansion of the private sector over this period took place in the context of an economy with a historically weak indigenous bourgeoisie.[36] Easy access to international capital and technology markets was also an integral part of the 'investment friendly' environment that facilitated expansion and diversification of the economy in the 1960s and 1970s. Meanwhile, the economy experienced an impressive growth by international standards.

The autonomy of the pre-revolutionary state was fostered by increasing revenues from oil in the 1960s and particularly in the 1970s. The independence of the state from a tax base, or the lack of a fiscal association between the state and the civil society, was accompanied by de-politicization of the latter and increasing centralization of the former.[37]

This is not to suggest that the pre-revolutionary Iranian state was a typical developmental state like those in Japan or Korea. I have already mentioned that industrial development in the pre-revolutionary period was primarily domestic market oriented without much attention to international competitiveness. Nevertheless, the pre-revolutionary state had substantial autonomy from social groups and was capable of providing an institutional set up and an incentive structure conducive to the development of the private sector. The state 'picked up the winners' and promoted them through the provision of cheap institutionalized credit and appropriate fiscal, monetary and commercial policies.

The role of the nature of the state altered radically with the Islamic revolution that questioned the existing pattern of economic development and placed emphasis on the redistribution of wealth and power. The crisis of the post-revolutionary state is closely linked to the redistribution order that has prevailed in the last two decades.

5. The 'Women Question' and the Ideological Orientation of the State

The change in the ideological orientation of the state since the revolution has been concurrent with a change in the social position of women. A very noticeable social-economic transformation in the post-revolutionary period has been a sharp decline in the share of women's employment, although this trend has been changing in more recent years.

Moghadam's article highlights the obstacles to and the limited share of female employment in the post-revolutionary period. She provides detailed analysis of government social policies, with emphasis on women's employment since the late 1980s. She notes that 'socio-economic rights, as well as socio-economic participation, were circumscribed for women during the 1980s.' The situation improved in the 1990s. However, female employment in the public sector, although growing during the 1990s, is still highly concentrated in education and health care. Female employment is very small in the private sector.

> Women's share of government employment grew during the 1990s – although this is perhaps as much a reflection of the deterioration of government wages and the increasing participation of men in the private sector as it is an indicator of the advancement of women. The number of public-service employees was nearly 2 million in 1994, of which 603,000, or about 31 per cent, were women. Again the ministries of Education and Health employed most of these women (43.8 per cent and 40 per cent, respectively), and 34 per cent of them had university degrees. Women were under-represented in the private sector. (Moghadam, this volume)

The article by Alizadeh explores the close relationship between the process of nation building and women's social participation. This close link arises from the specific role of women as transmitters of culture, tradition and educators of children. Thus control over the form and the extent of women's social participation is the principal concern of the state. Alizadeh examines this proposition in the context of data for female employment. In the post-revolutionary period, nationhood alongside the social position of women was redefined. Not surprisingly, 'economic development in Iran since the revolution has been accompanied by a decline in the share of female employment and increased occupational sex segregation.' This article also provides a comparative perspective on the pattern of female employment in Iran and several other Moslem countries.

Notes

1 For a comprehensive review of economic policies and their conse-quences see D. Rodrik, 'Trade and Industrial Policy Reform', in Behrman and T. N. Srinavasan (eds), *Handbook of Development Economics*, vol. 3, 1995, pp. 2925–82. For a recent World Bank view on policy reform see J. Page and L. Van Gelder, 'Missing Links: Institutional Capability, Policy Reform and Growth in the Middle East and North Africa', paper presented at the conference on 'The Changing Role of the State in the Middle East and North Africa', at the School of Oriental and African Studies, London, 6 May 1988. Both perspectives, despite different emphasis and orientation, high-light the importance of macroeconomic stability.
2 S. Fischer. 'Macro-Economic Factors in Growth', paper presented at the conference 'How Do National Policies Affect Long-term Growth?' The World Bank. Washington DC February 1993.
3 N. Yuval-Davis and F. Anthias (eds), *Women–Nation State,* London: Macmillan, 1989; D. Kandiyoti, 'Identity and its Discontents: Women and the Nation', in P. Williams and L. Chrisman (eds), *Colonial Discourse and Post-Colonial Theory,* New York, London: Harvester Wheatsheaf, 1993.
4 M. Karshenas, *Oil, State and Industrialization in Iran,* Cambridge: Cambridge University Press, 1990, Chapter 2. See also H. Katouzian, *The Political Economy of Modern Iran, Despotism and Pseudo-Modernism, 1926–1979,* London: Macmillan, 1981; H. Katouzian, 'Arbitrary Rule: A Comparative Theory of the State, Politics and Society in Iran', *British Journal of Middle Eastern Studies,* 24, 1997, pp. 49–73; A. Ashraf, 'Historical Obstacles to the Development of the Bourgeoisie in Iran', in M. A. Cook (ed.), *Studies in the Economic History of the Middle East from the Rise of Islam to the Present Day,* Oxford: Oxford University Press, 1970; A. Ashraf, *Mavane-ye Tarikhi-ye Roshd-e Sarma'i-dari dar Iran: Dowreh-e Qajarieh,* Tehran: Zamineh, 1350 (1980).
5 The rentier nature of the Iranian state is articulated by H. Mahdavi, 'Patterns and Problems of Economic Development in Rentier States: The Case of Iran', in Cook (ed.), *Studies in the Economic History of the Middle East.* See also A. Najmabadi, 'De-Politicization in a Rentier Society: The Case of Pahlavi Iran', in H. Behlawi and G. Luciani (eds), *The Rentier State,* London: Croom Helm, 1987.

Introduction

6   For the social-historical circumstances that shaped and conditioned the Iranian revolution see E. Abrahamian, *Iran Between Two Revolutions*. Princeton: Princeton University Press, 1983. Abrahamian emphasizes the lack of political development as an important factor in shaping the Islamic revolution. He argues that rapid economic growth was not accompanied by corresponding levels of political liberalization and development. Instead political development remained limited. It was the uneven development of these two factors that played a crucial part in igniting the revolution. A different perspective is presented by H. Katouzian, *The Political Economy of Modern Iran, Despotism and Pseudo-Modernism, 1926–1979*, London: Macmillan, 1981. The latter perspective is more concerned with the 'arbitrary rule' and despotism that dominated the Pahlavi era. For redistributive policies after the revolution see A. Mazarei, 'The Iranian Economy under the Islamic Republic: Institutional Change and Macroeconomic Performance (1979–1990)', *Cambridge Journal of Economics*, vol. 20, 1996, pp. 289–314.

7   For different perspectives on government policies in the post-revolutionary period see, for instance, H. Amirahmadi, *Revolution and Economic Transition: The Iranian Experience*, Albany: State University of New York Press, 1990; S. Rahnema and S. Behdad (eds), *Iran After the Revolution: Crisis of an Islamic State*, London: I.B.Tauris, 1995; J. Amuzegar, *Iran's Economy under the Islamic Republic*, London: I.B.Tauris, 1997.

8   For an interesting account of populist economic policies and their consequences see R. Dornbusch and S. Edwards (eds), *The Macroeconomics of Populism in Latin America*, Chicago: University of Chicago Press, 1991.

9   Although foreign trade is listed in Article 44 the Council of the Guardians opposed its nationalization in response to the pressure of powerful bazaar merchants who are traditionally linked with the religious establishment (see Behdad in this volume).

10   See D. C. North, *Structure and Change in Economic History*, New York: Norton, 1981, Chapter 1.

11   For a discussion of the role of the population in economic development see A. P. Thirlwall, *Growth and Development*, London: Macmillan Press, 1999, 6th edition, Chapter 8, pp. 193–213.

12   For an interesting discussion on the changing role of the state in the post-revolutionary period see Mazarei (1996).

13   See Ibid. For details on political structure and alliances see the article by Sohrab Behdad in this volume. Also see Amuzegar (1997), Chapter 3.

14 The approach to the role and function of the state in this paper conforms to an institutionalist interpretation. See, for instance, D. C. North, *Structure and Change in Economic History*. New York: Norton, 1981; D. C. North, *Institutions, Institutional Change and Economic Performance*, Cambridge: Cambridge University Press, 1990. The divergent literature on institutionalism makes it difficult to define the concept. However, by an institutionalist approach I mean the field of enquiry that examines the link between institutions, transaction costs, incentives, economic behaviour and outcomes. Institutions are a set of rules, compliance procedures, and moral and ethical norms that provide the framework within which individuals or firms interact and exchange (North 1981, p. 201). There is general consensus that decisive institutions are property rights, formal and informal rules and social authority. For a recent review of the institutionalist approach see T. Eggertson, 'The Old Theory of Economic Policy and the New Institutionalism', *World Development*, vol. 25, no. 8, pp. 1187–204, 1997. Also Page and Van Gelder (1998). The institutionalist approach differs from the neo-classical framework in which transaction costs are negligible and information is costless. Transaction costs, which are distinguished from production costs, are concerned with protecting and enforcing property rights to goods (North 1981:28). At the heart of the institutionalist approach is the making of rules and laws and their enforcement and adjudication, although informal rules and customs also matter. The state, as an organization that has the potential to use violence to gain control over resources, specifies and reinforces property rights. Hence the state can influence the institutional framework within which individuals interact. The institutionalist approach to economic performance highlights the centrality of the state in its capacity to increase or reduce transaction costs.

15 See for instance D. Rodrik, 'Credibility of Trade Reform: A Policy Maker's Guide', *The World Economy*, 1989, D. Rodrik, 'Policy Uncertainty and Private Investment in Developing Countries', *Journal of Development Economics*, vol. 36, 1991, pp. 229–42.

16 F. List, *The National System of Political Economy*, New York: A. M. Kelly, 1885/1996, p. 175.

17 I. Little, T. Scitovsky, M. Scott, *Industry and Trade in Developing Countries,* London: Oxford University Press, 1970.

18 A large number of cross-country and country studies have revealed the high costs of 'government failure' that were induced by the implementation of inward looking policies. The most instrumental are those by Little, Scitovsky and Scott, (1970); B. Balassa et al., *The Structure*

of Protection in Developing Countries, Baltimore: Johns Hopkins University Press, 1971; J. Bhagwati, *Foreign Trade Regimes and Economic Development: Anatomy and Consequences of Exchange Control Regimes*, Lexington, MA: Ballinger, 1978, and A. O. Krueger, *Foreign Trade Regimes and Economic Development: Liberalization Attempts and Consequences*, Lexington, MA: Ballinger, 1978. These studies, which undertook a quantitative evaluation of trade policies, especially protectionist policies in developing countries, concluded that highly interventionist trade and industrial policies had undesirable consequences for their growth prospects. The disagreeable effects of inward looking policies ranged from static efficiency loss of resource mis-allocation to dynamic costs of price distortions and resource cost of rent seeking activities. These studies strongly influenced the formulation of policy reforms by multilateral donor organizations, notably the World Bank. For an excellent review see Rodrik (1995).

19 For a comprehensive study of South Korean development see A. Amsden, *Asia's Next Giant: South Korea and Late Industrialization*, New York and Oxford: Oxford University Press, 1989.

20 For an excellent discussion on this issue see Rodrik (1995), pp. 2944–8.

21 Early explanations of the success of the East Asian NICs were based on the neo-classical perspective that emphasized the positive impact of market oriented policies. The noticeable growth rates of these countries combined with their ability to cope better in the face of negative external shocks in the second half of the 1970s (following the first oil shock, 1974–1978) were explained in terms of their export orientation and their less distortive policies. See, for instance, B. Balassa, *The Newly Industrializing Countries in the World Economy*. New York: Pergamon Press, 1981; B. Balassa, 'Adjustment to External Shocks in Developing Economies', World Bank Staff Working Paper No. 472, 1981. However, this interpretation, which was based on the neo-classical advocacy of 'getting factor prices right', has been challenged. Rodrik (1995) has pointed to two factors responsible for the amendment of the early consensus. The most important is the advent of a 'revisionist account' of the East Asian experience. The 'revisionist account' that was popularized by Amsden's (1989) study of South Korea and Wade's (1990) study of Taiwan, has revealed the positive role of the government in trade and industrial policies. This version of the narrative has disputed the validity of the earlier emphasis on minimalist state intervention. The second factor that has enhanced the case for intervention is the recent development of models of imperfect competition and 'new' trade theory which allow for strategic trade policy and increasing returns to scale.

23

22 See, for instance, C. Johnson, 'Introduction: The Taiwan Model' in J. S. Hsiung (ed.), *Contemporary Republic of China: The Taiwan Experience, 1950–1980*. New York: Praeger, 1981 and C. Johnson, *MITI and the Japanese Miracle*, Stanford, CA: Stanford University Press, 1982. See also Amsden (1989) and Wade (1990).

23 In the context of economic theory, there is no accord on the role, direction, and magnitude of state intervention in the economic sphere. See Rodrik (1995).

24 For an overview of economic inefficiencies in Sub-Saharan Africa see 'World Bank, Adjustment in Africa: Reform, Results, and the Road Ahead', Policy Research Department, October 1993. For an overall discussion concerning the lack of market and financial discipline in ex-Soviet style economies see D. Gros and A. Steinherr, *Winds of Change: Economic Transition in Central and Eastern Europe*, London, New York: Longman, 1995, particulary chapter 11, 'Beyond Stabilization'.

25 For a good review see A. Leftwich, 'Bringing the Politics Back In: Towards a Model of the Developmental State', *The Journal of Developmental Studies*, 31 pp. 400–28, February 1995. For further discussion see Johnson (1981) and (1982). Also G. White and R. Wade, 'Developmental States and Markets in East Asia: An Introduction', in G. White (ed.), *Developmental States in East Asia*, London: Macmillan Press, 1988. Also P. B. Evans, 'Transnational Linkages and the Economic Role of the State: An Analysis of Developing and Industrialized Nations in the Post-World War II Period', in P. B. Evans et al. (eds), *Bringing the State Back In*, New York: Cambridge University Press, 1985; P. B. Evans, 'Predatory, Developmental and Other Apparatuses: A Comparative Political Economy Perspective of the Third World State', *Sociological Forum*, vol. 4, no. 2, pp. 561–87, 1989; R. Charlton and D. Donald, 'Bringing the Economy Back In: Reconsidering the Autonomy of the Developmental State', paper presented at Political Studies Association Conference Panel on Contemporary State Theory, Belfast, 7–9 April 1992.

26 For an early study on the role of the state in 'backward' countries see A. Gerschenkron, *Economic Backwardness in Historical Perspective*. Cambridge, MA: Harvard University Press, 1962. In Gerschenkron's analysis the state's active role is in response to the 'lateness' of industrialization. Another early study on the role of the state is that of Myrdal, which distinguishes between the incapacitated or 'soft' state and the strong or 'hard' state. See G. Myrdal, 'The "Soft State" in Underdeveloped Countries', in P. Streeten (ed.), *Unfashionable Economics: Essays in Honour of Lord Balogh*, London: Weidenfeld and Nicolson, 1970.

27 Johnson (1982), p. 19.
28 Leftwich (1995).
29 Johnson (1981, 1982), Evans (1985), White & Wade (1988) and Leftwich (1995).
30 White and Wade (1988), p. 10.
31 Charlton & Donald (1995), p. 61.
32 Charlton & Donald (1995).
33 White and Wade (1988), p. 10. The weakness or control of civil society appear to have been a general condition for the emergence and continuity of developmental states. In East Asian NICs the civil society was weak to start with. In both South Korea and Taiwan neither the organized working class nor the industrial associations were an important factor in shaping economic and social policy. See Leftwich (1995).
34 Leftwich (1995), p. 401.
35 In the case of Iran, despite the rapid growth of manufactured output during the 1960s and the 1970s, non-oil exports remained limited due to the lack of a consistent policy vis-à-vis their development. Furthermore the rentier nature of the Iranian state provided ample opportunities for rent seeking activities by political and bureaucratic elites during this period. Industrialization policies entailed investment licensing and other forms of trade and investment restrictions that fostered rent seeking activities during these periods. See P. Alizadeh, 'The Process of Import-Substitution in Iran' (1960–1978). Unpublished D.Phil dissertation, Sussex University 1985. See particularly part 2, pp. 87–198.
36 For the historical weakness of the Iranian bourgeoisie see Ashraf (1970).
37 During the period 1962–78, which was an era of active industrial policy, the state had substantial autonomy from civil society. The latter signifies all privately organized interests, activities and groups above the family level. The Pahlavi state from 1953 onwards was charcterized by a growing concentration of power in the hands of a small political elite, which was ultimately reduced to the Shah and his court. See Najmabadi (1987).

Part One
Macroeconomic Policies and Performance

1

Dilemmas and Prospects for Economic Reform and Reconstruction in Iran

Hassan Hakimian and
Massoud Karshenas

1. Introduction

After more than a decade of revolutionary turmoil and external war (with Iraq), in the late 1980s the Iranian government embarked on an extensive economic reform and adjustment programme. The First Five-Year Development Plan, introduced in 1989, provided a framework for liberalizing the economy and dismantling the centrally-administered model of resource allocation that had evolved during the war years. The market reforms in this phase were intertwined with a broader, state-led, reconstruction drive to resuscitate the economy.

After a short success phase in the early 1990s, the liberalization effort stalled in the face of heightened macroeconomic instability and a severe foreign exchange crisis that came to a head in 1993. As emergency measures were adopted to deal with the debt crisis, the reforms were scaled back and the familiar spectre of stagflation – the malaise of the 1980s – came back to haunt the Iranian economy. Approaching the late 1990s, a combination of economic populism and another severe slump in international oil prices during 1997–99, has again blurred the prospects for economic reform in the country.

This chapter poses the question of Iran's economic reform prospects in the wider and comparative perspective of the problems of growth and diversification in an oil-exporting economy. While the recent abortive foray into market reforms is to some extent explicable in terms of economic mismanagement, lack of policy coordination and institutional inefficiency, the deterioration of Iran's relative economic performance, particularly since the 1980s, can be understood in relation to more-deep rooted structural characteristics of the economy. Addressing these challenges would require more fundamental economic and political reform than envisaged in the reform package of the early 1990s.

Section 2 examines the relative position of the Iranian economy in the world economy and its growth performance over the past four decades. The remarkable retrogression of the Iranian economy during the 1980s stands out both in regional and in international contexts. This prolonged period of economic retrogression, in addition to highlighting the adverse implications of misconceived policies and the need for economic reform, itself led to fundamental distortions in the economy with important implications for future reforms. These distortions are highlighted in Section 3, with particular emphasis on the industrial sector. Comparisons with Turkey and Korea are offered in order to highlight the perverse developments in Iranian manufacturing during the 1980s. With this background we proceed to discuss the economic reform programme and its shortcomings in Section 4. Section 5 concludes by offering some lessons from the recent experience of reform and highlighting the challenges the economy continues to face to date.

2. Iran's Economy in a Comparative Context

There has been a remarkable deterioration in the growth performance of the Iranian economy since the late 1970s, both relative to its past performance and compared to international standards. This is reflected in Figure 1, which shows comparative per capita GDP trends for Iran and various regions in the period 1955–92. It can be seen that the past two decades have witnessed a noticeable deterioration in the growth performance of the Middle East and North Africa region (MENA). Amongst the MENA region economies, however, the phenomenal decline in Iran's per capita GDP since the late 1970s stands out.

Figure 1: Per Capita GDP Trends in MENA and Other Regions, 1950–92

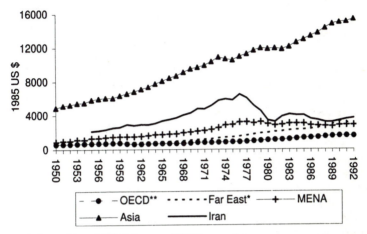

* Excluding China. **High Income OECD countries.
Source: Penn World Tables

Up to the late 1970s the Iranian economy showed impressive growth rates, paralleled only by a few other major economies in the MENA region or in Asia. Starting from higher per capita GDP levels in the 1950s, and growing at a faster rate, by the mid-1970s Iran's per capita GDP was nearly double that of the MENA region as a whole (Figure 1 and Table 1).[1] Iran's GDP growth rate during this period also exceeded that of the high income OECD countries, making her one of the few developing countries which succeeded in reducing its relative income gap with the industrial countries. The MENA region and Iran both showed a higher rate of growth of income per head compared to Asia over the 1955–75 period. In fact, by 1975 the GDP per capita in Iran was far above any of the newly industrializing countries in the Far East (Table 1). After the late-1970s however, the growth process slackened, in the MENA region as a whole and particularly in Iran. By the end of the 1980s, the per capita income gap with Asia had been considerably reduced, and the Far East (excluding China) had overtaken both Iran and the MENA region in this respect.[2]

Table 1: Per Capita GDP by Region, 1960–90

	1960	1975	1990
MENA	100	184	176
Iran	177	346	202
Turkey	96	169	222
Tunisia	65	122	173
Morocco	49	92	128
Egypt	48	76	114
East Asia	50	89	199
Korea	53	138	396
Malaysia	84	159	304
Singapore	97	319	695
Taiwan	75	181	479
Thailand	56	100	212
Asia	41	54	97
India	46	49	75
China	34	46	79
Bangladesh	56	57	83
Indonesia	38	57	117
High income OECD	387	622	885

Note: MENA 1960 = 100, at 1985 international prices in US dollars.
Source: PENN World Tables, Mark 5.

Comparing the growth performance of Iran with Turkey and Korea helps to further highlight the dramatic reversal of trends in the Iranian economy since the mid-1970s (Figure 2). During the two decades before 1975, per capita income in Iran grew faster than in Turkey and kept pace with Korea. By 1975, the level of per capita GDP in Iran was more than double those for Korea and Turkey (Table 1). However, since the late 1970s, income per head in Iran has witnessed a rapid decline, while the growth of the Korean economy has continued and that of Turkey has slowed down during a period of substantial industrial restructuring. By 1990, GDP per capita in Iran had declined by half, almost down to the levels prevalent in the early-1960s and falling behind Turkey and Korea (Korea's income was virtually double that of Iran's by then).[3] By the 1990s, per capita income levels in Iran had fallen closer to the MENA average, and matched the standards attained by Korea and other newly industrialized economies (NIEs) in East Asia in the mid-1970s.

Figure 2: Per Capita GDP Trends in Iran, Korea and Turkey, 1950–95

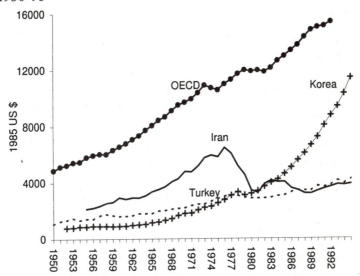

Source: Penn World Tables and World Bank (1998).

It would be wrong, however, to expect that Iran's growth potential would have matched that of the NIEs had she pursued similar economic policies. Such an expectation ignores differences in the initial conditions as well as the substantial changes that have come about in the international environment in the past two to three decades. However, in this chapter we are not concerned with the implications of the new international economic conditions for the growth potential of the Iranian economy.[4] We will instead focus on internal or structural conditions as the more important debilitating factors hindering the resumption of growth and resulting in prolonged stagnation in the Iranian economy.

The next section focuses on the industrial sector to highlight, again in a comparative context, structural rigidities that have been behind Iran's under-performing economy since the late 1970s.

3. Economic Policy and Industrial Structure

The rapid growth of the Iranian economy during the two decades preceding the 1979 Revolution took place in the context of an import substitution industrialization strategy. The paradoxical result of this strategy was to make the economy increasingly dependent on oil export revenues in order to finance the intermediate and capital goods imports needed by Iran's heavily protected industrial sector. Early signs of stress, indicating the need for industrial restructuring, occurred after 1975. However, the problems became most acute in the 1980s, when the rapid growth in oil export revenues finally came to an end. But in an environment marked by rapid economic and political change, far from embarking on fundamental economic reforms, the postrevolutionary government adopted policies throughout the 1980s that further exacerbated prevailing inefficiencies and the rigidity of the industrial structure inherited from the old regime.[5]

In the immediate aftermath of the revolution a considerable portion of large-scale modern industry, and the entire banking and insurance system were nationalized. These nationalizations were to some extent forced on the government as in many cases the owners and managers of factories had left the country and some enterprises were on the verge of collapse. During the 1980s, the role of the private sector and markets was continuously debated by the regime, and direct government controls over the economy were continuously increasing. This process was particularly spurred on by the exigencies of running a war economy. Throughout the war period, the government introduced an intricate system of rationing and direct subsidies for a large number of commodities. Government controls in other economic spheres also increased significantly during this period. Foreign exchange shortages, which became particularly acute from the mid-1980s, led to a policy of import compression and strict foreign exchange controls and rationing. The shortfall in oil revenues at a time of increasing demand on government resources led to substantial budget deficits that heightened inflationary pressures in the economy. This also intensified the growing shortages resulting from import restrictions, economic sanctions and war damage, encouraging further commodity rationing and government controls in the product markets.

The expanded government role in the post-revolutionary period was thus not solely or even primarily through a shift of balance from private to public ownership. It was manifested in direct interventions in the operation of markets – foreign exchange controls, maintenance of a system of multiple exchange rates, control on interest rates and bank credits – as well as direct price controls in a large number of product markets. Over time, substantial and entrenched price distortions developed in the economy, with serious consequences at all levels of economic activity from investment to production, trade, distribution, and consumption (see Karshenas and Pesaran, 1995). The keeping of an overvalued official exchange rate by the government during the 1980s has received much attention (see, e.g., Lautenschlager, 1986; Behdad, 1988; Pesaran, 1992, and Karshenas and Pesaran, 1995). The premium on the black market rate increased rapidly from low levels at the time of the revolution to 200–300 per cent by the early 1980s, 500–600 per cent by the mid 1980s, and exceeded 2000 per cent by the end of the decade. This twenty-fold premium in the parallel exchange markets was indicative of the enormous subsidies which the government was providing to a handful of institutions and individuals who benefited from its foreign exchange rationing system. Similar subsidies were granted, directly or indirectly, on various consumer goods and key producer goods (e.g., energy). The consumer price policy of the government during the war years consisted of a combination of measures, such as subsidization, direct control of prices and two-tier pricing based on coupon allocation for certain products. By the end of the war there had appeared an extensive network of official markets for some 300 price-controlled products. The prices of some key products such as energy and bread had fallen to well below 10 per cent of the corresponding international prices (see, e.g., Karshenas and Pesaran, 1995).

The problems associated with the exchange rate and other price and quantity controls, and the resulting disequilibria and inefficiencies, were all too clear to force the government to embark upon a comprehensive liberalization and restructuring programme from the end of the war (see Section 4 below). The exchange rate disequilibrium and the price distortions, however, reflected deepseated and more fundamental problems in the real economy which made the task of reform particularly challenging. This is best seen in a comparison of Iran's industrial structure and performance with those of Turkey and Korea.

3.1 Industrial Structure and Performance
Up to the mid-1960s, Iran, Korea and Turkey followed similar import substitution industrialization policies. By the early 1960s,

however, Korea started to combine this strategy with the pro-motion of manufacturing exports, which was soon to become one of its main engines of growth in the post-war period (see Amsden, 1989, and Wade, 1990). Although an understanding of Korea's industrial strategy and its outward orientation is the key to an explanation of its superior growth performance in recent decades, fundamental differences in its initial conditions should not be overlooked.

First, Korea had a much lower land/labour ratio in the 1960s compared to both Iran and Turkey. Table 2 shows that, this ratio was ten times higher in Iran, and over five time higher in Turkey, than in Korea in the early 1960s. Thus, despite the more intensive farming methods in Korea with much higher yields, the pro-ductivity of labour in Korea lagged behind both Iran and Turkey in this period. This meant that Korea's industrial sector benefited from abundant supplies of agricultural labour at early stages of its industrial take-off.[6]

A second important initial condition in Korea was the much higher levels of education and skills of the labour force. As can be seen from Table 2, literacy rates in Korea in the 1960s were higher than the rates prevailing in Iran and Turkey in the 1990s.[7] The combination of these two factors, namely abundant supplies of cheap and, at the same time, more skilled labour meant that after a relatively short period of learning the Korean manufacturing industries could become internationally competitive. By 1965, about 60 per cent of merchandise exports in Korea consisted of manufacturing exports, while a similar share in Iran and Turkey was no more than 2 to 4 per cent (Table 2). The existence of important cumulative learning effects from specialization in manu-facturing exports meant that Korean wages could grow at much faster rates than Iran and Turkey, along with the rapid rates of growth of labour productivity and increased technological sophis-tication of the economy, without impinging upon the profitability and competitiveness of the Korean industries. The same table shows that, by 1995, manufacturing wages in Korea had increased to over three times higher than wages prevailing in Iran and Turkey, while per capita manufacturing exports in Korea had reached levels 5 to 10 times higher than Turkey and Iran respectively.

Korea's ability to exploit profitable manufacturing export opportunities and her different resource endowment patterns contrast sharply with Iran's industrial performance and strategy,

Table 2: Selected Economic Indicators for Iran, Korea and Turkey, 1965–95

	Land Labour Ratio (ha/ worker)	Labour Produc- tivity*	Yields*	Manu- facturing Wages (US $)	Illiteracy Rate (% 15+ population)	Share of Manu- facturing Exports	Manu- facturing Exports per head ($)
1965							
Iran	4.3	7118	1638	461	77	4	na
Korea	0.4	3320	7984	229	21	59	na
Turkey	2.3	6034	2592	928	54	2	na
1975							
Iran	3.8	8618	2294	2062	64	1	131
Korea	0.4	4958	12682	964	10	81	157
Turkey	2.4	8453	3485	2780	40	23	135
1995							
Iran	2.7	14293	5256	5145[†]	28	3	271[†]
Korea	0.7	16947	24959	17129	2	93	2720
Turkey	1.9	10884	5660	6789	18	74	522

Notes: *Labour productivity and yields are in wheat-equivalent units in kg per person and per hectare respectively. † Refers to 1993.
Sources: FAO, UNIDO, World Bank Data Banks, and Karshenas (1998).

which became increasingly inward-oriented in subsequent years. By the late 1970s, Turkey, too, had adopted an extensive reform programme, with manufacturing export promotion as one of its key objectives. In Iran, by contrast, the old regime's import substi- tution industrialization policies were retained and intensified into the post-revolutionary period. In fact, the policy of import com- pression introduced as a response to foreign exchange shortages and the introduction of various forms of subsidies in the 1980s strengthened the protection given to the domestic manufacturing sector. An important new element introduced in the post- revolutionary period was the greater involvement of the public sector in industrial production, and the dominance of semi-public organizations in the form of various charitable foundations with strong political ties to the regime (such as the Foundation of the Oppressed and Disabled). This ensured the continued subsidiz- ation of the old manufacturing sector and the allocation of foreign exchange to old enterprises at highly undervalued official rates at a time of severe foreign exchange shortages. The outcome was to further exacerbate the existing distortions and inefficiencies in the manufacturing sector.

Table 3: Structure and Growth of the Manufacturing Sector, Iran, Turkey and Korea, 1963–90

| | Growth of Output | | Growth of Employment | |
	1963–77	1977–96	1963–77	1977–96
Iran	12.0	1.9	8.9	2.8
Turkey	7.9	5.5	6.6	1.5
Korea	18.7	8.1	11.3	2.5

| | Productivity Growth | | Growth of Real Product Wages | |
	1963–77	1977–96	1963–77	1977–96
Iran	3.1	-0.9	5.5	1.8
Turkey	1.4	4.0	3.2	-0.2
Korea	7.4	5.6	6.8	7.5

| | Industrial Markups | | | Share of Wages in Value Added | | |
	1967–75	1980–85	1987–96	1967–75	1980–85	1987–96
Iran	41.9	29.3	40.7	23.3	53.9	35.5
Turkey	42.6	36.1	47.5	27.1	24.8	22.5
Korea	41.0	32.7	43.9	24.1	27.2	26.7

| | Ratio of Intermediate Input Costs to the Wage Bill | | |
	1967–75	1980–85	1987–90
Iran	6.9	2.0	3.5
Turkey	5.4	7.6	6.3
Korea	6.8	7.2	5.3

Source: UNIDO, *INDSTAT*, 1994.

Figure 3: Manufacturing Output, Employment and Productivity in
Iran, Korea and Turkey, Selected Years

(a) Output

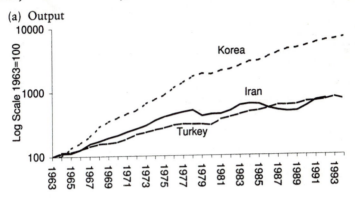

(b) Employment

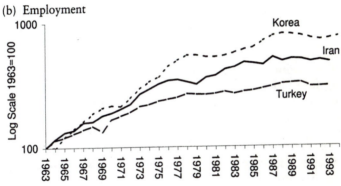

(c) Labour Productivity

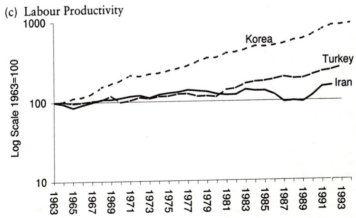

The trends in output, employment and productivity in the manufacturing sectors in Iran, Korea and Turkey during the 1963–96 period are shown in Figure 3. As can be seen, there was a considerable decline in the growth of manufacturing output in post-revolutionary Iran. The average annual rate of growth of output fell from 12 per cent per annum during the 1965–77 period to just over 1.9 per cent over the 1977–93 period (Table 3). What is particularly remarkable, however, is the continued growth of manufacturing employment and the phenomenal decline in labour productivity after the revolution. By 1990, the productivity of labour in the manufacturing sector in Iran had fallen to levels prevailing in the mid-1960s, and despite a revival during the 1990–93 reform period (see the next section), manufacturing labour productivity declined by about 1 per cent a year during the entire 1977–93 period (Figure 3 and Table 3). Part of this decline in labour productivity levels could be explained by low investment and lack of industrial renovation as well as the under utilization of capacity due to foreign exchange shortages and lack of raw materials. The major source of productivity decline, however, has been the continued growth of employment in the face of stagnant industrial output. Such a phenomenon could only take place in public enterprises, or in enterprises belonging to charitable foundations with access to sizeable state subsidies and with an employment policy geared to their role as charities rather than commercial profit making organizations. In private enterprises subject to commercial norms, such a pattern of development would be extremely unlikely, even if it could be afforded by large scale state subsidies. As we shall argue below, such extremes of inefficiency and low productivity in the manufacturing sector seem to have been major destabilizing factors for the attempted reforms by the government in the 1990s.

Another important aspect of the distortions in the manufacturing sector relates to the movement of wages and the cost-price structure in the sector. The trends in real product wages and labour productivity in the manufacturing sector in Iran, Korea and Turkey are shown in Figure 4. What is remarkable is that, despite the decline in labour productivity in the manufacturing sector during the post-revolutionary period, real product wages in 1993 were still higher than in 1977 when labour productivity in the manufacturing sector was at its peak. Real wages increased substantially just before the revolution when the old regime granted substantial wage awards to appease striking workers. Moreover, despite a rapid decline in productivity, real wage levels have been maintained at above 1977 levels in the large manufacturing sector. The outcome, as shown in Table 3, has been a substantial increase in the share of wages in value added in the manufacturing sector after the revolution. Wage shares increased from about a 23 per cent average during the 1967–75 period to about 54 per cent during 1980–85 and were somewhat reduced to 35.5 per cent during 1987–93 (Table 3). Again, Iran's experience contrasts sharply with that of Turkey and Korea.

Figure 4: Trends in Real Product Wages and Labour Productivity in Manufacturing in Iran, Korea and Turkey, Selected Years

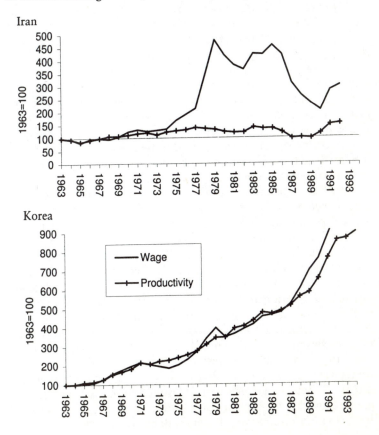

Turkey

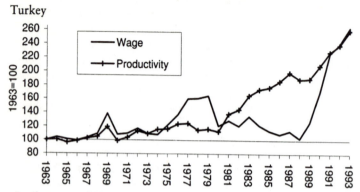

In the case of Korea, wage shares were kept relatively stable at a range of 24–27 per cent throughout the 1965–90 period, despite the rapid growth of real product wages. This was mainly because of an equally rapid growth of labour productivity. In the case of Turkey, wage shares declined from about 27 per cent on average during 1967–75 to about 18 per cent in the late 1980s. This was partly due to a relative improvement in the growth of labour productivity and partly due to real wage compression. Wage shares in the case of Iran, which were of similar order of magnitude in the pre-revolutionary period to those of Turkey and Korea, increased in the 1980s to almost double the levels prevailing in these two countries (Table 3).

What is even more significant, however, is that despite the phenomenal increases in the share of wages in value added during the 1980s, industrial mark-ups did not exhibit a commensurate decline. Industrial mark-ups declined from an average of about 42 per cent during 1967–75 to about 30 per cent in the first half of the 1980s climbing back to about 41 per cent in the 1987–93 period. What has made this apparently paradoxical outcome possible is the dramatic decline in the cost of intermediate inputs in the case of Iran. As can be seen from Figure 5 and Table 3, the ratio of intermediate input costs to the wage bill in the Iranian manufacturing sector declined from about 7 during the period prior to the revolution to just over 2 in the 1980s. This was to some extent due to the excessive growth of the wage bill as already discussed. But to a larger extent it resulted form the huge subsidies granted by the government to the manufacturing sector through the provision of substantially overvalued foreign exchange at the official rates, and other price subsidies on raw materials, e.g., cheap energy. In fact, it is not difficult to see that without such subsidization – other things including nominal and product wages and labour productivity being the same – mark-ups would have plummeted to no more than 10–12 per cent during the 1980s. It was precisely because of the provision of such large subsidies that the manufacturing sector could afford to finance the prevailing levels of real wages despite the rapid decline in labour productivity.

Figure 5: Ratio of Raw Material Costs to the Wage Bill in Manufacturing in Iran, Korea, and Turkey, 1963–96

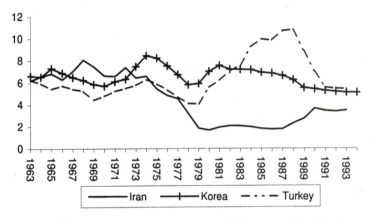

The ratio of the cost of intermediate inputs to the wage bill fell from 7 to 2 between the pre- and post-revolutionary periods. This ratio can be taken as a proxy for the real exchange rate (relative price of traded to non-traded goods) and signifies the substantial overvaluation of the exchange rate in the latter period.[8] This index also helps delineate the different sources of the overvaluation of the exchange rate: one resulting from the wage/price distortions and another arising from the low degree of production efficiency. The first source of overvaluation reflects allocative inefficiency in the economy and can be corrected by price and exchange rate reforms, e.g., a unification and devaluation of the exchange rate given money wages. The second source of overvaluation, however, requires a restructuring of industrial production to improve the production efficiency of the economy. When this latter source of overvaluation is predominant, there may be no exchange rate at which domestic industry would be competitive, because domestic output prices will always be excessive compared to international prices even at international input prices.

As we noted above, the overvaluation of the Iranian rial in the period after the revolution was related to both these factors, but predominantly the latter. On the one hand, given the productivity of labour, product wages seemed to be high relative to historical trends and so were money wages relative to the highly subsidized prices of other inputs. On the other hand, the apparent over-manning of the manufacturing sector and other production inefficiencies in the sector rendered industry non-competitive at international input prices. For a successful reform and restructuring programme both these problems have to be addressed adequately. To the extent that the latter problem – i.e., the problem of production inefficiency – is neglected, the adjustment programme may lead to excessive real wage compression which in the long run may further exacerbate prevailing production inefficiencies. Such a lopsided adjustment programme, whereby an excessive burden is imposed on real wage compression, is likely to fail even in the short run either due to political concern over declining real wages or due to financial instability and inflationary pressures resulting from real wage resistance on the part of the workers.

4. Restructuring and Economic Reform

The end of the war with Iraq in the late 1980s, opened up a new window of opportunity for economic reform and restructuring in Iran. The impetus for this new drive came partly from the long process of economic exhaustion Iran had suffered during the war years, and partly by the accumulation of long and deep-rooted economic problems since the early days of the revolution (as discussed above).[9] As we have seen, it was against a background of mounting economic difficulties, shrinking living standards and a contracting public sector resource base that the government was forced to embark on an ambitious reconstruction and economic reform programme within the framework of its First Five-Year Development Plan covering the period 1989–93.

The plan aimed at market liberalization through the dismantling of the intricate network of price and quantity controls that had evolved over the war years, the removal of quantitative trade restrictions and a gradual liberalization of foreign trade including the unification of the exchange rate system. It thus envisaged a general rolling back of the state's interventionist policies and postures. In practice, however, it became further caught up in the state's expansionary influence and its implementation was modified to make space for the latter's post-war reconstruction ambitions.

Despite the First Plan's mixed fortunes and the government's subsequent wavering commitment to reforms, the plan was a watershed in the development of Iran's post-war economy. First, it played a major part in dismantling the centrally-administered economy in the late 1980s. Second, it succeeded in establishing a new agenda for economic adjustment and reform with lasting, albeit moderated, effects to the present (through the Second Development Plan which covers the period 1995–99).

Understanding Iran's recent economic performance requires a critical appraisal and examination of the achievements and failures of this plan and the evolution of economic policy since its adoption in 1889. The next sections are devoted to this task.

4.1 Economic Performance
Iran's economic performance during the plan years, as judged by overall growth indicators, appears positive. During the 1989–93 period, the real average annual rate of GDP growth climbed to 7.3 per cent indicating an end to the reversals experienced during the war years (GDP had shrunk by almost 8 per cent in 1988, the last year of the war). Reflecting the surge in aggregate demand, private consumption and gross fixed investment also grew at 7.8 per cent and 14 per cent per annum in real terms respectively (for all macroeconomic data, unless otherwise specified, see the indicators in Table 4). Growth in this period was achieved with a two-digit consumer price inflation of 18.8 per cent per annum, which nevertheless compares favourably with both the war years and the more recent record (annual inflation rate averaged just under 20 per cent during 1980–88 and rose to 29 per cent for 1994–98).

Despite this broad favourable overview, a closer scrutiny suggests a much more uneven and lopsided pattern of growth during the plan years. Table 4 indicates that initially the plan succeeded in reinvigorating the economy with annual growth rate rising impressively to 11–12 per cent during 1990–91. Success on this scale, however, was short-lived as growth rate dropped back to about 5 per cent for 1992–93 followed by the slump of 1994, when the economy grew at a mere 1.6 per cent per annum.

Table 4: Macroeconomic Indicators of Iran, 1989–98

	1989	1990	1991	1992	1993	1994	1995	1996	1997	1998 (prel.)	Average 1989–93	Average 1994–98
Real Sector												
Real GDP Growth (% p.a.)	3.0	12.1	10.9	5.5	4.8	1.6	4.5	5.8	3.4	1.6	7.3	3.4
Non-oil GDP Growth (% p.a.)	*3.5*	*9.8*	*9.9*	*7.0*	*5.2*	*3.2*	*3.6*	*5.0*	*4.7*	*2.4*	*7.1*	*3.9*
Inflation (urban CPI)	17.4	8.9	20.7	24.4	22.9	35.2	49.4	23.2	17.3	20.0	18.8	29.0
Private Consumption (real growth % p.a.)	2.5	19.5	9.5	5.4	2.3	2.2	2.6	3.0	2.7	2.5	7.8	2.6
Fixed Investment (real % growth p.a.)	6.4	13.3	40.9	6.9	2.7	3.4	3.2	8.3	-0.2	-6.3	14.0	1.7
Public	*1.0*	*30.8*	*31.6*	*15.8*	*-4.8*	*4.3*	*4.2*	*10.9*	*-1.6*	*-14.5*	*14.9*	*0.7*
Private	*10.1*	*2.4*	*48.4*	*0.6*	*8.8*	*2.8*	*2.5*	*6.4*	*0.8*	*-0.2*	*14.1*	*2.5*
Fixed Investment (% GDP)	12.8	12.9	16.4	16.6	16.3	16.6	16.4	16.8	16.2	14.9	15.0	16.2
Public Sector												
Government Revenue (% GDP)	11.8	15.8	14.2	15.3	21.7	22.6	23.0	24.3	22.5	16.4	15.8	21.8
% Oil Revenue	*47.6*	*59.8*	*51.1*	*52.0*	*72.5*	*73.4*	*64.1*	*57.2*	*41.6*	*30.9*	*56.6*	*53.4*
Tax Revenue (% GDP)	4.4	4.7	5.7	5.9	4.3	4.2	4.0	5.3	6.2	34.8	5.0	5.1
Government Expenditure (% GDP)	16.0	16.9	16.6	16.7	22.3	22.4	22.9	24.1	23.6	21.8	17.7	22.9
Budget Deficit (% GDP)	-4.2	-1.2	-2.4	-1.4	-0.7	0.3	0.1	0.2	-1.0	-5.4	-2.0	-1.2

Continued . . .

Table 4: Macroeconomic Indicators of Iran, 1989–98 (continued)

	1989	1990	1991	1992	1993	1994	1995	1996	1997	1998 (prel.)	Average 1989–93	Average 1994–98
Monetary Sector												
M2 Growth (% year-end)	19.5	22.5	24.6	25.3	34.2	28.5	37.6	37.0	15.2	27.1	25.2	29.1
Wholesale Price Index (% growth)	18.5	23.9	26.6	33.4	25.3	42.4	60.2	25.1	9.9	11.6	25.6	29.8
Domestic Credit Growth (% year-end)	17.6	20.0	22.5	21.0	44.3	25.6	29.8	24.8	22.9	31.4	25.1	26.9
Net Credit to Central Gov't (% growth)	10.7	3.9	7.1	4.5	57.3	25.8	24.2	10.5	12.8	25.4	16.7	19.7
Credit to Official Entities (% growth)	12.5	76.8	27.8	60.5	73.7	33.8	68.5	41.3	40.2	36.4	50.2	44.0
Private Sector Credits (% growth)	29.7	35.7	38.2	29.1	30.3	23.4	24.4	30.9	23.5	33.1	32.6	27.1
Interest Rates[1]	8.5	9	9	10	11.5	11.5	14	14	14	14.0	9.6	13.5
External Sector												
Official Exchange Rate (Rls./$)	70.2	65.3	64.6	67.0	1758.6	1736.0	1747.5	1749.1	1754.3	n.a.	405.1	1746.7
Weighted Average Exchange Rate (Rls./$)[2]	299.1	394.2	511.7	655.1	890.1	1221.7	1725.8	n.a.	n.a.	n.a.	550.0	1473.8
Current Balance (m US$)	-191	327	-9448	-6504	-4215	4956	3358	5232	2213	-1895	-4006.2	2772.8
Oil Export Revenues (m US$)	12037	17993	16012	16880	14333	14603	15103	19271	15471	9942	15451.0	14878.0
Non-oil Exports (m US$)	1044	1312	2649	2988	3747	4831	3257	3120	2910	3040	2348.0	3431.6
Imports (cif, m US$)	13448	18330	25190	23274	19287	12617	12774	14989	14123	13608	19905.8	13622.2
External Debt (m US$)	6518	9020	11330	16033	23158	22737	21928	16835	12117	14089	13211.8	17541.2
% Short-term	71.4	80.1	81.8	88.9	76.1	29.5	20.7	27.1	27.1	43.2	79.7	29.5
Debt Service (% of Exports)	3.3	3.2	4.1	5.2	9.3	16.5	30.2	27.5	31.3	20.2	5.0	26.3

Notes: 1. Banking system's one-year deposit rate; 2. Trade weighted index of different exchange rates.
Sources: Bank Markazi Iran; World Bank (1998); IMF (1998), and PDS (1998).

Despite early successes, therefore, the plan did not manage to break out of the familiar boom and bust economic cycles that have so commonly plagued the Iranian economy following sudden oil price fluctuations in the past.[10] The deterioration of economic performance in the later years of the plan came in the wake of heightened macroeconomic instability, namely inflation and a severe external debt crisis. The pattern of boom and bust can be clearly seen in Figure 6, which shows annual changes in real consumption and investment in the decade after the war. Reflecting the reconstruction crusade unleashed by the First Plan, both these aggregate demand constituents rose sharply in the early years (1989–91), but neither proved to be sustainable and levelled off after 1992. For instance, pent up consumer demand which was unleashed rapidly after the partial liberalization of the economy in the early 1990s, led to an increase in private consumption by 19.5 per cent in 1990 and 9.5 per cent in 1991. There was a parallel rise in investment activity in the early stages of the plan. Propelled by the rapid expansion of domestic demand, and eased by access to cheap credit and greater availability of foreign exchange, private investment too shot up by nearly 50 per cent in 1991 alone. Similarly, public sector investment jumped by more than 30 per cent per annum during 1990–91 (after a fall of 18.5 per cent in 1988 and a mere 1 per cent rise in 1989; see Figure 6). While this was partly in response to the physical destruction of fixed assets and their dilapidation and disrepair during the long war with Iraq, it also signalled a spate of new and ambitious public sector investment projects unleashed to reverse the post-revolutionary stagnation and economic decline.

Figure 6: Growth of Real Consumption and Investment, 1988–96

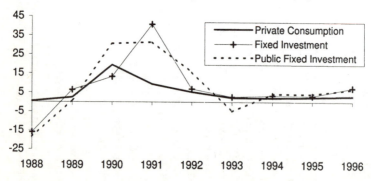

As so often in the past, economic boom was fuelled by a fortuitous increase in oil revenues. This was true of the early years of the plan, when government spending was boosted by a doubling of oil revenues. Foreign exchange revenues from oil sales rose from $9.7 billion in 1988 to about $18 billion in 1991, when they accounted for some 60 per cent of all government revenues (up from 39 per cent in 1988).[11] Although an important catalyst, oil was not the only factor behind the reconstruction drive. The government maintained its ambitious spending drive at times benefiting from certain budgetary procedures, which helped lessen its apparent deficit.[12]

A boom of this scale and nature was unsurprisingly short-lived as the pace of economic activity slowed down noticeably after 1991. GDP growth dropped to single figures (about 5 per cent) in the last two years of the plan (1992 and 1993). Moreover, the expansion of both private consumption and fixed investment slowed down considerably falling to just over 2 per cent per annum (with public investment contracted by 5 per cent in 1993). These years also saw a continuation of the inflationary build-up with the wholesale prices index jumping by about 33.5 per cent in 1992 and liquidity expansion (growth of M2) reaching about 25 per cent in the same year. The bust phase too coincided with sluggish oil revenues (oil revenues fell after 1992 and stagnated at just over $14 billion in 1993 and 1994). But this time, another crisis, affecting Iran's short-term foreign debt obligations, emerged abruptly and put it's newly introduced economic reform programme to a severe test.

4.2 From Liberalization to Debt Crisis

Macroeconomic instability came to a crunch with the rapid build-up of a foreign debt crisis in the latter part of the First Plan. The post-war reconstruction attempt, and the consumer boom mentioned above, had raised merchandise imports almost two-fold between 1989 and 1991 (up from $13.5 billion to $25 billion). This had been necessitated partly by the increased consumption after the war, but largely by the intermediate and capital goods imports needs of Iran's ailing industries.[13] The result was a sudden and massive deterioration in the current account balance with the deficit suddenly jumping to $9.5 billions in 1991 (a year before there had been a modest surplus). As stated before, the weakening of the oil market had exacerbated the situation as Iran's foreign exchange shortages deepened into 1992 and 1993.[14]

The result was a severe and unanticipated accumulation of external debt with a substantial short-term component. Total foreign debt stock reached a peak of more than $23 billion in 1993, over three-quarters of which was short-term. Rapidly mounting cash-flow repayment problems prompted Iran to embark on urgent and mostly bi-lateral debt rescheduling negotiations after 1993. This crisis was not so significant for the total size of debt Iran had accumulated *per se*. In fact, at its height in 1993, Iran ranked 21 among the top borrowing nations by the total stock of foreign debt (Brazil and Mexico each had six times more debts than Iran; see Table 5). As a proportion of GDP, too, Iran's relative standing was far from alarming (for instance, Iran's ratio was one-third compared to Egypt's and Venezuela's two-thirds and Nigeria's 133 per cent). Nevertheless, Iran's debt 'crisis' stood out in several respects. First, the debt trend edged upwards sharply over a short period of time during the liberalization of the early 1990s. For instance, total foreign debt rose six-fold between 1989 and 1993 (a jump of 40 per cent alone in 1992 over 1991). Second, this carried a significant short-term component, putting Iran top among the highest indebted nations by this criterion (short-term debt obligations were on average 80 per cent of the total debt volume during the First Plan period in 1989–93).

Apart from indicating the absence of adequate monitoring and debt management strategy on the part of the government, the debt crisis also exposed the high economic cost of the isolationist stance of Iran in the international arena. The inability of the country to raise long term credit in international markets meant that much of the debt consisted of suppliers' credit, suggesting that short-term finance had been used on a large scale for medium and long-term investment projects with long gestation periods.

Managing this largely unforeseen crisis proved to be costly for the Iranian economy in the coming years. In the short-term, the government embarked on urgent debt rescheduling negotiations to avoid default and to manage its arrears. In the medium term, however, it came to rely mainly on import controls to meet its new priority of paying back foreign dues. Although the measures taken were quite successful in reducing external debt consistently and rapidly over the next few years, they were not without costs. The reintroduction of import controls undermined the liberalization drive in the First Plan, and the process of growth was considerably slowed down after 1993. Evidently, the collapse of growth in this phase was as abrupt and intense as the short-lived boom of 1990–91.

Table 5: External Debt Indicators for the Highest-indebted
Countries, 1993

		Total Debt (Billion $)	As % of GDP	% Short-Term Debt
1.	Brazil	143.8	37.7	21.3
2.	Mexico	131.6	35.5	27.6
3.	Russian Federation	112.0	30.1	7.4
4.	India	94.5	40.5	3.8
5.	Indonesia	89.2	60.3	20.2
6.	China	85.9	21.8	17.8
7.	Argentina	70.6	n.a.	12.3
8.	Turkey	68.6	41.9	27.0
9.	Thailand	52.7	46.9	43.0
10.	Poland	45.2	n.a.	5.9
11.	Venezuela	37.6	65.6	12.5
12.	Philippines	35.9	73.5	14.0
13.	Nigeria	30.7	133.2	12.9
14.	Egypt	30.6	69.7	6.6
15.	Malaysia	26.1	44.6	26.6
21.	**Iran**	**23.5**	**33.1**	**76.1**
Iran's Ranking Among Top 21 Borrowing Nations		**21**	**16(a)**	**1**

Note: (a) Ranking excludes Argentina, Poland, and Vietnam among the 21
highest indebted nations due to data limitations.
Source: Based on World Bank, (1998) and Bank Markazi data.

4.3 Foreign Exchange Reform

Although reforming Iran's system of multiple exchange rates had
been a key objective of the First Plan, its implementation was
delayed until the last year of the plan, when conditions for its
successful implementation had arguably turned unfavourable. In
March 1993, the government sought to unify the exchange rate at
the prevailing free market rate. The attempt, however, failed in the
face of severe macroeconomic instability and the widening gap
between the free market and the spot exchange rates that
followed. The plan was thwarted in December of the same year,
when administrative measures for currency allocation were
reintroduced. In discussions of Iran's recent economic policy, few
issues have perhaps received as much attention as the unification attempt of 1993 and matters relating to its design and

implementation (see, e.g., Farzin, 1995, Karshenas and Pesaran, 1995, Mazarei, 1995).

Prior to March 1993, a number of measures were adopted to simplify Iran's elaborate multiple exchange rate mechanism, which had developed into an important consumer price stabilization instrument over the war years. These attempts included, for instance, the replacement, in 1991, of the complicated seven-rate system with a new, three-rate, system along with partial liberalization of foreign trade (Karshenas, 1998: 215).[15] Moreover, the effective exchange rate was allowed to devalue gradually in the 1988–92 period as various imported goods were shifted from the official to the 'competitive' exchange rate category, and others were shifted from the latter rate to the free market rate category.[16] As a result, the effective nominal exchange rate – weighted by share of trade conducted at various exchange rates – was devalued by over 100 per cent during the 1989–92 period (see Table 4). The impact of unification was, however, much more drastic. With the official floating rate raised to IR1,600 per US$, there was a massive and immediate devaluation of the rial, which exceeded 2,600 per cent.[17] This meant an implicit devaluation of the effective exchange rate, as the trade-weighted average rate increased by over a third to 890 Rials/$ in the same period.

It was hoped that the new system would undermine the parallel exchange market by stabilizing the currency close to the free market rate. This hope was, however, short-lived as the mounting debt crisis and its severe impact on Iran's currency reserves raised serious questions about the government's ability to manage the new system. In the wake of a widening gap between the free market and the official exchange rate, the government abandoned its unification policy, when it effectively fixed the official rate at IR1,750/$ in late 1993. Although adopting a 'managed unified rate' was, and remains, a stated government objective under the Second Five-Year Plan, it has, nevertheless, continued to use administrative measures for allocating foreign exchanges ever since.[18]

As mentioned above, the instability of the exchange rate and the failure of the unification programme has received much attention in recent discussions of macroeconomic policy in Iran. Some analysts, for instance, have questioned the level at which the new unified exchange rate was introduced in 1993 (Farzin, 1995). Others have questioned the choice of timing for unification at a time when the economy was beset by severe foreign exchange shortages (Nili, 1997: 374). It is also plausible that an earlier unification date would have averted the import boom of 1991–92, which preceded the expected unification of the exchange rate in 1993 (Mazarei, 1995).

Although clearly important in the context of Iran's unification attempt, the stability of the exchange rate system adopted required more than a sound technical design. Evidence suggests that even if the unification policy had been well-conceived (regarding its choice of timing and the parity level adopted), its success would still have required appropriate government policy to ensure macro-economic stability. On three accounts at least, the government's policy in fact increased inflationary pressures in the economy, further undermining the stability of the exchange rate.

First was the outbreak of severe foreign debt, as discussed above, and its macroeconomic consequences. This untimely development eroded the markets' faith in the government's ability to maintain its newly-unified exchange system. In handling it too the government resorted to deficit financing, which exacerbated inflationary pressures in the economy. The reason was that debt service obligations (including that of the private sector) continued to be honoured at the old preferential rate of 70 Rials/$. To deal with this, a special credit facility was set up at the Central Bank under a new 'reserve account for foreign exchange obligations' in early 1993. The deficit on this account, however, proved far more onerous than expected since the size of debt was severely under-estimated in the absence of adequate and reliable information (Roghani-Zanjani et al., 1997: 234–37). The result was increased borrowing from the Central Bank and even greater pressure on monetary aggregates after the unification.

Second, the government continued with the lax fiscal and monetary policy that characterized the First Plan years. In so doing, it continued to resort to accounting procedures which had helped it doctor its real budget deficits since the late 1980s. Faced with a budget deficit as large as 50 per cent of its revenue in the last year before the war ended, in 1988 it introduced new budget-ary legislation which allowed it to off-load the deficits of state-owned enterprises and key public sector industries onto the Central Bank (Nili, 1997: 21 and 376; Roghani-Zanjani et al., 1997: 255). The Central Bank was thus obliged to extend credits to these ailing industries to cover their annual deficits. This practice allowed the government to 'hide' its real budgetary financing requirements and helped keep these industries afloat, a practice that continued well into the First Plan years. In fact, a *prima facie* examination of the budget 'deficit' in these years can give a misleading impression about the pursuit of a restrictive fiscal policy as apparent fiscal deficit was reduced from 10 per cent of GDP in 1988 to less than 1 per cent by 1993, after which a modest surplus was attained (Table 4). The general government budget, however, does not include the accounts of public enterprises and the semi-public charity foundations, which were now financed directly by the Central Bank as suggested above.

The onus of this type of indirect deficit-financing rose with the unification of the exchange rate, as the state owned enterprises began to lose their access to foreign exchange at preferential rates.[19] Expansion of credit by the Central Bank to public institutions and corporations ('official entities') attests to this trend giving a better idea of the underlying process of deficit financing going on in these years. In the early years of the plan, for instance, this had risen as much as 77 per cent in 1990. A similar impact was made in 1993, in view of unification, when it jumped by a further 74 per cent (for the whole plan period the annual growth rate of net credit extended to public institutions by the Central Bank was as high as 50 per cent).[20] At a time when public investment had substantially slowed down, such pace of credit financing suggested overwhelming cost recovery problems of these industries.

The third inflationary undercurrent in the aftermath of unification also derived from the state of public finances. This reflected Iran's characteristic as an oil-exporting economy, where substantial foreign currency proceeds from oil sales feed directly into the government budget as its revenue. The immediate impact of devaluation was thus to boost government finances fuelling further aggregate demand and destabilizing the economy in the post-unification era.

Until unification, the existence of differential rates under the multiple exchange rates system allowed the government to make a 'profit' on its sale of foreign exchange at rates above the official rate. This source of income was explicitly shown in the general budget as proceeds from the 'sale of foreign currency'. Figure 7 shows this amounted to substantial sums and became an important source of income to the government. At its height in 1989–91, it amounted to some 5–6 per cent of Iran's GDP and a staggering

40 per cent of all government revenue. With exchange rate unification, this source dried up when exchange rate differentials disappeared. After 1995, the source reappeared again when the new two-rate system went into effect.[21]

Figure 7: Government Income From Differential Exchange Rates, 1988–96

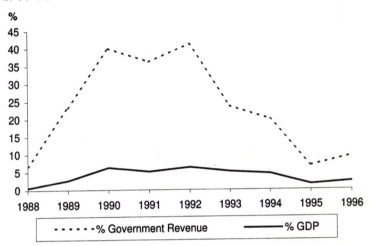

The immediate effect of devaluation was to raise substantially oil export revenues denominated in the *domestic currency* and, hence, bolstering government finances in general.[22] This seems to have provided the government with welcome fiscal relief particularly when its foreign (dollar) income from oil exports was falling and its large scale spending plans showed no signs of abating. Figure 8 shows that the dollar value of oil exports contracted by about 13.5 per cent between 1992 and 1994 (declining from about $16.9 billion to just over $14.6 billion). However, government oil revenues in domestic currency *increased* more than four-fold as a result of the unification and devaluations of 1993–94 (rising from IR5.1 trillion in 1992 to IR21.5 trillion in 1994). Of course part of this increase was neutralized with the disappearance of the profits on exchange rate differential accounts discussed above. The net result, however, was a large increase in government revenues in domestic currency as shown in Table 4. Reflecting this, currency devaluation raised the budgetary value of oil income for government as a whole: the share of oil jumped from 52 per cent of its total revenues in 1992 to a staggering 73 per cent in 1993 and 1994. This in turn provided the budget with a major boost between 1992 and 1994 when the share of government revenue rose from about 15 per cent of GDP to over 22 per cent.

Figure 8: Income from Oil in Foreign and Domestic Currencies Compared, 1992–94

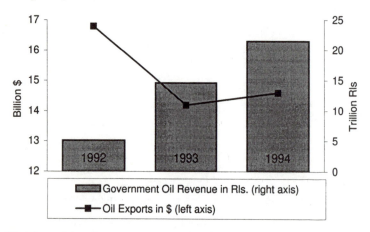

Clearly, what the government decided to do with its enlarged budget made a critical impact on the rest of the economy. As noted above, a large part of the enlarged revenues constituted a redistribution or revenue from state enterprises, and from the semi-public charity foundations, which hitherto benefited from access to foreign exchange at the overvalued official rate. Under these circumstances it would have been imperative to use these funds for rationalizing such loss making establishments. In the event, the devaluation funds were used to continue with an expansive policy which further exacerbated inflationary pressures. Figure 9 shows that devaluation in 1993 was accompanied with a more than 50 per cent rise in real government expenditure (the share of government expenditure in GDP jumped from 17 per cent in 1992 to 22 per cent in 1993). Underlying this rise was a huge expansion in the state's development expenditure, which nearly doubled in real terms in 1993 (its current expenditure expanding by 40 per cent). In this way, devaluation had directly flamed the government's ambitious reconstruction drive by inflating – overnight as it were – its budgetary resources. This was an ironic outcome of the post-war liberalization policies whose rationale was to stream-line the state activities and to scale down its size and command over economic resources.

Figure 9: Growth of Real Government Expenditure, 1989–97

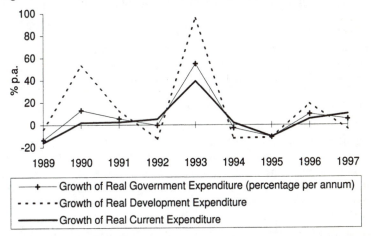

4.4 Beyond the First Plan

Iran's abortive attempt at liberalization and structural reform in the early 1990s has left its mark on economic policy and perform-ance after the First Plan. Following the foreign debt crisis and the failure of the exchange rate unification, a new economic era was ushered in, which has been characterized by low growth and high inflation. Breaking out of stagflation has proven difficult because of continued uncertainty over the direction of economic policy compounded by a severe slump in international oil prices in 1997–99.

In view of the seriousness of the external debt crisis and its adverse impact on Iran's international credit standing, paying back foreign dues was made a new government priority. The austerity measures introduced in 1994 were ultimately successful in dealing with the debt and balance of payments crises, but their wider impact on the economy has retarded growth and its short-term costs have been high.

By the end of 1997, a substantial part of the original debt stock had been repaid reducing the total to just about half of the peak volume in 1993 (falling to about $12 billion; the short-term debt component too was reduced to about a quarter from three-quarters).

Debt as a percentage of GDP too has continued to follow a sharp downward trend reaching less than 10 per cent between 1997 and 1998, and debt service payments were halved as a proportion of exports between 1995 and 1998 (down from 30 per cent to 20 per cent; Table 4).

Although improvements in oil prices and income helped this process, as stated before, it was principally through a policy of import compression that the repayment momentum could be maintained. After the austerity of 1994, an average annual current account surplus of $3.7 billion has been achieved. This compares sharply with a deficit of similar magnitude during the First Plan years. Underlying this was an upward trend of oil income until 1996 (when it peaked at $19 billion), and to some extent non-oil exports, which up to 1994 showed an encouraging trend, benefiting from devaluations of the exchange rate during the 1988–94 period. Nevertheless, controlling imports has played a key role in bringing about the required improvements in the current account balance and in the debt reduction strategy. Imports were slashed by 50 per cent in 1994 compared to their 1991 and 1992 levels. Although allowed to rise gradually since, they have not recovered their pre-boom levels and have on average been maintained at about a third lower than the First Plan years.

External adjustment and import compression used to achieve it have not been without costs. After the collapse of growth in 1994, recovery was sighted briefly in 1995–96, when the annual growth rate was restored to about 5 per cent. This was not sustained, however, as growth plunged back to 2.9 per cent again in 1997 highlighting the severe slump in international oil prices since late that year. With an average realized growth rate of just under 3.5 per cent since 1994, attaining even the Second Plan's more modest growth expectations appears far-fetched.[23] Reflecting the general weakness of the growth process, private investment too has grown at modest rates in sharp contrast to the early part of the First Plan (growing at 2.5 per cent during 1994–98 compared with 14.1 per cent during 1989–93). This picture of sluggish growth has been combined with persistent inflationary pressures that have continued to mar economic performance under the Second Plan. The height of the inflationary process came in 1995, when the wholesale price index grew by more than 60 per cent. Although falling gradually thereafter, the average for the period 1994–98 has, nevertheless, remained very high (30 per cent compared to 26 per cent during the First Plan), presenting the government with one of the most difficult challenges since the mid-1990s.

5. Conclusion and Perspectives

Iran's first post-revolutionary foray into market liberalization met with a Latin American style foreign debt and inflation crisis which tarnished its initial successes. The preceding sections have argued that the First Plan in fact failed to address the country's long-standing and deep-seated economic problems that were accentuated by the war with Iraq in the 1980s.

First, the reforms – or perhaps lack of sufficient commitment to them – failed to break the familiar cycle of 'boom and bust' commonly driven by external shocks and developments in the international oil markets. Second, the post-revolutionary malaise of stagflation (which was particularly acute in the war years) proved to be stubborn and has survived several attempts at reform and liberalization.

This study suggests that problems of slow growth and high inflation in the Iranian economy cannot be resolved without contemplating more fundamental institutional changes and a reform of the system of governance. As we have seen, the government has relied upon deficit financing (albeit in refined forms) to resolve the distributional tensions arising from the competing claims of powerful interest groups (including urban consumers and public and private sector producers). The problems have been compounded by the operation of semi-charitable organizations and foundations that have amassed considerable economic muscle without being subject to the usual rules and regulations concerning the accountability and transparency of similar commercial enterprises.

The international counterpart to this domestic scene has been the pursuit of an isolationist economic path in the last two decades with unduly high economic costs. Consequently, Iran's general economic performance has lagged severely behind international and regional standards as well as its own potential in a period marked by growing external opportunities in the world economy.

A decade after the introduction of the market reforms, the structural features of the Iranian economy are remarkably unchanged: a state of severe oil-dependency continues; the general investment climate is extremely weak and beset by uncertainty; public finances are fragile, and the economy continues to be highly inward-looking.

Whether and when these challenges can be successfully met will depend only partially on the design and adoption of appropriate economic policies, important though these are. The experience of the last round of economic reforms in fact points strongly to the need for an equally far-reaching and comprehensive package of political and institutional reforms. Delaying these reforms can only add to the eventual costs and pain of future adjustments.

Notes

1   The figures are in 1985 US $, and MENA refers to all the countries in the Middle East and North Africa including Turkey but excluding the oil-surplus countries in the Persian Gulf.

2   Far East refers to all the developing countries in east and south east Asia, excluding China and Japan. Asia refers to the developing countries in the Far East including China, and the developing countries in west and south Asia.

3   The per capita GDP levels reported in Figures 1 to 4 and Table 1 do not take into account the terms of trade effect. The magnitude of the terms of trade effect is sensitive to the base year adopted. But considering the substantial decline in the terms of trade of oil exporting countries during the 1975–90 period, real per capita income inclusive of the terms of trade effect in the 1980s is likely to be below the per capita GDP levels reported here.

4   For a discussion of the implications of the emerging global competition for the MENA region as a whole see, Riordan, et al. (1995), and Safadi (1997).

5   For a discussion of industrial policy in the post-revolutionary period see, Rahnema (1996).

6   Although data on agricultural wages are not available for these three countries, the much lower manufacturing wages in Korea in 1965 is an indirect reflection of the abundance of 'surplus' labour in agriculture (see Table 2).

7   Data on mean years of schooling for earlier years for the three countries are not available. But the existing data for the 1990s suggest even more of a glaring gap between Korea and Iran and Turkey. In 1995 the mean years of schooling for the male population (aged 15+) in Korea was 8.0 years as against 4.6 for Iran and 3.8 for Turkey. For the female population the mean years of schooling in Korea was 6.1 years as against 3.1 for Iran and 1.8 for Turkey. It is notable that in

Korea, and in fact in most East Asian and Latin American countries, the mean years of schooling for women are higher than the mean years of schooling for men in Iran and Turkey.

8   In countries with multiple exchange rates and huge subsidies on input prices this measure of real exchange rate is easier to calculate than the conventional measures, and is arguably more meaningful. For different measures of real official exchange rate in the case of Iran see, Pesaran (1992).

9   For an expanded discussion of the post-revolutionary economic crisis in Iran see, Behdad (1996).

10 For a discussion of similar episodes in the 1950s and the 1970s see, Karshenas (1990).

11 The rise in oil revenues was partly due to price increases in the wake of Iraq's invasion of Kuwait in 1990 and partly due to increased output. Crude oil exports rose by 43 per cent between 1988 and 1990, and by another 28 per cent between 1990 and 1993, as production and export facilities damaged during the war were gradually restored.

12 Since 1988, it had introduced budgetary legislation, which obliged the Central Bank to meet the financial requirements of the state-owned enterprises and key industries (this will be discussed in more detail below).

13 Raw materials and intermediate goods made up some 57 per cent of Iran's imports bill in the early 1990s with capital goods taking up another 30 per cent of the bill.

14 Despite a more than 20 per cent increase in crude petroleum export volumes between 1990 and 1993, oil export revenues declined from about $18 billion to $14.3 billion between these two years. The overall international terms of trade deteriorated by about 20 per cent between 1990 and 1993, which implied an income loss of over $3.7 billion for Iran.

15 The simplification involved a move from the complicated seven-rate system to a three-rate system; namely, the official exchange rate (at IR70/$), the 'competitive' rate (at IR600/$) and the free market rate. Moreover, the foreign exchange revenues from non-oil exports were allowed to be converted at the free market rate. Nevertheless, the gap between the official and the market rate stood at about 2,000 per cent in the early 1990s.

16 These were, of course, over and above the devaluation of the free market rate resulting from high inflationary pressures in the economy.

17 The average annual parity rate went up from IR67/$ in 1992 to IR1758.6/$ in 1993. Under this system, exceptions were still made for

essential imports and repayment of short-term foreign debt contracted previously, which were still calculated at the official rate of IR70/$.

18 The US sanctions against Iran and Libya introduced in May 1995 led to a major overnight run on the Iranian currency with a sharp drop in its parallel market value to about IR7,000/$. Although the unofficial rate was relatively quickly restored to about IR4,500/$, this episode showed again the relative fragility of the exchange system. The government responded by devaluing the official exchange rate for non-oil exports to IR3,000/$ and announcing foreign exchange transactions in the free market to be illegal.

19 Some public utilities (such as gas, water and electricity) were doubly squeezed since they continued to be subject to various price controls although they faced rising costs due to price deregulation in general and devaluation in particular. This resulted in a deterioration of their financing requirements, which was met by increased borrowing from the Central Bank (see, Nili, 1997: p. 375).

20 The growth of monetary aggregates tells a similar story in these years. In 1993, liquidity (growth of M2) shot up to more than 34 per cent (from around 20–25 per cent in previous years). A similar rate for the whole First Plan period was 25 per cent. Similarly, inflationary pressures heightened as the wholesale price index grew at an average annual rate of 25 per cent for the whole Plan period with annual inflation never falling below 20 per cent after 1990.

21 After 1995, however, the budget stopped including the sale of foreign exchange under revenue from oil and gas and included it under the 'others' category of revenue.

22 Devaluation affects the budget in other ways too: it raises government income from import duties and increases its subsidies bill for the basket of basic consumer goods for which the official rate was applied. Its net effect in the short-term is still likely to be a substantial income transfer to the government.

23 The average annual growth rate for the period 1994–98 has been 3.4 per cent (see Table 4). The Second Plan's target average annual growth rate is 5.1 per cent compared to the First Plan's projected and realized rates of 8.1 per cent and 7.3 per cent respectively.

2

Economic Trends and Macroeconomic Policies in Post-Revolutionary Iran[1]

M. Hashem Pesaran

1. Introduction

Two decades have elapsed since the 1979 revolution and the establishment of the Islamic Republic of Iran. During this period the economy has been subject to a number of major upheavals, disruptions and shocks, both internal and external in nature. These include the initial effects of the disruptions due to the revolution itself, the eight-year war with Iraq, and the ongoing economic and financial embargoes by the United States and, on occasions, by some of the European economies. Also, volatile international crude oil prices, the uncertainties surrounding the conduct of monetary, foreign exchange and trade policies, with abrupt switches between fixed and floating exchange rate regimes, open and closed foreign-trade policies, and private-owned and government-controlled enterprises also affected the situation. All these and many other factors have prevented the Iranian economy from exploiting its full potential. It failed to take full advantage of its unique geopolitical location, its abundant resources, and the new opportunities that have emerged in the world economy. These opportunities emerged as a result of rapid technological advances, the increasing globalization of the world economy, and the opening up of new markets in Eastern Europe and in Central Asia.

In this chapter we review some of the main trends in the Iranian economy over the past two decades and discuss the key economic policy issues that divide the reformist from the more conservative factions in Iran. In our analysis we primarily focus on economic factors. But this should not be taken to mean that we regard religious and other socio-political factors as of secondary importance. Clearly, there are complicated linkages and inter-actions between economic and non-economic factors which have to be taken into account. Although it may be worth bearing in mind that for a small open economy such as Iran, operating in an increasingly globalized world economic environment, the neglect of fundamental economic forces in favour of political vested interests can have dire consequences in the long run.

2. Main Economic Trends – The First Decade

The ending of the Iran–Iraq war in August 1988 signalled the beginning of a new phase in the development of the Iranian economy, and presented Mr Rafsanjani's newly elected government with an important opportunity to regenerate the Iranian economy, and to reverse the deteriorating trends of the previous decade. Over the period 1978–88, the real output and investment fell by average annual rates of 1.8 per cent and 6.6 per cent respectively, while the total real consumption expenditures had remained largely stagnant, with population growing at around 3.2 per cent to 3.9 per cent per annum.[2] Allowing for the population growth, one obtains annual average rates of decline of 4.2 per cent, 9.7 per cent, and 3.6 per cent for per capita output, investment and consumption expenditures, respectively. (Historical trends in these economic aggregates are displayed in Figures 1 and 2, covering the period 1961/62–1996/97. Figure 1 gives the per capita values, while the growth rates are presented in Figure 2.)[3] As a result the share of investment in aggregate output declined substantially from 22.2 per cent in 1978/79 to 10.8 per cent in 1988/89, while over the same period the share of consumption in aggregate output in fact rose from 66.0 per cent to 71.1 per cent, largely reflecting the populist economic policies of the regime.[4]

The unprecedented falls in output and investment were accompanied by a widening gap between the official and the black (or 'free') market exchange rates, and rapidly rising prices. See Figure 4 and 5.[5] Over the period 1978/79–1988/89 the exchange rate premium (defined as the ratio of the free to the official rate) rose by an average annual rate of 19.1 per cent, the Retail Price Index (RPI) rose by an average annual rate of 18.2 per cent and the money supply (the M_2 measure) by an average annual rate of 20.3 per cent.

Figure 1: Per Capita Output, Consumption and Investment in Iran

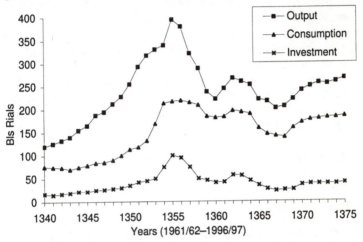

Figure 2: Growth Rates of Per Capita Output, Consumption and Investment in Iran

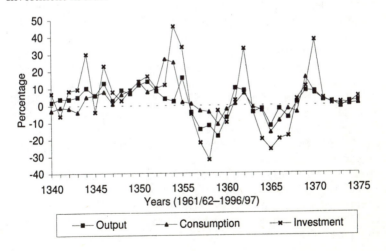

These adverse economic conditions (an acute form of 'stagflation') were due largely to the revolutionary upheavals and their aftermath already alluded to in the introduction. But they were further exacerbated by the regime's foreign policy adventurism with its adverse consequences for Iran's access to international capital markets, extensive nationalization of the entrepreneurial and the banking system, continued uncertainties over property rights and the role of the private sector in the economy, centralized and inward-looking government policies aimed at maintaining a highly over-valued official exchange rate through import compression, foreign exchange restrictions and generally interventionist economic policies with far reaching implications for resource allocation, particularly in the financial and industrial sectors. The result had been an economy in a state of acute disequilibrium with highly distorted prices signals. It was clear that the economic policies of the previous decade could not be continued, and a new approach to the management of the economy was needed.[6]

3. The Post-war Period of Economic Planning and Reconstruction

The First Five-Year Economic, Social and Cultural Plan, covering the period 1989/90 to 1993/94, represented the regime's manifesto for the reconstruction of the economy, and provided an important framework within which the government's reform and liberalization policies could be implemented. The primary aim of the plan was to regenerate the economy, carry out the reconstruction of the war-damaged regions, promote private investment, and initiate a reform and liberalization programme aimed at foreign exchange and trade policies. The plan's overall target was to achieve an average annual growth of 8.1 per cent in real GDP, 11.6 per cent in real investment, and an average annual growth of 5.7 per cent in real private consumer expenditures, seen to be rather ambitious at the time. Another important quantitative objective of the plan was to stabilize the economy's rate of monetary expansion to an average annual rate of 9.4 per cent and reduce the rate of inflation from 28.9 per cent in 1988/89 to an average annual rate of 15.7 per cent over the duration of the plan.[7]

However, the most significant aspect of the First Plan was in the area of foreign exchange and trade liberalization policies, attempting to reverse the autarchic and failed economic policies of the previous decade.

The breakdown of the plan's growth objectives by the main sectors of the economy, together with the associated realized growth rates, are given in Table 1. Under the plan, real output increased by an average annual rate of around 7.3 per cent, which is only slightly below the plan's overall target (at 8.1 per cent).

Table 1: Planned and Actual Sectoral Output Growths During the First Five-Year Plan (percentage)

Sectors	1989/90 (1368)		1990/91 (1369)		1991/92 (1370)	
	Plan	Actual	Plan	Actual	Plan	Actual
Agriculture	4.2	3.7	4.6	8.1	6.1	5.1
Oil	21.4	7.7	9.6	19.9	3.4	11.1
Industries and Mines	14.8	6.6	15.2	13.4	14.6	17.2
Water, Gas and Electricity	6.5	11.0	7.0	19.4	11.7	15.5
Construction	29.0	-1.7	15.7	2.9	12.4	16.0
Services	5.1	1.8	7.1	9.7	7.2	9.9
Gross Domestic Product (GDP)	7.9	4.2	9.2	11.5	6.8	10.1

Table 1: (continued)

Sectors	1992/93 (1371)		1993/94 (1372)		1989/90–1993/4 Average Growth	
	Plan	Actual	Plan	Actual	Plan	Actual
Agriculture	7.1	7.4	8.5	5.5	6.1	5.9
Oil	11.3	2.1	3.0	3.6	9.5	8.9
Industries and Mines	16.4	4.7	13.8	1.3	15.0	8.7
Water, Gas and Electricity	5.3	8.5	47.8	9.4	9.1	12.7
Construction	10.0	7.9	6.5	2.4	14.7	5.5
Services	7.0	8.0	7.1	7.5	6.7	7.4
GDP	8.5	6.0	8.4	4.8	8.1	7.3

Source: *Bank Markazi Jomhuri Islami Iran.* Actual figures are based on gross domestic product at factor cost in constant 1982/83 (1361) prices. The planned growth rates are from Iran Centre for Statistics, Plan and Budget Organization, *The First Five-Year Plan.*

The situation is different, however, when one considers the growth performance of individual sectors in particular years. For example, while actual average growth rates under the plan for the agriculture, oil and service sectors are generally in line with those envisaged in the plan, the same is not true of the other, mainly industrial and construction, sectors. The average annual growth rates of value added in industries and mines and in construction were below their target values by 6.3 per cent and 9.2 per cent respectively, while the growth of value added in the water, electricity and gas sectors (at 12.7 per cent) exceeded the plan's target by 3.6 per cent. These discrepancies, perhaps not surprisingly, were even more pronounced in the case of the growth rates in particular years. The actual growth rates exceeded the target rates over the years 1990/91 and 1991/92, and then significantly fell short of the planned rates over the last two years of the plan.

The high growth achieved during the first half of the plan largely reflected the initial effects of the trade and foreign exchange liberalization and the utilization of unused capacity in the economy, and was accompanied by an unprecedented surge in private consumption expenditures. With the removal of trade and foreign exchange restrictions, the private consumption expenditures at constant prices, which had shown only a modest growth of around 2.5 per cent in 1989/90, grew by the staggering rates of 19.5 per cent and 9.5 per cent over the years 1990/91 and 1991/92 respectively, followed by more moderate rates of 5.1 per cent and 2.6 per cent for the last two years of the plan. (See Table 2 and Figure 2). The huge increases in real private consumption expenditures during the years immediately following the Iran–Iraq war can be explained, at least partly, in relation to the pent up demand created over the war years. However, the government failure to moderate the rate of consumption growth during 1990/92 played a significant role in bringing about the exchange rate crisis that in fact followed. (See below for more details).

A similar pattern can also be seen in investment growth. Over the years 1990/91 and 1991/92 gross fixed capital formation at constant prices rose by 13.3 per cent and 40.9 per cent respectively, while during the last two years of the plan real investment grew by 7.1 per cent in 1992/93 and by only 2.7 per cent in 1993/94.[8] Over the course of the plan real private consumption expenditures rose by an average annual rate of 8.3 per cent which is well in excess of the plan's average annual target of 5.7 per cent.

In contrast, the average growth of real investment was in line with the plan's target, although once again there are important discrepancies between the actual and planned investment growth over the different years of the plan. Public sector consumption expenditures at constant prices also grew very much in line with their target values, and averaged to around 4.0 per cent as compared to the planned figure of 3.8 per cent. (See Table 2).

The high growth of output and the excessively high private consumption growth during the first three years of the plan were primarily achieved through increased utilization of existing capacities and increased imports, particularly final consumer goods imports. The imports of goods and services rose from 13.5 billion dollars in 1989/90 to around $25 billion in 1991/92. (See Table 3.) Given Iran's limited capacity to export, these high levels of imports could not be sustained and led to a substantial deterioration of the country's external current account, creating major difficulties for the government in meeting the repayment of the country's foreign debt, estimated to have been around $23.2 billion at the end of 1993/94.[9] Ordinarily, this amount of foreign indebtedness for a major oil producing country such as Iran would not have been a real problem. But in view of US economic embargoes and the inability of international organizations such as the IMF and the World Bank to help (again due to the threat of US vetoes) and the fact that as much as 76.1 per cent of the $23.2 billion were in the form of short term debts, it appears that the Iranian authorities were left with no choice but to make a U-turn; reverting back to the 'closed door' policies of trade restrictions and foreign exchange controls.

We shall discuss this policy reversal and its likely consequences for the future development of the Iranian economy later. But first we need to consider the evolution of the monetary sector and its relationship to the real economy.

4. Monetary Growth and Inflation

In addition to output, consumption and investment targets, the First Plan also stipulated upper bounds on the average rate of monetary growth and the inflation rate. The plan was to limit the rate of expansion of the total private sector liquidity (namely the M_2 measure of money supply) to an average annual rate of 9.4 per cent, and the rate of increase of the index of retail prices to an average annual rate of 15.7 per cent.[10] However, as can be seen from Table 5, money supply (the M_2 measure) grew by an average annual rate of 25.2 per cent, thus substantially exceeding the plan's target. The M_1 measure of money supply grew slightly less at around 23.8 per cent, mainly reflecting the move from cash and non-interest bearing deposits to term-investment deposits paying returns of between 7 to 15 per cent per annum. The Retail Price Index rose by an average annual rate of 18.7 per cent during the plan, which was much closer to the plan's target of 15.7 per cent.[11] However, it is important to note that due to direct and indirect government subsidies on essential food stuffs, energy and transportation, the index of retail prices does not fully reflect the extent of inflationary pressures that have been present in the economy over the past five years. A more appropriate overall measure of inflation is the rate of change of the implicit deflator of the Gross Domestic Product. According to this measure the average rate of inflation over the plan has been around 25.3 per cent, which is substantially higher than the rate of increase in the Retail Price Index.[12] This discrepancy is, however, of a short-term nature and largely reflects the time delays involved in the transmission of inflationary pressures to the final goods prices, and the fact that, with the substantial depreciation of the exchange rate, the level of government subsidies (direct and indirect) on consumer goods has been rising; largely neutralizing the adverse effects of the devaluation on a number of essential commodities such as bread, fuel, water and electricity.[13] But one would expect that in the long-run most of the excess of the inflation in the implicit GDP price deflator over the inflation in the Retail Price Index to show itself in a higher rate of increase in the level of consumer prices in the future. In fact, historically, the average rate of increase of the three main general price indices, namely the Retail Price Index, the wholesale price index and the implicit price deflator of GDP, have all been of the same order of magnitude. For example, the averages of these indices (per cent per annum) over the pre- and post-revolution periods have been as follows:

Different Measures of Inflation across Different Sub-Periods

	1959/60–1978/79	1979/80–1996/97	1959/60–1996/97
Retail Prices	6.5	21.8	14.1
Wholesale Prices	5.7	24.4	15.1
GDP Deflator	7.9	21.3	14.6

Source: Bank Markazi Jomhuri Islami Iran, *Annual Reports*, various issues.

Table 2: Planned and Actual Growth of Real Investment and Consumption Expenditures during the First Five-Year Plan (percentage)

Years	Gross Fixed Capital Formation		Private Consumption Expenditures		Public Consumption Expenditure	
	Plan	Actual	Plan	Actual	Plan	Actual
1989/90 (1368)	26.4	6.4	2.6	2.5	-4.1	-14.8
1990/1 (1369)	31.9	13.3	4.7	19.5	9.0	12.4
1991/2 (1370)	2.9	40.9	6.7	9.5	2.8	8.5
1992/3 (1371)	-0.2	7.1	7.3	5.4	5.2	7.0
1993/4 (1372)	1.2	2.7	7.6	4.6	6.7	17.3
Average Growth during First Plan (1989/90–1993/4)	11.6	14.1	5.7	8.3	3.8	4.0
1994/5 (1373)	6.2	3.4	4.0	2.2	-0.9	4.3
1995/6 (1374)	6.2	3.2	4.0	2.6	-0.9	3.0
1996/7 (1375)	6.2	7.4	4.0	3.1	-0.9	6.0

Sources: Actual growth rates are from the Bank Markazi Jomhuri Islami Iran, and are computed from the national income statistics at constant 1982/1983 (1361) prices. The figures for the years 1993/94–1996/97 are taken from *Economic Trends*, Third Quarter 1997, Bank Markazi. The figures for 1996/97 are preliminary. The planned growth rates are from Iran Centre for Statistics, Plan and Budget Organization, *The First Five-Year Plan*.

Table 3: Balance of Payments (million US dollars)

	1988/89 (1367)	1989/90 (1368)	1990/91 (1369)	1991/92 (1370)	1992/93 (1371)	1993/94 (1372)	1994/95 (1373)	1995/96 (1374)	1996/97 (1375)
Trade Balance	101	-367	975	-6,529	-3,406	-1,207	6,817	5,586	7,402
Exports	10,709	13,081	19,305	18,661	19,868	18,080	19,434	18,360	22,391
Oil and Gas	(9,673)	(12,037)	(17,993)	(16,012)	(16,880)	(14,333)	(14,603)	(15,103)	(19,271)
Others	(1,036)	(1,044)	(1,312)	(2,649)	(2,988)	(3,747)	(4,831)	(3,257)	(3,120)
Imports (FOB)	-10,608	-13,448	-18,330	-25,190	-23,274	-19,287	-12,617	-12,774	-14,989
Services	-1,970	-2,324	-3,148	-4,919	-5,094	-4,508	-3,059	-2,224	-2,633
Receipts	467	798	892	881	846	–	–	–	–
Payments	-2,437	-3,122	-4,040	-5,800	-5,940	–	–	–	–
Transfers	–	2,500	2,500	2,000	1,996	1,500	1,198	-4	463
Current Balance	-1,869	-191	327	-9,448	-6,504	-4,215	4,956	3,358	5,232

Sources: *Annual Reviews*, 1991/92 (1370) and 1992/93 (1371), and *Economic Trends*, Economic Research Department, 1997. Bank Markazi Jomhuri Islami Iran.

Table 4: Iran's External Debt*
(Million dollars, End of the Period)

	Short-Term	Medium- and Long-Term	Total	Changes in International Reserves
1992/93 (1371)	–	–	–	-166
1993/94 (1372)	17,616	5,542	23,158	232
1994/95 (1373)	6,707	16,030	22,737	921
1995/96 (1374)	4,536	17,392	21,928	2,868
1996/97 (1375)	4,557	12,278	16,835	2,346
1997/98 (1376) (first nine months)	2,883	9,680	12,563	-2,967

*Source: *Economic Trends*, Bank Markazi Jomhuri Islami Iran, No. 10, 1997.
The figures in this table exclude contingent claims, opened letters of credit not yet consigned and future interest payments.
Total external obligations (actual and contingent) amount to $24.5 billion at the end of December 1997 (Azar, 1376).

The plan's overall monetary growth target of 9.4 per cent per annum has clearly been out of line with economic realities. But, more importantly, it has not even been consistent with the plan's own inflation target of 15.7 per cent per annum. In a developing economy such as Iran, one would expect the money supply growth to exceed the inflation rate and not vice versa. This is confirmed by the price and money supply rate given in Table 5. Over the period 1979/80–1996/97, the average annual growth of money supply exceeded the growth of retail prices by 2.2 per cent, and that of the GDP price deflator by 2.7 per cent. A similar result also follows if attention is confined to the period after the revolution and before the start of the First Plan. Over the period 1979/80–1988/89, money supply (M_2) and the index of retail prices grew by average annual rates of 20.1 per cent and 19.0 per cent, respectively. The smaller rate of increase in the real money balances (the difference between the money supply growth and the inflation rate) over this period is largely explained by the negative output growth experienced at that time (see Table 5).

4.1 Determinants of Money Demand in Pre- and Post-Revolutionary Periods

It is, however, important to note that the revolution seems to have significantly affected the relationship between money supply growth, output and inflation which could have important consequences both for the efficacy of monetary policy in relation to the control of inflation, and for the economy's future financial development.

Using annual observations we estimated autoregressive distributed lag (ARDL) models in real per capita money balances, per capita output and inflation over the (pre-revolution) period 1960/61–1978/79. The lag orders of the ARDL (q_1,q_2,q_3) model were selected according to the Schwarz Information Criterion using the automatic lag-order selection procedure in *Microfit 4.0*. Given the few observations available for estimation we set the maximum lag order of the various variables in the model equal to unity.[14]

$$\log(M_2/P)_t = -\underset{(0.346)}{2.36} + \underset{(0.069)}{0.576}\log(M_2/P)_{t-1} + \underset{(0.098)}{0.441} + \log y_t + \underset{(0.130)}{0.344}\log y_{t-1}$$

$$-\underset{(0.072)}{0.725}\Pi_t + \hat{\varepsilon}_{1t}, \tag{1}$$

$$\overline{R}_v^2 = 0.888;\ \chi_{sc}^2(1) = 4.25;\ \chi_F^2(1) = 0.01;\ \chi_N^2(2) = 0.15;\ \chi_H^2(1) = 2.27,$$

where M_{2t} is the per capita broad definition of money, P_t is the implicit price deflator of GDP at market prices, y_t is the per capita real GDP measured at constant 1982/83 (1361) market prices, $\Pi_t = \Delta\log(P_t)$ is the rate of price inflation used as a proxy for the nominal interest rate, and $\hat{\varepsilon}_{1t}$ is the residual. The standard errors of the estimates are given in brackets, $\overline{R}_v^2$ is the adjusted squared multiple correlation coefficient computed for changes in $\log(M_2/P)_t$, $\chi_{sc}^2(1), \chi_{FF}^2(1), \chi_N^2(2)$, and χ_H^2, are Lagrange multiplier statistics for tests of residual serial correlation, functional form mis-specification, non-normal errors and heteroskedasticity, respectively. These statistics are distributed as Chi-squared variates with degrees of freedom in brackets.[15]

The regression passes all the diagnostic tests, although there is some evidence of residual serial correlation at the 5 per cent significance level but not at the 10 per cent level. All the estimated coefficients have the expected signs and are statistically significant. Furthermore, they imply a long run income elasticity of demand for money of around 1.85 (0.067), and a long run inflation (interest rate) elasticity of -1.71 (0.289).[16] These estimates are robust to the possibility of unit roots in real money balances, output and inflation and yield the following error correction specification:[17]

$$\Delta\log(M_2/P)_t = -\underset{(0.069)}{0.424}EC_{t-1} + \underset{(0.098)}{0.441}\Delta\log y_t - \underset{(0.072)}{0.725}\Delta\Pi_t + \hat{\varepsilon}_{1t}, \tag{2}$$

where the error correction term Ec_{t-1} is defined by

$$EC_{t-1} = \log(M_2/P)_{t-1} - \underset{(0.067)}{1.85}y_t + \underset{(0.289)}{1.711}\Pi_t + \underset{(0.326)}{5.56}.$$

Applying the same estimation procedure to the data over the period after the revolution (namely 1979/80–1996/97) we obtained the following estimates based on a slightly simpler ARDL (1,0,0) model:

$$\log(M_2/P)_t = -\underset{(0.961)}{0.590} + \underset{(0.137)}{0.735}\log(M_2/P)_{t-1} + \underset{(0.114)}{0.141}\log y_t$$
$$- \underset{(0.162)}{0.295}\Pi_t + \hat{\varepsilon}_{2t}, \tag{3}$$

$$\overline{R}_v^2 = 0.190; \chi_{sc}^2(1) = 0.01; \chi_F^2(1) = 0.03; \chi_N^2(2) = 0.25; \chi_H^2(1) = 1.56.$$

Once again the regression passes all the diagnostic tests even more readily than the one estimated over the pre-revolutionary period.

However, apart from the coefficient of the lagged money variable, $\log (M_2/P)_{t-1}$, none of the other estimates are statistically significant at the 5 per cent level. The short run output and inflation elasticities are now estimated to be around 0.141 (0.114) and -0.295 (0.162), as compared to 0.441 (0.098) and -0.725 (0.072) obtained using the time series observations from the pre-revolutionary period. The post revolution estimates are much smaller (in absolute values) and less precisely estimated. The same also applies to the long run estimates. The long run output and inflation elasticities for the post revolution period are estimated to be 0.532 (0.526) and -1.111 (0.720), which are smaller in magnitude and are much less precisely estimated. Finally, the error correction specification of the money demand equation for the post 1978/79 period is given

$$\Delta \log(M_2/P)_t = \underset{(0.137)}{-0.265} EC_{t-1} + \underset{(0.114)}{0.141} \Delta \log y_t - \underset{(0.162)}{0.295} \Delta \Pi_t + \hat{\varepsilon}_{1t}, \qquad (4)$$

where the error correction term EC_{t-1} is defined by

$$EC_{t-1} = \log(M_2/P)_{t-1} - \underset{(0.526)}{0.532} y_t + \underset{(0.720)}{1.111} \Pi_t + \underset{(2.844)}{2.222}$$

The above estimates show clear evidence of a structural break in the money demand equation. They suggest a rapid adjustment of real money balances to money market disequilibria during the period before the revolution, but not after. Also the long run output elasticity of demand for money is estimated to be substantially higher during the pre- as compared to the post-revolutionary period. This finding is in line with the strong trends in financial deepening during the period before the revolution. In fact as can be seen from Figure 5, the indices of financial deepening, measured as the ratios of money to income, have been rising steadily during the period 1960/61–1978/79, while an opposite trend is in evidence when the period after the revolution is considered. In fact the ratio of M_2 to nominal GDP in 1996/97 was almost the same as it had been in 1978/79. The low output elasticity of money demand and the declining trend in money-output ratio over the past two decades are likely to have undesirable consequences for the country's growth potential and the ability of monetary authorities to harness inflationary pressures through money supply controls.[18]

In the regressions for both sub-periods the inflation variable has the correct sign, indicating that a rise in inflation has the desired dampening effect on the demand for real money balances.

But once again the quantitative effect of inflation on demand for real money balances seems to have declined substantially after the revolution. Consequently, the same rates of expansion in private and public sectors liquidity are likely to have more inflationary consequences after than before the revolution. This point can also be clearly seen in Figure 6 (and Table 5) where there is a much closer association between growth of money supply and inflation over the post-revolutionary period as compared to that which existed before the revolution. As a result, relatively more stringent restrictions on credit expansion are required if the authorities are to succeed in controlling inflation.[19]

4.2 Determinants of Money Supply Growth

The factors contributing to the growth of the private sector liquidity are, however, highly complex and in the case of Iran involve an important political dimension. Given the rather under-developed nature of the capital and bond markets in Iran, almost all financing needs of the public and the private sectors are met through the banking system. Therefore, the expansion of credit to the private and the public sectors is among the most important driving forces behind money supply growth, and hence inflation.[20] The annual rates of change of the private and the public sector indebtedness to the banking system are given in Table 5. Over the post-revolution period the indebtedness of the private and the public sectors to the banking system has increased by average annual rates of 24.6 per cent and 20.7 per cent respectively, as compared to an average annual rate of 23.8 per cent for the money supply growth. Using a simple regression of money supply growth on the growth of the public and private sector indebtedness to the banking system (estimated over the period 1979/80–1996/97) we obtained:

$$\Delta\log(M_{2t}) = \underset{(0.034)}{0.045} + \underset{(0.129)}{0.487}\,\Delta\log(PRCR_t) + \underset{(0.091)}{0.360}\,\Delta\log(PUBCR_t) + \hat{\varepsilon}_{3t}, \qquad (5)$$

$$\overline{R}^2 = 0.600; \chi^2_{SC}(1) = 0.133; \chi^2_F(1) = 6.10; \chi^2_N = 0.81; \chi^2_H(1) = 2.52,$$

where $\Delta\log(PRCR_t)$ and $\Delta\log(PUBCR_t)$ represent the growth rates of private and public sector indebtedness to the banking system, respectively. We did try a dynamic (ARDL) specification first, but did not find any statistically significant dynamic effects between private and public credit expansions and the money supply growth.[21] Changes in private and public sector credits tend to be fully reflected in money supply growths within the same year. The above regression also demonstrates that both sources of credit expansions are almost equally responsible for monetary expansion. Although the point estimate of the elasticity of money supply to private sector credit (0.487) is slightly larger than that of the public sector credit (0.360), the hypothesis that the two elasticities are the same cannot be rejected.[22] In principle there could also be feedbacks from increases in money supply to credit expansions. But in the case of post-revolutionary Iran, where credits to the private and public sectors are strictly regulated, it is not the availability of funds (through increases in money and quasi-money) that determine credits, but rather the political resolve of the government and the Bank Markazi which determine the growth of credits and hence money supply growth. The situation could have been different if a more active and timely interest policy had been followed in Iran.

A closer examination of the annual growth rates in Table 5 also reveals a highly uneven expansion of credits to the private and public sectors. The rate of growth of private sector credit peaked in 1991/92, while the growth in public sector credit was successfully controlled at around 9.6 to 12.8 per cent over the first four years of the plan, but shot up to 60.7 per cent in 1993/94. This uneven pattern is closely related to the pace and timing of government liberalization and exchange rate unification policy. The substantial increase in private sector credit of around 39 per cent in 1991/92 was a direct consequence of the removal of the credit ceilings and the application of the floating exchange rate to a wider class of private sector imports. The effect of the exchange rate depreciation on public sector borrowing requirements did not, however, become fully transparent due to substantial increases in government's rial revenues from the sale of foreign exchange at preferential rates in the free market.[23] But such increases in government revenues are short-lived and can only be maintained by a continual process of exchange rate depreciation, which is clearly undesirable as well as being ineffective in the long run.

4.3 Control of Inflation: Economic and Political Considerations

The money demand and supply equations estimated over the post revolution period (namely equations (3) and (5), have two important features: (i) the response of money demand to output seems to have become very much muted after the revolution, and (ii) money supply growth is largely determined by the growth of private and public sector credits. Therefore, to control inflation, the Bank Markazi must be able to control the economy's rate of credit expansion, a task complicated by political factors and the Bank's apparent inability to raise deposit or expected profits rates above the prevailing (or expected) rates of inflation. The Keynesian policy of creating output slacks to reduce inflation is also unlikely to be effective in the longer run, unless of course it is accompanied by appropriate credit and interest rate policies.

In the final analysis the main causes of the excessive monetary expansion and inflation have to be found in the government's unwillingness to oppose the credit demands of politically powerful groups (both inside and outside the government). In Iran these political considerations are more critical for the conduct of monetary and credit policies both because of the size and political importance of the semi-public enterprises, and the relatively non-responsive nature of interest rates to changes in the economy's inflationary environment. The large state subsidies on essential food items, fuel and public services also present the government with further political problems:[24] the reduction of public sector indebtedness through the elimination or substantial cuts in subsidies will be difficult politically and in the short run will most likely result in higher rather than lower rates of inflation. The anti-inflationary effect of reduced subsidies will materialize in the longer run as the higher relative prices of subsidized commodities start to reduce their consumption, and only if the government (in conjunction with the Bank Markazi) is able to reduce the rate of growth of credits in the economy.

The rates paid on bank (term-investment) deposits have changed little in comparison to high and rising rates of inflation.[25] As Tables 5 and 6 show over the period 1992/93–1996/97, the deposit rates have ranged between 7.5 per cent (on short-term deposits) to 18.5 per cent (on five-year investment deposits), while the average inflation rate (the RPI measure) over this period has been well in excess of 30 per cent per annum, thus yielding negative *ex post* real rate of returns of between 12 per cent and 22 per cent per annum. This degree of 'financial repression' inevitably has undesirable implications. It discourages the mobilization of domestic savings, promotes the development of an unofficial (curb) money market that lies outside the control of monetary authorities, increases capital flights, promotes speculative activities in land, real estate and foreign currencies, and generally retards financial development with possible adverse consequences for the country's growth potential. (See also below).

The Bank's lending rates were also well below the rate of inflation and over the period 1991/92–1996/97 ranged between 9 per cent to 18 per cent for productive activities and exports, and were only marginally higher (between 18 per cent and 25 per cent) for trade and services, as compared to an average annual rate of inflation of around 30 per cent over the same period. The inevitable consequence of such low lending rates is excess demand for bank credits and credit rationing, with undesirable rent seeking implications. The rent seeking aspects of credit rationing can be particularly troublesome in the case of semi-public corporations (such as the enterprises under the auspices of the Foundation for the Oppressed). The semi-public (semi-private) nature of these enterprises, and their ready access to centres of political power in the country, weakens the political resolve of the banking system in their efforts to control the level of bank credits, and tends to alter the composition of credits in favour of the foundations and the public sector.[26]

Even when 'investment' deposit and bank 'profit' rates are increased in response to rising inflation, there is a clear tendency for these increases to be too little and too late. As a consequence, the relationship between the real interest rate and inflation has become perverse with real interest rates becoming more negative when inflation has been rising and less negative when the inflation rate has been falling! For market forces to have an equilibrating effect on money and credit markets, real interest rates need to rise when inflation is rising and not the reverse. Otherwise, excess demand for credits will increase even further; thus making the task of credit control that much harder and politically more vulnerable.

Prolonged periods of negative real interest rates have also had adverse consequences for the country's financial development. As can be seen in Figure 5, the ratio of broad money to output (M_2/Y), often used in the literature as an index of financial development, shows a strong downward trend during most of the two decades after the revolution.[27] Such a downward trend in money-income ratio can have important adverse consequences for investment and growth in the long run. In fact, one of the key objectives of the Second Five-Year Development Plan has been to

'... set rates at levels that would ensure positive real return on bank deposits.'[28] Clearly this objective is far from being met. The Iranian financial system is in need of major reforms if it is to achieve the dual objectives of price stability and financial development. The abolition of credit ceilings and other restrictions on bank credits would be desirable and effective only if accompanied by deposits and bank profit (lending) rates that are responsive to market forces and fully reflect the inflationary expectations that are present in the economy. An effective policy of financial liberalization also requires a competitive banking system where the lending policies of the banks are based on commercial considerations rather than on political factors. Such reforms should also take account of the developments in foreign exchange markets and the complicated interactions that exist between monetary and foreign exchange policies.

5. Foreign Exchange and Trade Policies

5.1 Background
One of the major objectives of the First Five-Year Plan was to rationalize the foreign exchange market, promote non-oil exports and achieve a more efficient allocation of foreign exchange resources. Rigid adherence to a fixed official exchange rate during most of the 1980s, when the economy had been subject to a number of large negative shocks accompanied by relatively high domestic inflationary pressures, had resulted in a highly overvalued currency. The observation of the official exchange rate became particularly serious over the latter half of the 1980s, and led to substantial premiums on the black market rate. The premium rose from 200–300 per cent in the early 1980s to 500–600 per cent by the mid-1980s and then reached phenomenal rates of over 2000 per cent by 1989. The existence of these enormous premiums introduced gross distortions in relative prices, encouraged rent-seeking at the expense of productive activities, and masked large government subsidies to consumers and producers with easy access to the country's foreign exchange earnings at the official rate.[29] With income from oil exports dwindling and import requirements rising, particularly during the initial years of the plan, rationalization of the foreign exchange market became a top economic priority.

Figure 3: Investment-Output Ratio in Iran

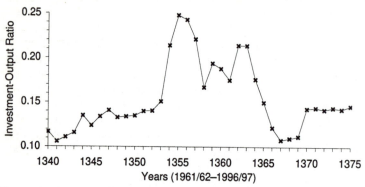

Figure 4: 'Free' Market and Official Rate of Exchange in Iran

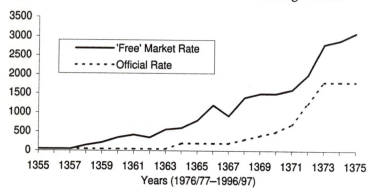

Figure 5: Money Supply Growth (M$_2$) and Inflation (RPI) in Iran

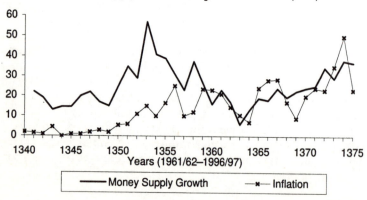

Figure 6: Indices of Financial Development in Iran

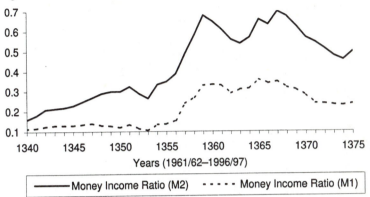

Years (1961/62–1996/97)

———— Money Income Ratio (M2) · · · · · Money Income Ratio (M1)

In 1988/89, Iran's total foreign exchange receipts from goods exports at current prices amounted to $10.7 billion, which was less than half of Iran's foreign exchange receipts before the revolution. The fall in the country's foreign exchange revenues would be even more pronounced if one allowed for increases in import prices over the period and Iran's rising population. Per capita foreign exchange revenues from oil exports measured in constant 1990 dollar prices shrunk from $842 in 1978/79 to $160 in 1988/89, namely less than one-fifth of its value before the revolution.[30] Nevertheless, exports of oil and gas still accounted for the bulk of the foreign exchange receipts, with non-oil exports amounting to around 1 billion dollars (see Table 3). Furthermore, it was not expected that oil exports could be expanded significantly, due to limited production capacities and the rapidly rising domestic oil consumption, largely brought about by artificially low, and in real terms declining, domestic energy prices. The oil production and oil export targets envisaged in the plan have all been met. Under the plan oil exports were to rise from around 1.99 million barrels per day (b/d) in 1989/90 to 2.29 million b/d in 1993/94. As it turned out, oil exports rose from 1.82 million b/d in 1989/90 to 2.40 million barrels in 1992/93, thus over-shooting the plan's target (see Table 7). However, due to lower than expected prices of oil exports over the last three years of the plan, foreign exchange receipts from oil and gas exports have fallen short of their targets. This shortfall amounted to 25 per cent for 1993/94, though for the whole plan period it was only 7 per cent.[31]

Table 5: Trends in Monetary Aggregates and Inflation in Iran
(Rate of change, per cent)

Year	Money (M₁)	Money and Quasi-Money (M₂)	Private Sector Credit[1]	Public Sector Credit[2]	Retail Price Index	GDP Price Deflator[3]
1979/80 (1358)	34.7	37.7	17.2	44.2	11.4	27.0
1980/81 (1359)	32.3	27.0	18.8	60.3	23.5	23.4
1981/82 (1360)	22.9	16.2	5.2	26.6	22.8	24.5
1982/83 (1361)	28.7	22.8	8.2	23.9	20.3	14.6
1983/84 (1362)	11.1	16.9	22.1	18.0	14.8	12.3
1984/85 (1363)	17.8	6.0	5.7	14.9	10.4	10.1
1985/86 (1364)	8.1	13.0	12.9	8.3	6.9	4.7
1986/87 (1365)	18.1	19.1	9.8	23.6	23.7	13.2
1987/88 (1366)	16.6	18.1	13.8	16.7	27.7	22.9
1988/89 (1367)	14.5	23.8	17.8	20.2	28.9	17.0
1989/90* (1368)	15.8	19.5	29.7	10.8	17.4	19.3
1990/91* (1369)	24.6	22.5	35.7	9.6	9.0	18.6
1991/92* (1370)	21.8	24.6	39.1	9.7	19.6	23.6
1992/93* (1371)	20.0	25.3	28.9	12.8	24.4	25.4
1993/94* (1372)	36.9	34.2	29.9	60.7	22.9	38.6
1994/95 (1373)	35.8	28.5	23.4	27.6	35.2	36.1
1995/96 (1374)	34.6	37.6	24.4	34.8	49.4	33.8
1996/97 (1375)	37.4	37.0	30.9	19.7	23.2	22.8
Average (1358–75)	24.0	24.0	24.6	20.7	21.8	21.3

Sources: Bank Markazi Jomhuri Islami Iran, various publications.
1. Private sector debt to the banking system.
2. Public sector debt to the banking system.
3. Implicit price deflator of Gross Domestic product at market prices, base year 1982/83 (1361).
The years of the First Five-Year Plan are shown with an *.

Table 6: Bank Profit (Interest) Rates in Iran
(per cent, per annum)

	Term-Investment Deposit Rates				
	Short-term	One-year	Two-year	Three-year	Five-year
1992/93 (1371)	7.5	10	11.5	13	15
1993/94 (1372)	8	11.5	13.5	14.5	16
1994/95 (1373)	8	11.5	13.5	14.5	16
1995/96 (1374)	8	14	15	16	18.5
1996/97 (1375)	8	14	15	16	18.5

Table 6: (continued)

	Expected Rate of Profit on Facilities				
	Manufacturing and Mining	Construction and Housing	Agriculture	Trade and Services	Export
1992/93 (1371)	13	12–16	9	18 & over	18 & over
1993/94 (1372)	16.8	12–16	12–16	18–24	18
1994/95 (1373)	16–18	15	12–16	19–24	18
1995/96 (1374)	17–19	15–16	13–16	22–25	18
1996/97 (1375)	17–19	15–16	13–16	22–25	18

Source: Bank Markazi Jomhuri Islami Iran, *Economic Trends*, Third Quarter 1376 (1997).

5.2 Attempted Reforms

Faced with the realities of capacity constraints on oil production and the vagaries of the international oil market, a large and increasing part of the plan's foreign exchange requirements had to be met from other sources, such as further increases in non-oil exports, a more efficient use of oil and gas revenues and foreign borrowing. Reform of the foreign trade and exchange system was therefore essential for a successful implementation of the plan. As a first step towards meeting this goal, in 1989/90 surrender requirements applicable to several non-oil exports were significantly reduced or eliminated, and a special 'service' exchange rate of Rls 845 = US$1 was introduced for certain payments by qualified individuals. The multitude of exchange rates were in effect replaced by three main rates: the 'official' rate (Rls 70 = US$1), primarily applicable to the foreign exchange transactions of the public sector, a 'competitive' rate for certain essential private sector imports, and a 'floating' rate for other approved private sector imports.[32] The proceeds from non-oil exports were allowed to be converted into rials at the preferential floating rate, an Export Development Bank for the promotion of non-oil exports was founded in 1991/92, barter agreements were cancelled with a number of countries in the old Soviet Bloc, obligation on incoming passengers to declare the importation of foreign exchange for the equivalent of $5,000 was removed, and out-going passengers were permitted to export foreign currency up to the equivalent of $10,000 per person, lists of goods to be imported at the 'competitive' and at the 'floating' rates were gradually extended.[33] Largely as a result of these policies, and the substantial increases in private and public sector credits,[34] imports of goods and services more than doubled between 1989/90 and 1991/92, rising from $13.5 billion to $25.2 billion (see Table 3). Non-oil exports also responded vigorously to the favourable new economic climate and rose steadily from $1 billion in 1988/89 to $3.7 billion in 1993/94. Despite these substantial increases in non-oil exports, because of stagnant oil and gas revenues, and in particular due to much higher than expected imports of goods and services, the current account of the balance of payments showed a deficit of $9.5 billion in 1991/92, followed by a further current account deficit of $6.5 billion in 1992/93, and 4.2 billion in 1993/94 (see Table 3). These deficits were substantial both in the context of the Iranian economy as well as in comparison with other economies. The ratios of current account deficits to GDP over these three years amount to 9.6 per cent, 6.7 per cent and 5.5 per cent respectively, if we use GDP estimates converted to US dollars at the official rate of exchange. Using the 'free' exchange rate to carry out the conversion we would obtain the substantially higher ratios of 28.9 per cent, 15.9 per cent and 8.9 per cent. These are much higher than the current deficits to GDP ratios experienced by the countries involved in the 1997 Asian currency crises. In 1996, the ratios of current account deficits to GDP for Thailand, Malaysia, the Philippines, Korea and Indonesia were 9.1 per cent, 5.9 per cent, 5.8 per cent, 4.9 per cent and 3.4 per cent respectively.[35]

5.3 External Debts and Currency Crisis

As a result of these large deficits Iran's external debt, which was almost non-existent at the end of the Iran–Iraq War, started to grow very rapidly and according to the official statistics amounted to \$23.2 billion by the end of 1993/94.[36] Furthermore, as much as 76 per cent of this amount was in the form of short-term (up to one year) debt, thus making the economy highly vulnerable to foreign exchange crises, particularly given the hostile international economic relations under which Iran operates. This level of dependence on short term capital inflows has been unprecedented in Iran's history and is also well above the level experienced by the countries involved in Asian currency crises. At the end of June 1997 the share of short term foreign liabilities of Thailand, Malaysia, Philippines, Korea and Indonesia stood at 65.7 per cent, 56.4 per cent, 58.8 per cent, 67.9 per cent and 59 per cent, respectively.[37]

In spite of these large and continued balance of payments deficits, and the clear evidence of the government's difficulties with external debt repayments, Bank Markazi decided to go ahead with the next stage of its exchange rate unification policy and in April 1993 announced that from then on all private and public foreign exchange transactions (except for about \$4 billion of government imports of essential commodities) would be conducted at a new 'floating' rate, to be determined daily on the basis of the balance of supply and demand for foreign currency. Initially, the policy proved to be quite effective and the gap between the new 'floating' rate used in bank transactions outside the banking system virtually disappeared. From April to September 1993 the two rates differed by less than 0.5 per cent. But with deficits on the balance of payments continuing, and evidence of the government's inability to meet its external debt mounting throughout, the two rates started to widen in late October 1993. In December 1994, the free market rate for one US dollar stood at 2,680 rials and was some 50 per cent higher than the so-called 'floating' rate, which was kept unchanged at its level of 1,750 rials per US dollar.[38] A new 'black' market for foreign exchange started to develop only a few months after the announced move towards the unification of the exchange rate system. The black market rate started to rise very rapidly, reaching 3,240 rials per US dollar in mid January 1995 and then climbing to 6,800 rials (albeit for a short time) in May 1995.

5.4 Imposition of Trade Restrictions and Foreign Exchange Controls

The rapidly unfolding foreign exchange crisis and the highly short-term nature of Iran's external debt, in conjunction with the country's limited access to international capital markets, left the government with no choice but to abandon the exchange rate unification and the foreign exchange and trade liberalization policies in favour of trade restrictions and foreign exchange controls. In May 1995 foreign exchange transactions outside the official network were announced 'illegal' and a dual exchange rate system was officially put into effect composed of:

i. an official rate, known as the 'floating' rate, was fixed at 1,750 rials per US dollar. This rate applies to oil and gas export receipts, imports of essential goods and services, and imports for use by large national projects, and
ii. an 'export' rate fixed at 3,000 rials per US dollar was announced for non-oil exports and all other official current account transactions not falling under the essential import proceeds for direct sales to the banking system at the 'export' rate.

Since 1995 other exchange rates have emerged. In order to promote non-oil exports, in July 1997 exporters were allowed to use the non-oil export proceeds to import certain goods from an approved list, or to receive 'import certificates' which could be traded on the Tehran Stock Exchange.[39] Initially the eligibility rate of non-oil export proceeds for importation purposes differed according to the type of exports (industrial, hand-woven or other categories). But from March 1998, 100 per cent of all non-oil export proceeds could be used for imports or to receive import certificates. As a result a new 'effective exchange rate for non-oil exports' came into effect which is equal to the sum of the 'export' rate and the 'import certificate' rate. Not surprisingly, alongside the above official rates an illegal 'black' market rate for foreign exchange, transactions outside the banking system have also come into existence.

5.5 The Aftermath

The abolition of the free market for foreign exchange, the pegging of the 'official' and the 'export' rates to the US dollar, and the imposition of strict controls on trade and capital flows combined with stringent credit controls, resulted in drastic cuts in imports. The level of goods imports decreased from an average annual figure of $22.6 billion over the period 1991/92–1993/94 to the level of $13.5 billion during the subsequent three years, or a fall of 67.8 per cent.[40] Thanks to rising oil prices foreign exchange revenues from oil exports rose significantly and amounted to $19.3 billion in 1996/97, an increase of around 32 per cent over the previous years.[41] Also, due to the continued favourable treatment of non-oil exports, proceeds from non-oil exports showed only moderate declines during 1995/96–1996/97. As a result, the balance of payments on current accounts showed large surpluses during 1994/95–1996/97, and Iran's external debt declined steadily from $16.8 billion at the end of 1996/97 (see Table 4). Naturally, most debt repayments were those with short term maturity, thus reducing the proportion of short term debts in Iran's total foreign liabilities from 76.1 per cent at the end of 1993/94 to 27.1 per cent at the end of 1996/97.

The drastic cuts in imports and the continued uncertainties over exchange rate policies affected prices adversely and the rate of price inflation (the RPI measure) jumped from 22.9 per cent in 1993/94 to 35.2 per cent in 1994/95 and then to 49.4 per cent in 1995/96. But the stabilization of the currency markets and, more importantly, the stringent control of private and public sector credits during the period 1994/95–1996/97 started to have the desired effect on inflation. Despite an average rate of inflation of around 42.3 per cent over the period 1994/95–1995/96, the average rates of private and public credit expansions were kept to

23.9 per cent and 31.2 per cent, respectively (see Table 5). As a result, the rate of inflation fell from 49.4. per cent in 1995/96 to 23.2 per cent in 1996/97. The more recent evidence, based on the first nine months of 1997/98, also suggests that this downward trend is continuing.[42]

Given the lagged response of domestic production to import changes, the full effects of the trade and foreign exchange restrictions on domestic production only started to be felt in 1994/95 when, according to the latest estimates published by the Bank Markazi, GDP (at factor costs and at constant 1361 prices) grew only by 1.6 per cent, against the rate of population growth of 2.4 per cent–2.8 per cent. The GDP estimates for the years 1995/96 and 1996/97 portray a more optimistic picture and put Iran's output growth over these two years at 4.5 per cent and 5.2 per cent, respectively. These relatively high growth rates are even more impressive considering that the oil sector grew in real terms by 1.2 per cent per annum over the same period.

However, it seems unlikely that without major economic reforms such GDP growth could be maintained. At the time of writing (August 1998) the shortfall in oil income has forced the Bank Markazi to draw $2.967 million from foreign exchange reserves to pay for the badly needed imports during the first nine months of 1997/98. (see Table 4).

Further substantial withdrawals from reserves could de-stabilize Iran's precarious foreign exchange rate system. The authorities must either resort to foreign financing (for example through the postponement of debt repayments) and implement economic reforms, at least on a limited scale, or to compress imports and credits even more. Once again, the Iranian economy stands at the crossroads. Given the political uncertainties and the opposing approaches to economic reforms, both inside and outside of the government, a decisive outcome seems unlikely.

6. Concluding Remarks

After many years of revolutionary upheavals and wars, the First Five-Year Plan provided Mr. Rafsanjani's government with an important opportunity for regeneration of Iran's war-damaged and ailing economy. It also provided the government with a reasonably cohesive framework for the formulation and implementation of badly needed reforms of the trade and foreign exchange systems. The plan's growth objectives were, however, rather ambitious and attempts at achieving them led to substantial balance of payments deficits and, given Iran's unfavourable international position, created serious external financing difficulties for the government. These developments were further exacerbated by hasty and badly-timed moves towards unification of the exchange rate. In consequence, the pace of economic growth slowed down, inflation reached new heights and the country faced the daunting task of servicing and repaying large foreign debts. Faced with these difficulties, the government had no choice but to abandon the exchange rate unification and foreign exchange and trade liberalization policies in favour of the 1980s policies of pegged exchange rates, import compression, trade restrictions, foreign exchange controls and credit restrictions.

The macroeconomic evidence so far seems to suggest that the new policies are having the desired effect of stabilizing the currency market and bringing down the inflation rate without undue negative consequences for output growth. A substantial part of the foreign debt has been repaid. Rates of growth of public and private sector credits have been moderated, and the rate of inflation has started to decline from its peak of 49.4 per cent in 1995/96. There are, however, a number of important factors that point to troubled times ahead. Oil prices that had been rising over the period 1994/1996, started to stabilize in 1997 and have fallen substantially during 1998. This has already forced Bank Markazi to make substantial withdrawals from foreign exchange reserves, and is likely to have important adverse effects both for inflation and output growth, particularly if oil prices fail to recover over the next two years. The import compression policy while effective in the short run is not sustainable if output growth is to be maintained (even at the relatively low levels of 3–4 per cent per annum). Iran's manufacturing industries depend heavily on imports of raw materials and equipment and there are no indications that this dependence has been reduced in a structural manner. The success in reducing the rate of inflation has been largely based on government and Bank Markazi's resolve in curtailing credits. But the rate of growth of private sector credits has started to rise again and in 1996/97 amounted to 30.9 per cent as compared to the inflation rate of 23.2 per cent. The evidence from the first nine months of 1997/98 suggests that this rate of expansion is continuing despite further falls in the inflation rate.

Such high rates of real credit expansion will most likely pose further difficulties for the import compression policy and could place greater strains on the exchange rate system. Already the black market rate of exchange has risen substantially and currently stands at around 5,250 rials per US dollar and given present policies and weak oil prices is likely to increase further. It seems possible that the high black market exchange rate premia of the 1980s could be repeated. A pegged exchange rate regime is not generally sustainable unless it is coupled with stringent import controls and credit restrictions. However, such controls, even if feasible politically, can have harmful consequences for financial development and growth in the long run. The economic policy dilemma of whether or not to liberalize the economy has not gone away and very much lies dormant.

Postscript

This paper was written in August 1998 and it may be useful to consider some of the main trends in the Iranian economy over the two years 1997/98 (1376) and 1998/99 (1377). As was predicted, output growth has decelerated from 4.5 and 5.8 per cent in 1995/96 and 1996/97 to 3.4 and 1.6 per cent during the years 1997/98 and 1998/99.[43] The inflation rate (measured by the percentage change in the consumer price index), after falling to 17.3 per cent in 1997/98, has begun to rise again and was reported to be around 22 per cent during the first half of 1999/2000 (1378). The exchange rate has deteriorated substantially on the free market (now legal again, having been illegal from May 1995 until June 1997). The US dollar rate in August 1999 stood at 8,902 rials, an almost two-fold increase from its value at the end of 1997/98 (1376). The presidency of Mr Khatami is beginning to lay the foundations of a more tolerant society, both politically and socially. But it is yet to deal with the structural problems that face the Iranian economy in a new world economy dominated by technological innovations and global competition.

Table 7: Production, Exports and Domestic Consumption of Oil, 1990/91–1996/97[1] (thousands of barrels per day)

	1988/89 (1367)	1989/90 (1368)	1990/91 (1369)	1991/92 (1370)	1992/93 (1371)	1993/94 (1372)	1994/95 (1373)	1995/96 (1374)	1996/97 (1375)
1. Crude oil production	2,557	2,947	3,231	3,366	3,692	3,603	3,609	3,612	3,595
2. Crude oil exports	1,647	1,823	2,224	2,460	2,397	2,184	2,220	2,290	2,620
3. Net crude oil exports in the form of consignment	–	–	136	149	274	280	185	–	–
4. Net exports of refined products	–	52	-64	-29	-77	-31	29	9.9	–
5. Domestic consumption	839	881	918	980	1,077	1,125	1,159	1,118	975*
6. Discrepancy[2] (1) – (2+3+4+5)	71	191	-47	-223	21	45	16	105	–

1 Fiscal years ending March 20. * Preliminary.
2 Discrepancy includes changes in inventories, crude oil flowing in the pipelines and refining wastage.
Source: Bank Markazi Jomhuri Islami Iran, *Annual Reports*, various issues.

Table 8: Subsidies Effected through the Organization for the Protection of Consumers and Producers, 1990/91–1995/96[1] (billions of Iranian rials)

	1990/91 (1369)	1991/92 (1370)	1992/93 (1371)	1993/94 (1372)	1994/95 (1373)	Budget 1995/96 (1374)
Fertilizer	46.1	78.6	85.1	238.5	522.0	558.0
Sugar	106.1	102.6	243.9	238.6	296.2	495.0
Wheat	171.0	250.2	512.5	1,154.4	2,095.4	2,632.8
Milk and cheese	20.1	30.0	32.0	102.8	129.0	230.0
Rice and vegetable oil[2]	–	–	–	–	371.0	632.0
Others[3]	60.6	53.5	170.2	391.6	272.6	610.8
Total	403.9	514.9	1,043.7	2,125.9	3,686.2	5,158.6
As per cent of GDP	1.1	1.0	1.6	2.3	2.8	3.0

1 Fiscal years ending March 20. Does not include transfers for commodities whose transactions are self-liquidating.
2 Prior to 1994/95 this category was self-liquidating as it benefited from implicit subsidies as these items were imported at the official exchange rate of Rls 70 = US$1. Since then, these goods have been imported using an exchange rate of Rls 1,750=US$1. Hence the subsidies to this category have become more explicit.
3 Includes transfers to agro-industry complexes, and the Agricultural Products Insurance Fund, as well as subsidies for meat and seeds In 1995/96; also includes subsidies for pesticides.
Source: Bank Markazi Jomhuri Islami Iran.

Notes

1 The present work builds on my paper, 'Planning and Macroeconomic Stabilization in Iran' published in Persian in a special issue of *Iran Nameh*, on the Iranian Economy edited by Jahangir Amuzegar, vol. 13, Winter/Spring 1995. I am grateful to Parvin Alizadeh and Adnan Mazarei for helpful comments.

2 The real output is measured by the Gross Domestic Product (GDP) at market prices, the real investment is measured by the Gross Fixed Capital Formation. All figures are in 1982/1983 (1361) constant prices, and are obtained from the *Bank Markazi Jomhuri Islami Iran*.

3 The primary source of the historical observations displayed in Figures 1-6 is the various issues of the Annual Reports of the *Bank Markazi Jomhuri Islami Iran*.

4 See Figure 3. It is also worth noting that only 28% of countries in Summer and Heston's Penn-World Tables had investment rates below 10% over the years 1988-89.

5 The source of the official exchange rate data is the International Financial Statistics Databank of the International Monetary Fund. The 'free' or the 'black' market rates are obtained from various issues of the World Currency Yearbook. For further details see M. H. Pesaran, 'The Iranian Foreign Exchange Rate Policy and the Black Market for Dollars', *International Journal of Middle East Studies*, 1992, 24, pp. 101–25.

6 For a more detailed account of the economic conditions during this period see, for example, M. H. Pesaran, 'The System of Dependent Capitalism in Pre- and Post-Revolutionary Iran', *International Journal of Middle East Studies*, 1982, 14, pp. 501–22; M. H. Pesaran, 'Economic Development and Revolutionary Upheavals in Iran' in H. Afshar (ed.), *Iran: A Revolution in Turmoil*: London, Macmillan 1985; S. Behdad, 'Foreign Exchange Gap, Structural Constraints, and the Political Economy of Exchange Rate Determination in Iran', *International Journal of Middle East Studies*, 1988, pp. 1–21; H. Amirahmadi, *Revolution and Economic Transition: The Iranian Experience*, Albany: State University of New York Press, 1990; J. Amuzegar, *Iran's Economy Under the Islamic Republic*, London: I.B.Tauris, 1993; A. Mazarei Jr., 'The Iranian Economy Under the Islamic Republic: Institutional Change and Macroeconomic Performance, 1979–1990', *Cambridge Journal of Economics*, 1996, pp. 289–314.

7 Also see 'An Evaluation of the Performance of the Country's Real Economy in 1992/93' (in Persian), Department of Economic Accounts,

Bank Markazi Jomhuri Islami Iran, Mordad, 1372. Note that the target and realized growth rates given in this publication refer to the first four years of the Plan. Also the GDP figures at constant prices published by the Bank Markazi include an adjustment for the changes in the terms of trade, while our figures do not.

8 The differences in year-to-year movements of planned and actual growth rates also demonstrate the difficulties surrounding planning/forecasting of annual changes in sectoral output in an economy such as Iran, where it is still highly dependent on the developments in volatile international oil markets, and raises serious doubts about the utility of detailed sectoral planning in Iran.

9 See Table 4. It appears that the full extent of Iran's foreign indebtedness became known to the authorities only after the crisis had erupted; a feature also shared with the recent foreign exchange crises experienced by some of the East Asian economies during 1997.

10 The M2 measure is defined as the sum of money (the M1 measure) and quasi-money. The M1 measure is defined as notes and coins in circulation plus sight deposits of the private sector with the banking system. Quasi-money is defined as the sum of time and saving deposits of the private sector with the banking system.

11 See Table 5.

12 A similar discrepancy also exists between the rate of change of the wholesale and the retail price indices. Under the plan the wholesale price index rose by an average annual rate of 25.5%, as compared to the average annual rate of change of the retail prices of 18.7%. Also note that the rate of increase of the wholesale prices almost exactly matches the rate of change of the GDP deflator over the period of the plan.

13 For a discussion of the extent of government subsidies on bread and energy see M. Karshenas, and M. Hashem Pesaran, 'Economic Reform and the Reconstruction of the Iranian Economy', *The Middle East Journal*, 1995. See also Table 8.

14 See M. H. Pesaran, and B. Pesaran, *Working with Microfit: Interactive Econometric Analysis*, Oxford: Oxford University Press, 1997.

15 For a more detailed description of these test statistics see ibid., Chapter 18.

16 As before, the figures in brackets are the standard error of the estimates.

17 See M. H. Pesaran, and Y. Shin, 'An Autoregressive Distributed Lag Modelling Approach to Cointegration Analysis', in S. Strom (ed.), *Econometrics Theory in the 20th Century: The Ragnar Frisch*

Centennial Symposium, Chapter 11, Cambridge: Cambridge University Press, 1999.

18 The econometric evidence linking financial deepening to economic growth is reasonably well established, but the evidence is much less clear cut when the direction of causality between the two variables is considered. For early discussions of the possible links between financial development and economic growth see R. McKinnon, *Money and Capital in Economic Development*, Brooking Institutions, Washington, 1973; and E. S. Shaw, *Financial Deepening in Economic Development*, Oxford: Oxford University Press, 1973. More recent developments in this literature are surveyed by R. Levine, 'Financial Development and Economic Growth: Views and Agenda,' *Journal of Economic Literature*, 1997, 35, 688–726. In the case of Iran the causal nature of the relationship between financial deepening and economic growth is further complicated due to the importance of oil exports in the economy, which is likely to be the primary cause of the changes in real output and real money balances.

19 A better understanding of the policy implications of the results reported here requires a separate empirical examination of the likely factors behind the observed structural change in the money demand equation in Iran. This is, however, beyond the scope of the present chapter.

20 Another important source of money supply growth is the non-neutralized part of increases in the country's foreign exchange reserves. This factor has not, however, been very important over the period under consideration.

21 Other variables such as legal reserve requirements and interest rates could also exert significant influences on the money supply process. But in the case of Iran, where interest rates are administrated and variations in legal reserves are rather limited, these variables do not seem to be important.

22 The Wald statistic for testing this hypothesis is 0.71 which is well below the 95% critical value of the chi-squared distribution with one degree of freedom.

23 For instance, 41% of total government revenues in 1992/93 originated from the sale of foreign exchange at preferential rates. See *Annual Review*, Bank Markazi Jomhuri Islami Iran, 1992/93.

24 Government subsidies on some of the main food and agricultural items over the period 1990/91–1995/96 are summarized in Table 8. These do not include implicit subsidies on fuel, air transport, utilities and other public services.

25 Under the arrangement of Islamic banking, interest paying deposits with the banking system are viewed as participation in the investment activities of the banking system. Such deposits are subject to two (profit) rates. An initial rate, known as the 'provisional' (*ali al-hesab*) rate which is announced at the time deposits are placed with the banks; and a final or actual rate which is computed on the basis of the bank's operations at the end of the year. However, in practice the provisional and actual returns are very close. For a more detailed account of Iran's financial and banking system see H. Pourian, 'The Experience of Iran's Islamic Financial System and Its Prospects for Development', in *Development of Financial Markets in the Arab Countries, Iran and Turkey*, Cairo: Economic Research Forum for Arab Countries, Iran and Turkey, 1995.

26 The average annual rates of increase in bank credits advanced to private and public sectors over the period 1979/80–1996/97 have amounted to 20.7% and 24.6% respectively.

27 It is also worth noting that, despite substantial nominal increases in private sector credits, the real value of credit extended to the private sector in fact declined slightly over the period 1979/89–1996/97.

28 The Second Five-Year Plan covers the period 1994/95–1998/99, but because of delays in its approval by the Majles and the financial difficulties of the government its implementation was delayed by one year and begun in March 1995. For the details of this plan see the Law of the Second Five-Year Economic, Social and Cultural Plan of the Islamic Republic of Iran, *The Official Gazette of the Islamic Republic of Iran*, vol. 50, no. 14515, (8/10/1373). Also see the documentations of the Second Plan for Economic, Social and Cultural Development of the Islamic Republic of Iran, vols 1–5, Plan and Budget Organization, Islamic Republic of Iran, Azar 1372 (1993/94).

29 See W. Lautenschlager, 'The Effects of an Overvalued Exchange Rate on the Iranian Economy, 1979–1989', *International Journal of Middle East Studies*, 1996, 18, pp. 31–52; S. Behdad, 'Foreign Exchange Gap Structural Constraints and the Political Economy of Exchange Rate Determination in Iran', *International Journal of Middle East Studies*, 1988, 20, pp. 1–21; and M. H. Pesaran, 'The Iranian Foreign Exchange Rate Policy and the Black Market for Dollars', *International Journal of Middle East Studies*, 1992, 24, pp. 101–25.

30 Per capita oil revenues in constant dollars were computed by dividing foreign exchange receipts from oil exports by population by the index of export prices of the industrialized countries. The export price index (1990=1.0) was obtained from the International Financial Statistics Annual Data Bank, IMF.

31 The planned target for foreign exchange receipts from the oil and gas sector was $19.2 billion for the year 1993/94, and $83.1 billion for the whole five-year period.

32 In 1992/93, out of the total foreign exchange allocation of $23.2 billion, $12.1 billion was transacted at the official rate, $4.2 billion at the competitive rate, and $6.9 billion at the floating rate. This allocation brought the share of foreign exchange allocated at the official rate to 52%, down from 71% in 1991/92. (See *Annual Review*, Bank Markazi Jomhuri Islami Iran, 1992/93).

33 See *Annual Report and Balance Sheet*, Bank Markazi Jomhuri Islami Iran, 1991/92, Chapter 9.

34 In real terms during the three years 1989/90–1991/92 the private and public sector credits rose by average annual rates of 17.1%, respectively. See Table 5.

35 See, for example, G. Corsetti, P. Pesenti, and N. Roubini, 'Paper Tigers? A Preliminary Assessment of the Asian Crisis', a paper presented at NBER-Bank of Portugal International Seminar on Macroeconomics, Lisbon, June 14–15, 1998.

36 It is worth noting that the cumulated sum of deficits on current accounts over the three years 1991/92–1993/94 was as much as $20,167 million, showing that almost all of the country's external debt at the end of 1993/94 had been incurred over a relatively short time period.

37 See 'The Maturity, Sectoral and Nationality Distribution of International Bank Lending, First Half 1997', *Bank for International Settlements*, Basle, January 1998.

38 See Table 2 in M. Karshenas and M. Hashem Pesaran, 'Economic Reform and the Reconstruction of the Iranian Economy', *The Middle East Journal*, 1995.

39 In February 1998, 100% of non-oil export proceeds could be used for imports or to receive import certificates.

40 These average estimates are computed using the annual figures provided in Table 3.

41 The average price of Arabian Light crude has increased from $14.8 per barrel in 1994 to $16.09 per barrel in 1995, and to $18.56 per barrel in 1996. The average crude prices fell slightly to $18.14 in 1997, but fell substantially during 1998. See *British Petroleum Statistical Review of World Energy*, 1998.

42 *Economic Trends*, Bank Markazi Jomhuri Islami Iran, no. 10, Third Quarter, 1376 (1997).

43 *Economic Trends*, Bank Markazi Jomhuri Islami Iran, no. 17, Second Quarter, 1378 (1999).

3

From Populism to Economic Liberalism: The Iranian Predicament

Sohrab Behdad[1]

For two decades, since the revolution of 1979, Iran has been suffering from an acute economic crisis. This has been a crisis of the post-revolutionary type, the outcome of open social confrontations over the defining of a new social order when the old order has been negated by a revolution.[2] Three distinct phases depict the evolution of the post-revolutionary economic crisis in Iran. They are:

Phase I: Revolutionary disruptions, from the height of the revolutionary movement in 1978 to the purge of President Banisadr in 1981;

Phase II: Islamic populism, from the establishment of the rule of Islamic revivalist clerics in the Islamic Republic of Iran (IRI) in 1981 to the death of Ayatollah Khomeini in 1989; and

Phase III: Liberalism of the post-Khomeini era, which began in 1990, was accelerated in 1993, and was impeded by public opposition and factional disputes within the government, and came practically to a halt with the election of Mohammad Khatami as the president in May 1997.

I have previously studied phases I and II of the crisis and the reciprocal interconnection of the economic crisis with the

100

transformation of politics in the IRI in these years.[3] Here I will focus on phase III of the crisis and will examine the economic liberalization policy of the IRI. My main contention is that the IRI halted its economic liberalization policy because it would have necessitated the unequivocal negation of its revolutionary claims and would have implied the formal abandonment of its remaining popular base. The responses of the IRI to the popular reaction to its economic policies, as well as the factional disputes within the regime over the implementation the liberalization policy, indicate that the post-revolutionary character of the economic crisis is not yet completed and that the IRI has not been able to formally define and legitimize a new social order. Hence, I conclude that under the existing circumstances there is little chance for an economic liberalization policy to achieve its objectives in Iran. In particular, I argue that, in any case, instituting a floating exchange rate for the rial is too disruptive and costly for the IRI to accept. Although Khatami's presidency may be viewed as a step toward mitigating the cultural crisis in the IRI, a resolution of the economic crisis is not on the horizon.

I will first outline briefly the general features of phases I and II of the economic crisis and will note the impact of these general economic conditions on the structure of the Iranian economy. Then I will examine the aborted attempt of the IRI in pursuing a liberalization policy in phase III of the post-revolutionary economic crisis. In particular, I will examine the attempts of the IRI to unify exchange rates, decontrol prices and privatize state-owned enterprises. Lastly, I will state my conclusions about the predicament of the IRI in pursing an economic liberalization programme.

Phase I: Revolutionary Disruptions

Economic disruptions began in the fall of 1978. Strikes in large enterprises were the prelude to the revolutionary disruption. Soon, takeovers and confiscations began. Some of the takeovers were 'natural' as the newly formed workers' councils took charge of the enterprises whose owners had fled the country.[4] In the summer of 1979, the Provisional Revolutionary Government nationalized and brought under the state's ownership banks, insurance companies and many large manufacturing enterprises. Meanwhile, the Revolutionary Islamic Courts confiscated the assets of the 'anti-revolutionaries'. This brought under the domain of 'public' ownership a large collection of economic assets. 'Public' ownership in Islamic jurisprudence is distinct from state ownership. 'Public' properties are at the disposal of the Imam to be used in strengthening Islam and society of Muslims.[5] The Foundation for the Oppressed was formed in 1979, with the directive of Ayatollah Khomeini, to hold and manage 'public' assets. Soon, other foundations, such as the Martyr's Foundation and the Fifteenth Khordad Foundation were formed.

The takeovers were extensive.[6] A popular wave had brought the sanctity of property rights and security of capital under attack.[7] The newly formed Islamic state, while defending the principle of private ownership, endorsed, and even at times promoted this popular wave as a means of mass mobilization. The ethos of the IRI cast further doubt on the security of property. The constitution asserts that 'the Iranian Revolution ... has been a movement aimed at the triumph of all oppressed and deprived persons over the oppressor,' condemns 'concentration and accumulation of wealth and maximization of profit,' and diminishes the place of the private sector in the economy as a residual that will supplement the state and cooperative sectors (Article 44).[8] Although the constitution recognizes 'legitimately acquired' private property (Article 47), the criteria (Article 49) are so vague that any property may be declared illegitimate. To these were added statements by Ayatollah Khomeini, such as: 'We will deal with these capitalists, whose capital and wealth could not have become so large from legitimate sources.'[9] Or, 'even if we assume someone has legitimate properties but the Islamic judge or *vali-ye faqih* realizes that an individual having so much will adversely affect the welfare of Muslims, he can expropriate those properties.'[10]

In this environment, production was severely disrupted. By 1980 there was a 20 per cent decline in industrial output (Table 1) and investment of the private sector in machinery, a sensitive index of business outlook, declined to only 23 per cent of the 1977 level (Table 2). When in 1979 the Provisional Revolutionary Government provided 80 billion rials of easy credit (at the interest rate of 4 per cent) for resumption of industrial activities, only 25 billion rials were borrowed by private enterprises.[11]

Table 1: Value Added Index in Major Economic Activities in the Three Phases of the Economic Crisis 1977–96 (in 1982 prices)

| | Phase I | | | | | Phase II | | | | | | | |
| | Total value added index (%) | | | | | | | | | | | | |
	1977	1978	1979	1980	1981	1982	1983	1984	1985	1986	1987	1988	1989
Agriculture	100	107	113	117	119	127	134	143	155	162	166	161	167
Industry	100	90	76	80	80	81	97	101	96	87	89	85	91
Services	100	99	111	102	97	99	113	116	119	103	97	89	91
Non-oil GDP	100	102	118	125	122	124	141	147	147	125	124	110	113
GNP (at market prices)	100	88	93	84	82	93	105	106	106	90	91	83	86

| | Phase III | | | | | | | | Per capita value added (%) | |
| | Total value added index (%) | | | | | | | | | |
	1990	1991	1992	1993	1994	1995	1996	%Δ* 1977–96	Index 1996	%Δ* 1977–96
Agriculture	181	190	204	216	220	225	233	4.5	133	1.5
Industry	103	120	126	127	134	141	150	2.2	86	-0.8
Services	97	108	119	128	132	135	141	1.8	81	-1.1
Non-oil GDP	124	137	146	154	159	168	178	3.1	102	0.1
GNP (at market prices)	97	109	115	118	116	121	128	1.3	73	-1.6

* Average annual growth rate (%Δ = percentage change).
Sources: Bank Markazi, *Hesabha-ye Melli-ye Iran 1353–1366* (Tehran, 1991); *Hesabha-ye Melli-ye Iran 1367–69* (Tehran, 1992); idem, *Economic Report and Balance Sheet*, various issues; and idem, *Annual Review*, various issues.

Phase Two: Islamic Populism

The mobilization for the Iran–Iraq war and the need for increased output brought the IRI to extend some protection to property and encourage the private sector to resume production. At the same time, as the price of oil increased, Iran's oil revenues reached the $20 billion mark in 1982 and 1983 (Table 3). Consequently, by 1984, value added in manufacturing reached the pre-revolutionary level, although investment remained substantially lower than in 1977. Thus there was a move towards the normalization of economic conditions.

The IRI, however, did not possess an economic programme for post-revolutionary economic reconstruction. In the midst of the government's slogans on anti-dependency and economic justice, two factions dominated the debate. One faction, with a populist-statist tendency aimed for extensive control of the state over the economy, and the other, with a *laissez-faire* market orientation, opposed the populist-statist tendency. After the fall of President Banisadr in June 1981, the clerics attained complete control of the state, and the confrontation between two factions of clerics came into the open, in a debate obfuscated by their vague scholastic discourse of Islamic jurisprudence. This battle was most clearly seen between the First and the Second Majles, dominated by populist-statist deputies, and the Council of Guardians, empowered by the constitution to ratify laws passed by the Majles and dominated by the proponents of a *laissez-faire* policy. The Majles kept passing laws and the Council of Guardians kept rejecting them as un-Islamic. Ayatollah Khomeini continued to oscillate in his support of these tendencies until his death in 1989.

Meanwhile, the IRI pursued only ad hoc economic policies to alleviate the most serious manifestations of the economic crisis, to provide for the war supply and the basic staples of mass consumption. The economic crisis was aggravated by the oil glut that began in 1985. It is no secret that the Iranian economy is highly dependent on oil revenues, which have accounted for 85 to 95 per cent of the annual exchange earnings of the country in the past decades. Any notable decline in the oil revenues imposes a serious real constraint upon the economy, in addition to the budgetary limitation that the government would face. More than 80 per cent of Iranian imports are intermediate products and capital goods (Table 3). These imports are the life-line of Iranian manufacturing industries. Foreign exchange earnings determine Iran's ability to import.[12] The economic crisis in the war economy intensified when oil revenues plummeted from $21 billion in 1983 to only $6 billion in 1986. Consequently, imports declined from an average of $16 billion between 1981 and 1984 to $11 billion between 1985 and 1988. The value of intermediate and capital goods, which had reached $17 billion in 1983, declined to only $8.7 billion in 1986. Consequently, the current account balance began showing a deficit, reaching $5 billion in 1986 (Table 3), and Iran began relying on foreign borrowing to finance its import bill.

The impact of the decline in imports on the Iranian economy was overwhelming. Between 1984 and 1988 all major economic activities suffered a decline. The only exception was agriculture, which because of its lower reliance on imported inputs managed to grow at the average annual rate of 1.3 per cent (in constant prices) between 1985 and 1988. Nevertheless, in this three-year period, non-oil GDP and GNP declined by 25 per cent and 22 per cent respectively. The most serious effect of the decline in imports was on manufacturing enterprises with more than 50 workers, which rely most heavily on imported intermediate products and capital goods. Their output and productivity in 1988 was about one-third less than what it was in 1984.[13] The impact on investment was also acute. Between 1984 and 1988 total investment declined by 56 per cent, and investment in machinery (mostly imported) decreased by 70 per cent (Table 2).

Structural Involution
In these circumstances, political instability and turmoil continued to disrupt the accumulation process, and capitalist relations of production in general. Low investment rates, low rates of capacity utilization, and the decline in output were manifestations of these interruptions. The impact of the crisis on the economic structure must be seen, however, in the context of the contradictory articulation of capitalist and pre-capitalist modes of production in economies like Iran.[14]

I contend that the post-revolutionary crisis involves more than just an economic decline. The inability of the state to facilitate the production process, and the antagonism expressed toward capital and property, cause a general retrenchment of capital and capitalist relations of production. The other side of the coin is an expansion of petty-commodity production in the economy.

Table 2: Gross Domestic Fixed Capital Formation in the Three Phases of the Economic Crisis 1977–1996 (in 1982 prices)

Sohrab Behdad

Investment index (%)

| | | | Phase I | | | | | | Phase II | | | | |
	1977	1978	1979	1980	1981	1982	1983	1984	1985	1986	1987	1988	1989
Total	100	81	56	57	53	57	79	79	67	51	42	35	38
Private	100	60	62	68	59	60	97	102	87	61	55	47	52
Machinery	100	18	14	23	28	20	56	74	44	8	13	23	38
Construction	100	84	89	93	76	73	120	118	111	90	78	60	59
Government	100	98	51	48	49	59	64	61	50	43	32	26	26
Machinery	100	107	65	51	60	79	91	95	83	59	38	28	33
Construction	100	95	47	48	45	52	55	48	38	37	30	26	24
Machinery, Total	100	60	38	36	43	48	73	84	62	32	25	25	36
Construction, Total	100	91	64	66	58	61	82	77	68	59	50	40	39

Table 2: (continued)

| | Investment index (%) | | | | | | | Average annual investment in 1978–96 relative to 1977 (%) |
| | Phase III | | | | | | | |
	1990	1991	1992	1993	1994	1995	1996	
Total	43	60	64	66	68	70	76	60
Private	52	78	79	86	88	90	98	73
Machinery	45	95	97	112	108	110	115	55
Construction	57	69	68	71	77	79	88	82
Government	34	45	52	50	52	54	58	50
Machinery	49	61	74	61	65	67	70	65
Construction	29	40	45	46	48	50	54	45
Machinery, Total	47	79	86	87	88	90	94	60
Construction, Total	41	52	55	57	60	62	68	60

Sources: See Table 1.

Table 3: Balance of Payments 1977–1996 (in US$ million)

	1977	1980	1981	1982	1983	1984	1985	1986	1987
Exports, merchandise	21,521	12,338	10,959	22,082	21,587	17,087	14,175	7,171	11,916
Oil and gas	20,926	11,693	10,619	21,797	21,230	16,726	13,710	6,255	10,755
Non-oil products	595	645	340	284	357	361	465	916	1,161
Imports, merchandise	17,968	10,888	15,515	14,345	20,603	14,494	12,006	10,585	12,005
Intermediate and capital goods (%)	82	73	77	77	84	84	86	82	82
Trade balance	3,553	1,450	-4,556	7,737	984	2,593	2,169	-3,414	-89
Current account balance	1,293	-2,434	-4,815	7,368	445	1,924	-476	-5,156	-2,090

Table 3: (continued)

	1988	1989	1990	1991	1992	1993	1994	1995	1996
Exports, merchandise	10,709	13,081	19,305	18,661	19,868	18,080	19,434	18,360	22,391
Oil and gas	9,673	12,037	17,993	16,021	16,880	14,333	14,600	15,103	19,271
Non-oil products	1,036	1,044	1,312	2,649	2,988	3,747	4,834	3,257	3,120
Imports, merchandise	10,608	13,448	18,330	25,190	23,274	19,287	12,617	12,774	14,989
Intermediate and capital goods (%)	82	82	87	88	88	88	87	na	na
Trade balance	101	-367	975	-6,529	-3,406	-1,207	6,817	5,586	7,402
Current account balance	-1,869	-191	327	-9,448	-6,504	-4,215	4,956	3,358	5,232

Sources: Bank Markazi, *Economic Report and Balance Sheet*, various issues; idem, *Annual Review*, various issues.

This is a degenerative process, creating tangles within the existing economic structure, obstructing the accumulation process and aggravating the economic crisis. This gives rise to what I have called 'structural involution'.[15] Structural involution is manifested in sectoral shifts in production and employment, in the increased peasantization of agriculture, the de-proletarianization of the labour force, and a huge expansion of service activities in a myriad of occupations such as those held by small retailers, street vendors and moonlighting cabbies.

Between 1976 and 1986, the number of 'small' manufacturing enterprises (with less than 10 workers) increased by 100 per cent, to about 330,000.[16] In 1987, these enterprises made up about 97 per cent of all manufacturing establishments. On the other hand, 10,000 'medium-sized' firms (with 10–49 workers) and 1,300 'majors' (with more than 50 workers) produced 61 per cent of the manufacturing output and employed about 50 per cent of manufacturing workers. Between 1976 and 1987, the average size of small enterprises increased from 1.9 to 2.3 workers (a 21 per cent increase), while the size of the majors increased from 294 to 407 workers (a 38 per cent increase). In the same period, however, medium-sized firms became smaller, on average, from 29 to 18 workers (a 37 per cent decrease).[17] Thus, in spite of an increase in the number of these firms, their share of employment in manufacturing decreased from 18.5 to 13.2 per cent. The fall in the output share of these firms was larger than the decline in the share of all large industries (with 10 and more workers). That is, between 1976 and 1987, as the share of large industries in total manufacturing output fell from about 84 to 60–70 per cent, the share of medium-sized firms in the output of large industries declined from 28 to 24 per cent. Hence, as industrial output stagnated between 1976 and 1987, the medium-sized enterprises were squeezed from both sides, by a mass of small workshops on one side and the huge state-owned corporations on the other.

Structural involution is manifested in the changes of the occupational stratification of the work force. These changes reflect, more than anything else, a process of de-proletarianization of the working class. Between 1976 and 1986 the number of industrial wage workers (including government employees) declined by 11.3 per cent, from 1,051,000 to 932,000. On the other hand, the number of self-employed workers engaged in industrial activities increased from 309,000 to 444,000 (43.7 per cent) (Table 4). In the urban areas, the number of industrial wage workers declined from 713,000 to 651,000 (8.7 per cent), and the number of urban self-employed workers in industrial activities increased from 178,000 to 289,000 (62.4 per cent).[18] That is, the proportion of self-employed industrial workers increased from 17 to 28 per cent of the urban industrial labour force. The increase by more than 100,000 in the number of urban self-employed industrial workers accounts for most of the growth, indicated above, in the number of small manufacturing establishments between 1976 and 1987. Therefore, the majority of small manufacturing enterprises were no more than one-worker workshops that mushroomed around a battered capitalist economy. These workshops are simply a reservoir for unemployed workers.

The main area of increase in employment was in services. Between 1976 and 1986, total employment grew by about 2.2 million to 11 million (Table 4). Ninety-one per cent, or about 2.0 million of these newly employed positions, were in the service sector, and the government accounted for 68 per cent of the new jobs in services. Meanwhile, industrial employment declined by 13 per cent to 1.6 million. Similar to the pattern of change in industrial employment, the overall employment structure shifted from wage labour to self-employed workers. In 1976, self-employed workers made up 32 per cent of the total labour force; in 1986 they accounted for 40 per cent (Table 4). The number of self-employed workers in all major urban and rural activities increased substantially. In the same period the number of wage workers in the private sector declined by more than one million workers. The decline in the number of wage workers was not the consequence of the increase in the number of government employees in this period. Less than 300,000 of the 1.8 million increase in the number of government workers were for non-service activities which might have replaced the activities of the private sector, and potentially brought wage workers of the private sector into government employment (about 220,000 in manufacturing). In 1986, the other 1.5 million new government workers were employed in activities that traditionally have not competed with the private sector, including an addition of 900,000 in the various military and paramilitary activities. A slower expansion in government employment would have increased the number of self-employed or unemployed workers. Therefore, the increase in the number of self-employed workers

Table 4: Changes in Occupational Categories 1976, 1986, 1996 (In 1,000 workers)

	1976			1986				1996			
	Total	%	Industry*	Total	%	1976-86 %Δ	Industry*	Total	%	1986-96 %Δ	Industry*
Govt employees	1,673	19.0	265	3,454	31.4	106.5	491	4,258	29.2	23.3	743
Entrepreneurs	182	2.1	50	341	3.1	87.3	67	528	3.6	54.6	126
Self-employed	2,810	31.9	309	4,398	40.0	56.5	445	5,199	35.7	18.2	653
Family workers†	1,021	11.6	411	462	4.2	-54.7	65	797	5.5	72.5	242
Wage workers††	3,072	34.9	786	1,882	17.1	-38.7	440	3,327	22.8	76.8	966
Not specified	41	0.5	2.4	464	4.2	1041.6	67	463	3.2	-0.3	92
Total	8,799	100.0	1,824	11,002	100.0	25.0	1,575	14,572	100.0	32.5	2,822

Censuses of 1976 and 1996 include the working population 10 years and above, whereas the census of 1986 includes working population 6 years and above. I have subtracted the workers aged 6–9 in the 1986 census to have the data for the three years comparable.

* Includes manufacturing, mining, water, gas and electricity.
† Includes unpaid trainees.
†† Includes all wage and salary workers in the private sector.

Sources: Markaz-e Amar-e Iran, *Sarshomari-ye 'Omumi-ye Nofus va Maskan, 1355* (Tehran, 1980); idem, *Sarshomari-ye 'Omumi-ye Nofus va Maskan, 1365* (Tehran, 1988); and idem, *Sarshomari-ye 'Omumi-ye Nofus va Maskan, 1375* (Tehran, 1997).

and the decline in the number of wage workers reflect a change in the organization of production independent of the increase in government employment.

In services, the increase in the number of self-employed workers is greater than can be accounted for by the increase in non-governmental activities in this sector. The number of self-employed workers in services nearly doubled between 1976 and 1986 to 1.2 million, 929,000 of whom were in cities. Out of this, no fewer than 600,000 were shopkeepers. Another 300,000 were 'taxi' drivers of various sorts. These are the occupations that have traditionally attracted otherwise unemployed workers.

End of Populism?

Structural involution, above all, reflects retardation of the accumulation process by the state and the private sector. It leads the economy into decay. Between 1977 and 1988 national income per capita declined by nearly 50 per cent and urban unemployment increased from 4.4 to 18.9 per cent. The populist policies of the IRI reduced the impact of this decline on the level of consumption of the population. In this period, private consumption expenditure per capita in the urban areas fell by 30 per cent and that of the rural areas by only 19 per cent.[19] The cost of this populist policy was a decline in capital accumulation. The investment of the private sector in 1987–90 was about half the level in 1977 and state investment was about one-quarter of the 1977 level (Table 2). Once capital depreciation is accounted for, little net investment was made throughout these years.

In the midst of the economic crisis a new monopolistic structure began to replace the one that was made dysfunctional by the revolution. The conglomerate network of the 'revolutionary foundations,' and the group of emerging entrepreneurs, who were close associates of the regime and benefited from the many privileges of this association, dominated the market. For example, the volume of transactions of the Foundation for the Oppressed in 1994 was 6,000 billion rials (the total tax revenue of the government in that year was 5,500 billion rials). Through 400 companies, the Foundation for the Oppressed produces 70 per cent of glass containers, 53 per cent of motor oil, 43 per cent of soft drinks, 27 per cent of synthetic fibre, 26 per cent of tires, 20 per cent of sugar, 20 per cent of textiles, and 30 per cent of dairy products in Iran. It owns 43 per cent of the hotel capacity of the country and in 1994 produced 2.4 million square meters of construction. It is also the contractor for building a highway between Tehran and the Caspian Sea. It is the largest economic entity in the Middle East.[20]

The giant 'revolutionary foundations' and the networks of their affiliated enterprises have benefited from special privileges and have reaped extremely attractive profits over the years. The foreign exchange gap and the shortages that developed in the market accentuated the monopolistic position of these networks. Meanwhile, the 'un-affiliated' enterprises were deprived of the essentials for keeping their business running. The battered and denigrated bourgeoisie that had survived the revolutionary turmoil was no match for state enterprises, 'revolutionary foundations', or even the merchants who had a close association with the regime. Realizing that the normalization process held little promise for its rejuvenation, the bourgeoisie took its battle to the political arena and raised the banner of economic liberalism, demanding denationalization (privatization) of industries and deregulation of the market.

Two other concurring developments helped to advance the cause of economic liberalism. First, the public had become disillusioned with revolutionary rhetoric and worn out by the prevailing state of siege. Its standard of living had been declining and it had become a seemingly unlimited supply of martyrs for a war whose senselessness was becoming everyday more apparent.[21] The foreign exchange gap had intensified this state of public disenchantment. With the shortage of foreign currency and the persisting need for war mobilization, imports of items of mass consumption, which were relied upon to mitigate domestic shortages, declined by nearly 50 per cent between 1983 and 1988.[22] As if this were not enough, the economic burden of the public increased as the government began raising indirect taxes and the price of services that it provided in order to ameliorate its budget deficit, which had increased by the declining oil income and the falling revenues from import taxes. As the economic burden increased, and the revolutionary fervour subsided, people's longing for a programme of peace and prosperity intensified

Second, the acute foreign exchange crisis and the chronic deficiency in the level of domestic investment brought the IRI to abandon its cardinal revolutionary principle of rejecting foreign capital. As it was revealed subsequently, in these years the IRI had begun borrowing to finance its imports. The matter was kept secret to avoid public embarrassment. By 1989, the IRI owed $12 billion on account of its short-term borrowing.[23] Moreover, the First Economic Plan, approved by the Majles for implementation in the years 1989–93, projected $28 billion external borrowing for the duration of the plan.[24] This estimate was made with the unrealistic assumption that Iran's export earnings for these years would reach $17.8 billion.[25] Attracting this large sum of foreign capital to a country that had suffered from economic sanctions and other forms of international financial isolation is an overly optimistic expectation, if not wishful thinking. Nevertheless, Iran began normalizing its international relations by accepting, on 20 July 1988, the UN Cease Fire Resolution 598 to stop the eight-year war with Iraq. Furthermore, the IRI sought the economic consultation and policy advice of the World Bank and the IMF (International Monetary Fund) in anticipation of borrowing from these institutions and with the expectation of acquiring their seal of approval to enhance its borrowing potential with other lenders.

In June 1990 the World Bank-IMF mission visited Iran and was impressed by Iran's 'determination' to commence an economic liberalization policy.[26] The approval of the World Bank for Iran's move toward 'opening up its economy' was expressed by extending to the government a series of loans amounting to $850 million, before U.S. opposition in May 1994 blocked any loans to Iran, including a $400 million proposal on the table.[27]

Phase 3: Economic Liberalization

The liberalization policy of the IRI began in 1990, coinciding with the fortunate increase in Iran's oil revenues to $18 billion in that year (Table 3). This increase in oil revenues was the combined outcome of an increase in Iran's output, from 2.2 barrels a day in 1986 to 3.5 barrels a day in 1990 (due to reconstruction of the production capacity after the cease-fire agreement with Iraq) and an increase in the world price of petroleum, from $8 in July 1986 to an average of $20 in 1990 (because of the Persian Gulf war and the exclusion of Kuwait and Iraq from the oil market).[28] By 1991, Iran's imports had increased to the unprecedented figure of $25 billion and the import-dependent economy expanded. Non-oil GDP grew by 8.5 per cent, 10.4 per cent and 7.2 per cent in constant prices in 1990, 1991, and 1992 respectively. This expansion was an added encouragement for the IRI to pursue economic liberalization with its three essential components: (i) exchange rate unification and floating the currency, the rial; (ii) decontrolling prices and eliminating subsidies; and (iii) privatization of the state owned enterprises.

The logic of the liberalization policy is that when state control over the exchange rate, production and prices is eliminated, scarce resources (including foreign exchange) would be allocated by the forces of the market. That is, the highest bidders, presumably the most productive (profitable) enterprises, would receive the available resources and those who could not match the higher bids would have to leave the market empty handed. Thus, some activities, or even sectors, would contract and others would expand. This is the 'structural adjustment' that is expected. The outcome would be more exports, less imports, higher output and less unemployment. The proponents of economic liberalization and structural adjustment note that this is a policy toward adding transparency (*shaffafiyat*) to market transactions, meaning that it would become clear why resources are moving toward any particular pole. It also means that the situation would reflect the logic of the working of the market: those who have the means would get all they want, those who do not are out of luck. This is the controversial dimension of any structural adjustment policy, and any politician would attest to the political dangers of plunging into its seemingly attractive arms. Let us consider the complexities of the liberalization policy in Iran.

Foreign Exchange Liberalization

The most crucial aspect of the liberalization policy is foreign exchange realignment. In 1982, with the first appearance of current account deficits in 1980 and 1981 ($2.4 billion and $4.8 billion, respectively), some experts in the Planning and Budget Organization proposed the devaluation of the rial to close the foreign exchange gap. This view was opposed by the economists of Bank Markazi, but the issue was kept out of the public arena for the obvious reason that a devaluation of the rial would have meant a serious setback for the IRI. In 1986 the issue was raised in print, I believe for the first time, by Patrick Clawson (with the pen name of Wolfgang Lautenschlager) in an article in the *International Journal of Middle East Studies*.[29] There, Clawson suggested that the overvalued rial has had a strong adverse effect on the Iranian economy. His main point was that the inflow of cheap imports resulting from the overvalued rial had caused a decline in the market share of Iranian industries. He maintained that 'if Iranian industry had not lost this market share, its output would possibly have been as much as one-third higher.'[30] Clawson saw the overvalued exchange rate policy of the IRI as a ploy 'to meet the interest of bazaar merchants' against 'their major competitor ... namely, modern industry.'[31]

In an article in the same journal in 1988 I argued that Clawson's analysis, or what I call the 'devaluation thesis', understates the complexities of the Iranian economic structure and Iran's economic conditions.[32] My main argument was that maintaining an overvalued rial and a multiple exchange rate system has been an instrument of the IRI's industrial and social policy. The overvalued exchange rate policy makes it possible for the IRI to run a highly import-dependent industrial structure and to minimize, at least in the short-run, the deterioration of the standard of living of the Iranian population. I maintained that the implications of a devaluation, to the extent necessary for overcoming the foreign exchange gap, are much more grave for the IRI than the 'devaluation thesis' suggests. At that time, I asserted that the IRI would continue to maintain exchange control with a system of multiple exchange rates because it did not dare face the economic and political consequences of a floating currency.

The artificially low foreign exchange price has provided Iranian industries with low-cost imported inputs. Many Iranian manufacturing enterprises were established between the mid-1960s and the mid-1970s, when 'cheap' foreign exchange was becoming ever more abundant, thanks to the increase in the volume and price of Iranian oil exports. Since the largest portion of Iranian imports are industrial inputs with few domestic substitutes, Iran's demand for imports (thus for foreign exchange) has a relatively low price elasticity. That is, only a large devaluation would have any appreciable effect in reducing imports. At the same time, the impact of devaluation on export earnings is minimal because Iran's main source of foreign exchange earning is from the export of oil, which is independent of the rial's rate of exchange. Oil prices are determined in dollars in the international market, and the volume of Iran's exports of oil depends on international market conditions (determined by the OPEC quota, or on its own) but not on the rial cost of production of oil. The non-oil exports constitute such a small fraction of the total value of exports that only major increases in their earnings could have an appreciable effect on the foreign exchange gap.

The issue is accentuated by the fact that non-oil exports have a large import content. According to a report by the Ministry of Agriculture, for example, the foreign exchange requirement for producing a ton of apples is $460, for oil seeds $319, and for almonds $981.[33] The same is true for many manufactured exports. For example, Jamegan, which produces TOC-TOC jeans and shirts solely for export to Europe, needs to import two-thirds of its required material.[34] The production and export of these goods is profitable because in the system of multiple exchange rates the producers pay for foreign exchange (to import their inputs) at a fraction of the price that they get from selling their foreign exchange earnings (from exporting their products). The IRI managed to increase non-oil exports after 1990 by maintaining a high spread between the cost of foreign exchange that is available to the 'export' enterprises for buying their imported inputs and the price that these enterprises can fetch for their 'earned' foreign exchange.[35] Therefore, the net foreign exchange earning of non-oil exports is significantly less than the value of these exports indicates. In other words, some of the non-oil exports are no more than 'exports of the oil revenues, repackaged in another form.'[36]

With these supply and demand considerations for foreign exchange one can conclude that to overcome even a small foreign exchange gap would necessitate a very large devaluation. This is not to say that a devaluation does not have a positive impact on the size of the foreign exchange gap. It does. Hashem Pesaran shows that the Marshall-Lerner condition is indeed satisfied in the case of an oil exporting country such as Iran.[37] That means that a devaluation will reduce (*and will not increase*) the size the foreign exchange gap. The fulfilment of the Marshall-Lerner condition (also referred to as the stability condition) is not the problem. The issue is that because of low elasticities on the in-payments and out-payments sides, the foreign exchange market has a low degree of responsiveness to exchange rate changes. That is, devaluation will reduce the foreign exchange gap, but only at very small increments for any given rate of devaluation. Furthermore, any small fluctuation in the supply of foreign exchange (most frequently in the oil revenues, resulting from a change in the price of oil) or in the demand for foreign exchange (resulting, for example, from an increase in domestic output and higher need for imported inputs) would give rise to large changes in the equilibrium price of foreign exchange. Therefore, not only is devaluation minimally effective, but also it is needed in frequently very high doses in order to rectify short term fluctuations. Thus the impact of such a high and frequent devaluation on the economic structure and the political landscape are factors that creep into the equation for maintaining economic and political stability in the oil/import dependent economy of Iran.

Devaluation has drastic effects on an economy so dependent on imports. A 100 per cent devaluation of the rial would increase by as much as 50 per cent the input cost of an average manufacturing establishment in Iran, which imports half of its inputs.[38] This is without taking into account the increase in the cost of domestic inputs resulting from the devaluation. Such a large increase in production cost cannot be possibly absorbed by any increase in the efficiency in production, be it from privatization of these enterprises, or any downsizing efforts at the factory level. Simply put, many enterprises depending on imported inputs will have to shut down if they cannot receive their dose of subsidized foreign exchange. A sharp increase in the rate of inflation is the inevitable outcome of the devaluation.

In March 1993, after some gradual moves toward economic liberalization (decontrolling some prices and reducing some subsidies), and with optimism reflecting the high oil revenues of the previous three years (Table 3), the IRI floated the rial. Previously, the principal rates of exchange were $1=IR70 for governmental and defence orders, and $1=IR600 for favoured enterprises which received foreign exchange quotas. There were also a myriad of rates for exports, travellers and students abroad, etc. The rial initially floated at the rate of $1=IR1,540. But even this huge depreciation of the rial (an increase of 157 per cent in the price of foreign currency) was not sufficient to close the foreign exchange gap.[39] In the following months, the price of oil, and thus Iran's oil income, decreased as the demand for imports began to increase (after the initial decline due to depreciation of the rial) when domestic prices escalated (Table 5). Obviously, with a fall in supply and an increase in demand, the price level would rise. So did the price of foreign exchange, and the rial depreciated further. Meanwhile, the need to pay off the short-term loans accumulated in the years of high imports (1990–92, see Table 3) put Bank Markazi under an additional pressure. These together pushed up the value of foreign exchange. In December 1993, Bank Markazi fixed the 'float rate' at $1=IR 1,750. But as the rial continued to depreciate, the spread between the 'float rate' and the free market rate increased. In October 1994, the U.S. dollar was traded in the free market for 2,500 rials, and in March 1995 for 4,500 rials. By early May 1995, the speculative demand for foreign exchange caused the value of the rial to fall to 7,000 rials per dollar. In response, Bank Markazi, while maintaining the fixed value of the 'floating' rial at 1,750 per dollar (for those who have import licenses), raised the official value of the dollar for export earnings to 3,000 rials.

Thus, the experimentation with a floating currency was officially over, although, in reality, it did not last any more than a few weeks. Bank Markazi retreated from its foreign exchange liberalization policy and imposed a complete exchange control. The non-official free (black) market rate outside Iran in December 1996 was around $1=IR 4,900 and it stayed within that range over subsequent months, until the spring of 1998, when the fall in oil income pushed the foreign exchange value to around IR6,000 per U.S. dollar. On 12 April 1998, the dollar appreciated in the black market to 6,300 rials, but returned to 5,500 in the early days of May.[40]

The new system of multiple exchange rates: Faced with the failure of the floating exchange, the IRI has been reconstituting an elaborate system of multiple exchange rates. The main features of this system are explained in a 1997 official publication of Bank Markazi.[41] The official exchange rate, fixed at $1=IR1,750, is 'applied to oil exports receipts, imports of essential goods and services, debt service, and imports related to large national projects.'[42] The exchange rate for exporters 'is fixed from time to time,' but has remained at $1=IR3,000 since May 1995.[43] Exporters were required to repatriate and sell to Bank Markazi all of their foreign exchange earnings. But even a rate more than 70 per cent higher than the 'official rate' was not sufficient to promote non-oil exports, which declined from nearly $5 billion in 1994 to about $3 billion in 1996 (Table 3).

In 1996, a new provision made it possible for the exporters of manufactured products to use 50 per cent of their foreign exchange earnings for importing items on the 'authorized' list.[44] Exporters of other non-oil exports could use only 30 per cent of their export earnings for buying imports. Rug exporters, however, managed to acquire the special advantage of being able to use 100 per cent of their earnings for imports. To give a further boost to non-oil exports, in June 1997 exporters were allowed to transfer, through the Tehran Stock Exchange, their foreign exchange allotment to others who would pay a premium to buy their 'right to import'. In July 1997 the premium was about IR1,700 which would bring the exchange rate for the traded currency to $1= IR4,700.[45] In January 1998, the government extended the 100 per cent privilege of the rug exporters to all other exporters. Meanwhile, the enterprises that manage to receive foreign exchange quotas at the official rate pay only 1,750 rials per dollar to import their industrial inputs and capital goods. If the price of foreign exchange traded on the Tehran Stock Market is an approximate reflection of the true rate of exchange in Iran, these lucky enterprises were paying in January 1998 only 37 per cent of the true cost of the foreign exchange that they received. By early 1999, when the value of dollar in the 'black market' passed the 8,000 rials mark, and the dollar exchanged in the stock market reached 6,000 rials, this percentage was even less.

Iran's multiple exchange rate system includes special rates for tourists and students as well as for those seeking medical treatment abroad. The decline of foreign exchange revenue in the spring of 1998 brought the government to devalue some of these rates. For example, Iranian tourists, entitled to $1,000 at the official export rate, after 21 March 1998 had to purchase their foreign exchange allotment at the rate of 4,720 rials per dollar.[46] Similarly, the price of airline tickets for travelling abroad, purchased domestically, was raised by about 60 per cent to account for the devaluation of the exchange rate for Iranian travellers.[47]

It is doubtful that the IRI would submit itself to a free market for foreign exchange. The brief experimentation in the working of a floating currency showed that the market is too erratic and the political stakes are too high to warrant the risk of submitting to a free or even a managed float. The 'free market' of foreign exchange has already regained its old and dubious title of a 'black market'. The operators in this market are no longer referred to as 'dealers' or 'agents' but as 'smugglers' and 'disruptive, opportunist elements', 14,000 of whom were arrested and fined by government agents in May 1998.[48] With an expected 25 per cent decline in Iran's foreign exchange earnings in 1998–99, more restrictions, more devaluations, and a more elaborate system of multiple exchange rates are expected. In October 1998, Bank Markazi made it clear that it would not consider floating the rial before March 2000.[49]

The Politics of Wage and Price Liberalization

Devaluation has an inflationary impact on the domestic economy. The price of imports increases, and so too does the price of those goods with an import content. If the devaluation has any notable impact on the international demand for exports, the domestic price of the exportables would increase too, especially when capacity expansion is limited by various internal economic constraints. Nearly all prices change to accommodate the changes in the price of tradeable goods. In the two years (1993 and 1994) following the devaluation, the wholesale price index increased by 78 per cent, and the consumer price index by 96 per cent. As expected, products with a higher import content had a higher rate of increase in their prices. The rise in the price of chemicals and transport equipment, the most import dependent industry groups in Iran, far exceeded the rise in the general wholesale price index (Table 5).

The price effect is expected to remedy the foreign exchange gap along two avenues. First, with the price increase for imported goods and goods with a high import content, domestic demand would shift toward the domestic alternatives, provided that the price of these products does not increase in step with the increase in the price of imports and those with high import content. Second, if the rate of inflation in consumer prices is not matched by the increase in nominal wages, real wages would decline, reducing real income of the largest group of urban consumers, and consequently causing a fall in the demand for domestic and for imported products. The lagging wage rate effect appeals to the policy makers because it is anti-inflationary and would, at least partially, compensate the increase in the demand for imports due to the rising domestic prices, and would help to promote exports by containing the labour cost of production.

It is in this context that one may view the emphasis of the proponents of liberalization policy on cutting subsidies and raising the price of products of mass consumption offered by the government. These policy measures would not only divert some resources from producing these products, whose cost of production is higher than their subsidized market price, but also help to reduce the real income of a large mass of the population and thereby reduce the demand for other products, many of which are imported, have high import content, or are exportable. For example, as the fare for the subsidized urban transportation is increased, or the subsidy for bread is cut, the typical urban dweller ends up allocating a larger share of his or her household budget for these expenditures, in spite of taking, say, fewer bus rides and buying less bread.[50] To the extent that urban dwellers pay more of their income for taking bus rides or buying bread, they would have less to spend on buying a new television set, or a hand woven Persian rug. Thus the demand for televisions, which have a high import content, and the domestic demand for Persian rugs, which are an export product, falls and as a result the demand for imported goods will decrease and more rugs may be exported.

But all this is achievable at the cost of reducing the standard of living of the general population, which, as the proponents of liberalization policy see it, is in itself a blessing for the economy. This is so because the inflationary trend, and subsequently the decline in real wages and standard of living, reduces the distributive share of labour and augments the share of capital (profit) in the economy. Consequently, as the argument goes, private consumption would decrease and the possibility for investment would increase. This would potentially increase productive capacity, employment and output. As attractive as these possibilities seem, it is the mass of the population that must pay the cost of the increased investment today, in return for uncertain benefits for the wage earners of tomorrow.

In 1993 and 1994 the liberalization of the market was accelerated. Many prices were let free and the government began raising the price of the goods and services that it provided. The prices of natural gas, telephone, post, electricity, inter-city trains, airlines and urban public transportation increased, some by more than 100 per cent. The rate of inflation in 1994 was officially marked at 59.6 per cent (Table 5), although the Tehranis and the inhabitants of other large cities may have felt a sharper reduction in the purchasing power of their rials. The adverse impact of the liberalization policy on the urban population raised the level of public discontent and intensified the factional discord within the regime. Fearful of the political impact of the inflation, Majles deputies spoke out in opposition to the liberalization policy and its effects on the 'ordinary people'. A deputy declared that the 'mismanagement of the government has provided a fertile ground for hoarding and profiteering.'[51] The Majles began obstructing the government's attempt to raise the price of the services and products that it provided, and it even passed the first draft of a bill to dissolve the Supreme Economic Council (which had approved price increases) and to have the Majles take over the matter of prices.[52] Although that bill never became law, the government seemed to have welcomed the concern of the Majles deputies. By October 1994, programmes were announced to combat inflation by controlling prices and every government official and leader of the Friday prayer condemned profiteering and price gouging. The minister of justice declared that the death penalty could be the punishment of big retailers if they gouge prices.[53] In November, Ali Khamene'i, the Supreme Leader of the Revolution, expressed his support for the anti-profiteering policies of the government.[54] Two days later, President Hashemi Rafsanjani, leading Tehran's Friday prayer, underscored his government's commitment to a battle against inflation. He stated that anyone who opposed these effort would be 'annihilated'.[55] Yet, on the same days, the Majles, in spite of being dead-set against price hikes, approved, as a part of the Second Development Plan, a 100 per cent increase in the price of gasoline, and annual increases of 20 per cent for the next five years in the price of gasoline and other petroleum products. Thus, the price of gasoline increased from 50 rials to 100 rials per litre (15 cents per gallon) beginning March 1995.[56] Although there was much reaction to the energy price hike (taxis increased their fares by as much as 50 per cent), the price increase could hardly match the rate of inflation and remains significantly lower than the international price. The government pays $400 to $900 million a year to import additional amounts of petroleum products to satisfy domestic demand. The effective subsidy for maintaining energy prices is currently about $11 billion a year.[57]

In this way the IRI began a zig-zag strategy to pursue economic liberalization. It pushed forward where it could, mainly in the arenas that were inconspicuous, and gave in when public discontent mounted. As riots and demonstrations in opposition to government policies (e.g., in Mashhad, Qazvin, Arak, Akbarabad and Islamshahr) became elements of political negotiation, the parameters of public tolerance gained higher importance in the equation of political stability. Demands for wage increases were

Table 5: Wage Rates and Prices 1990–96

	1990	1991	1992	1993	1994	1995	1996
Price Indices							
Wholesale	100.0	126.6	168.9	211.7	301.4	482.7	604.0
Chemicals and petrochemicals	100.0	122.6	187.2	376.6	539.1	726.7	884.9
Machinery and transport equipment	100.0	130.6	201.2	256.7	381.4	640.2	824.3
Consumer price	100.0	120.7	150.1	184.4	294.3	372.4	458.8
Consumer price inflation rate	8.9	20.7	24.4	22.9	59.6	26.5	23.2
Wage Rate Indices							
Minimum wage rate (nominal)	100.0	166.7	226.7	299.4	389.4	533.3	690.7
Minimum wage rate (real)	100.0	138.1	151.0	162.4	156.2	143.2	150.5
All construction workers wage rate (nominal)	100.0	113.6	136.9	161.4	200.4	278.2	372.1
All construction workers wage rate (real)	100.0	94.1	91.2	87.5	68.1	74.7	81.1
Large enterprises (50+ workers) wage rate* (nominal)	100.0	137.4	179.3	231.5	295.2	403.5	535.2
Large enterprises (50+ workers) wage rate (real)*	100.0	113.9	119.4	125.6	100.3	108.3	116.6

* Includes benefits.

Sources: Bank Markazi, *Economic Report and Balance Sheet*, various issues; idem, *Annual Review*, various issues; and idem, *Natayej-e Barresi-ye Kargaha-ye Bozorg-e San'ati-ye Keshvar, 1375* (Tehran, December/January 1997/1998).

accommodated under pressure and ignored otherwise.[58] Thus, the salaries of government workers (4.25 million workers out of a 14.6 million working population – see Table 4) were increased occasionally to partially catch up with consumer inflation. The official minimum wage rate was also increased periodically to compensate for rising prices (Table 5). Ironically, the main beneficiaries of the increase in the minimum wage rate are workers in state enterprises and large corporations, who generally receive higher wages and in addition are entitled to a series of fringe benefits, which are calculated based on the official minimum wage rate. At the low end of the wage scale, little is gained because the minimum wage rate is substantially lower than the prevailing rate for unskilled workers.

Figure 1 presents the changes in the nominal wage rate of construction workers (skilled and unskilled), the official minimum wage rate, the wage rate (including benefits) of workers in large (50 plus workers) enterprises, in contrast with the changes in the consumer price index. It is distinctly clear (see also Table 5) that while the minimum wage rate and the wage rate (including benefits) of the workers in large enterprises increased substantially faster than consumer prices, wages of construction workers lagged behind the inflationary trend, in spite of an urban construction boom in these years. In 1996, about 563,000 workers were employed in enterprises employing more than 50 workers,[59] and 1.65 million were employed in construction activities.[60] Although the wage rates for all major groups of workers are not available, the indications are that some groups among the urban workers have managed to stay in pace with the price increase, while some clearly have not. The overall effect should be reflected in the changes in consumption expenditure, which we will examine below.

Privatization
The third component of the liberalization policy was privatization of state owned enterprises, to increase their efficiency by making them subject to the forces of the market. Employment, production and pricing decisions in state-owned enterprises are made according to political considerations. Thus, these enterprises may hire more than the optimum number of workers, pay them higher than market wages, produce more or less than the optimum output and price it lower than the profit-maximizing firm would.

All of this would generate economic inefficiency and would inhibit capital accumulation in the economy.

Figure 1: Wage Rates and Inflation, 1990–96

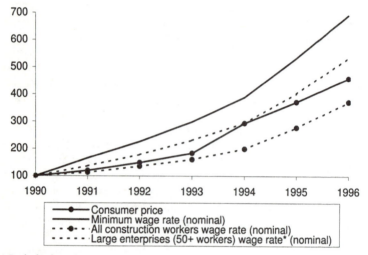

* Includes benefits.
Source: Table 6.

Between 1976 and 1986, the number of government employees increased by 107 per cent, hence, in 1986, almost one-third of workers were employed by the government (Table 4). The dominance of the state in the economy was also reflected by the state's share in manufacturing production, noted at the outset, and its share in capital formation. In 1990, when the early attempts for liberalization began, investment (in machinery and construction) by the public sector was 46 per cent of the total in the economy. In the same year, the share of public current expenditures in Gross Domestic Expenditures (GDE) was 11 per cent (Table 6). Altogether, the state accounted for 28 per cent of the GDE.

In 1991 the government announced its intention to privatize 400 nationalized enterprises.[61] The initial limitations on the privatization policy of the IRI were the legal and political constraints on offering various state enterprises for privatization. First, the Constitution of the Islamic Republic specifies a number of major activities as the monopoly of the state. Article 44 of the constitution declares that 'the state sector is to include all large-scale and major industries, foreign trade, major mineral resources, banking, insurance, energy, dams and large-scale irrigation net-works, radio and television, post, telegraphic and telephone services, aviation, shipping, roads, railroads and the like.'[62] Although foreign trade is listed among these activities, the Council of Guardians opposed all attempts of the Majles to promulgate a law for the nationalization of foreign trade. With this major exception, all activities named in Article 44 are off limit to the private sector. Any attempt at the privatization of nationalized enterprises in the above list would require a revision of the constitution. About 30 enterprises (of the 2,400 owned by the state), mainly in oil, petrochemicals, steel, water and electricity, constitute about 90 per cent of the state sector.[63]

Second, 'revolutionary foundations' have been, de facto, exempted from the privatization policy since they claim to be under 'public' ownership.[64] These colossal conglomerates are neither subject to the forces of the market, nor to the budgetary and accounting scrutiny of the government. They operate under the direct supervision of the Supreme Leader of the Revolution and manage their activities and their profits to promote the welfare of the Muslim community, as they and the Supreme Leader of the Revolution see fit. They dispense their profit by paying the families of martyrs, veterans of the IRI's wars, and engaging in activities that they believe would advance the cause of Islam, such as allocating a reward for the assassination of Salman Rushdie, and financing Islamic movements in various parts of the world. Their sheer economic and political power has prevented any discussion about imposing even the slightest limit on their expanding domain of activities, much less privatizing them. The Foundation for the Oppressed in particular has expanded its activities into spheres that have been set aside for the state sector, like trans-ocean shipping and air transport, and is trying to enter the arena of finance to compete directly with the state owned banking system.[65]

The privatization of the 400 enterprises encountered major obstacles. The initial criticism of the policy was the consideration of 'economic justice' and the absence of any limits on the concentration of ownership over these enterprises. In at least two cases the government agreed to take back the privatized enterprises

Table 6: Composition of Gross Domestic Expenditure 1988–96 (current prices)

	1988	1990	1991	1992	1993	1994	1995	1996
Share in Gross Domestic Expenditures %								
Private consumption expenditures	66.8	65.7	63.2	62.0	55.1	56.1	60.9	61.7
Public current expenditures	14.3	11.1	10.7	10.4	14.6	12.6	12.9	13.4
Gross domestic investment	13.3	15.5	21.6	22.0	22.1	23.2	23.2	25.6
Change in inventories	5.8	13.2	11.6	13.3	6.9	1.0	-3.6	-5.7
Net exports	-1.1	-3.8	-4.6	-3.7	1.3	7.1	6.7	5.0
Share in investment %								
Private	59.4	53.8	60.9	59.0	51.7	55.3	54.8	55.9
Public	40.6	46.2	39.1	41.0	48.3	44.7	45.2	44.1

Sources: Bank Markazi, *Economic Report and Balance Sheet*, various issues; idem, *Annual Review*, various issues.

after workers protested the privatization of their companies.[66] In July 1994, the Majles passed a law to stop offering shares in these enterprises in the Tehran Stock Exchange until conditions could be determined for offering the shares first to the families of martyrs of the revolution and veterans of the war.[67] Yet when all these matters were resolved, the enthusiasm for purchase of these enterprises was limited and, ironically, much of what was sold was purchased by the 'revolutionary foundations'. There is, however, no clear account of the degree of success of the government in selling off these enterprises and the new structure of their ownership. An amendment to the 1998 budget requires the government to complete the privatization of the enterprises under its ownership within that budgetary year. As of this writing, there has been no indication of any new developments on this issue.

Structural Adjustment
With oil revenues averaging over $19 billion in 1990–96, Iran experienced one of its more prosperous periods. The IMF, which regards this an ideal condition for pursing a liberalization policy, has expressed its displeasure at the zig-zag strategy of the IRI and its limited success in opening the market to the private sector.[68] After seven years of pursuing a privatization policy, the state (including the 'revolutionary foundations') remains the dominant actor in the economy. Between 1986 and 1996, the number of government employees, instead of declining, increased by 23 per cent.[69] Of the 804,000 new government employees, 251,000 were added to state industrial enterprises, where privatization is expected to have been pursued most vigorously (Table 4). Meanwhile the state's share in allocation of domestic output has also increased. Public current expenditures, in current prices, increased from about 10–11 per cent of GDE in 1990–92, to around 13 per cent in 1993–96. At the same time, a notable increase is shown in the share of the public sector in investment. In 1994–96 public investment, at current prices, accounted for no less than 44 per cent of the total (Table 6). One of the objectives of the liberalization policy, as I have noted above, is to increase the level of investment in the national economy, generally by reducing the share of private consumption and government current expenditures in the GDE. The total amount of investment increased (at constant prices) in the years of economic liberalization (Table 2), most significantly as the result of the economic expansion brought

about by increasing oil prices. The share of gross domestic investment in GDE, too, increased in the initial years of liberalization as a result of two concurrent changes. First, the share of private consumption expenditure in GDE declined from 66 per cent in 1990 to 55 per cent in 1993. This indicates that overall the wage/income of the population had lagged behind prices. Second, in these years the value of imports increased substantially, even more than the increase in oil revenues, therefore part of the increase in investment was provided for by negative net exports. Thus, instead of paying fully for the increased investment in 1990–92 by reducing either private or public expenditures, the reliance on imports was increased. Starting in 1994, the impact of the IRI's policy in accommodating wage demands is observed in the upward movement of the share of private expenditures in GDE (Table 6). But in these years, as net exports are kept positive (to pay for foreign debts incurred in the years of high imports), the changes in the inventories declined from 13 per cent of GDE in 1993 to 1 per cent in 1994 and -6 per cent in 1996.

Overall, in the years of economic liberalization, 1990–96, any growth of the private sector (at constant prices) has been mainly due to the general expansion of the economy and not to a decline in the activities of the public sector. The private sector's investment has increased, but mainly because the economy has expanded and not as the result of either a reduction in government expenditures and investment in the economy, or because of a decline in the share of consumption expenditures. The increase in the activity of the private sector in the expanding economy has increased the number of wage workers outside the public sector. In 1996 they constituted 23 per cent of the working population, compared to only 17 per cent in 1986, but still much less than the 35 per cent recorded in 1976. The increase in the ratio of wage workers in total employment was mainly the result of a reduction in the rate of growth of self-employed workers, where much of the unemployment is disguised (Table 4). The changes in the sectoral distribution of employment have been along the trend observed in the first post-revolutionary decade. In the decade 1986–96 the relative size of agricultural employment decreased from 29.1 per cent to 23 per cent, while that of industry increased from 14.3 per cent to 19.4 per cent, almost approaching the ratio prevailing in 1976. Service employment continued to increase from 43.1 per cent of total employment in 1986 to 46.3 per cent in 1996, in comparison to only 31 per cent in 1976.[70] In general, we can see that the decline in the share of agricultural employment over the last two decades has been offset principally by the increase in the relative size of the service sector.

Wither Liberalization? Whither the Economy?

For two decades the Iranian economy has suffered from disruptions and stagnation. In spite of some expansion in the past few years resulting from increases in oil revenues, in 1996 non-oil GDP per capita just reached the level it was at twenty years ago. That is, the oil sector aside, the economy has, at best, stagnated. Industrial value added per capita has declined, and so has the service sector, which now employs nearly one half of the working population. GNP per capita in 1996 was only 73 per cent of the 1977 level. This indicates a substantial decline in the standard of living. The result would be even more disheartening if one were to consider the bias of the GDP deflator, which underestimates the extent of inflation. The foreign exchange rate is still fully regulated, with multiple exchange rates providing highly favourable rates for the import dependent manufacturing enterprises, many under the ownership of the 'revolutionary foundations'. By 1996, the devaluation of the rial by 192 per cent (from \$1=IR 600 to \$1=IR 1,750) and other liberalization measures had raised the wholesale price index by 258 per cent, and the consumer price index by 206 per cent (in comparison to 1992). This is hardly a success story. Contrary to the aims of the liberalization policy, the state still dominates the economy. Prices are controlled, government bureaucracy has grown, and privatization has been limited. To pursue the path of liberalization the IRI had to implement a tight austerity policy. This would have entailed the complete abandonment of the IRI's populist stature and loss of the political base that it still claims to represent.

In the course of the revolutionary movement, the Islamic contenders for leadership tried to outdo their principal rivals on the left, Marxist or otherwise, who had shaped the ideology of the opposition in the previous two decades. Even the idols of many Muslim activists, Ali Shari'ati, Ayatollah Taleqani and the People's Mojahedin Organization, were ideologically, if not epistemologically, on the left.[71] A manuscript left behind after the May 1979 assassination of Morteza Mottahari, Shari'ati's major critic and the guru of Muslim conservatives, indicates that he, too, was evolving toward an involuted variation of the Marxist view about capital, labour and surplus![72] Ayatollah Khomeini and his master tactician, Ayatollah Beheshti, skillfully manoeuvred to take ownership of the slogans of the left. They condemned the 'blood-sucking capitalists' (*sarmayeh-daran-e zalusefat*) and damned dependent capitalism (*sarmayeh-dari-ye vabasteh*). They did so by relying on the authority of the Qur'an, the Tradition of Muhammad, and the deeds and thoughts of Imam Ali and Imam Hossein (the Martyr). The Constitution of the Islamic Republic was so close in many respects to the demands of the left that the young activists of the Tudeh Party would gleefully brag to their Marxist rivals that their leader, Nuraldin Kianuri, served as an advisor to Ayatollah Beheshti in drafting the constitution. Maybe he did. But it was Khomeini who promised land to the peasants; jobs, ownership and prosperity to the dispossessed; a dwelling and free electricity to every urbanite, and even a dowry to new brides and subsidized pilgrimages to the holy shrines for needy Muslims. The promises became obligations when millions took part in the *jihad*s of the IRI, first against the 'infidel' contenders for power in Kurdistan and Turkman Sahra, and the 'hypocrite' followers of Mojahedin in the streets and the back alleys of the cities, and later, in an eight-year deadly campaign against Iraq, to reach Qods (Jerusalem) via Karbala.

Rivals were defeated. The left was suppressed and disappeared from the political scene in Iran, and vanished in the international arena. The IRI, entangled in its struggle with its self-definition, is still left with the mass of the 'oppressed' who were promised the opportunity to establish their rule, and an oil market which is at least as sensitive to the winter temperature in Europe as it is to the supply adjustments of the Saudis. The oil revenues have been used more for augmenting consumption and mitigating the erosion in the standard of living than for capacity expansion and economic development. The policy of economic liberalization was a way of getting out of the deadlock of populism. But the IRI carries a heavy ideological baggage. The earlier condemnations of capitalism, exploitation and economic inequality in the heyday of the revolution, by the same leaders of the IRI who are now trying to come out of the capitalist closet to promote entrepreneurship, high profit and capital accumulation, were too explicit and vociferous to be easily hushed up today. Rejection of what the IRI now regards (still within its closed circles) as its early 'juvenile leftism' is in the works. Nematzadeh, a former minister of industries and a proponent of economic liberalism, made the following comments in 1996:

> In 17 years of debate we have not succeeded in explaining investment, capitalism, and capital. ... But we must distinguish between capitalism (*sarma'i-dari*) and making capital investments (*sarma'i-gozari*). An investor (*sarma'i-gozar*) is someone like a learned person who benefits the society with his knowledge ... and with whatever else he has accumulated as scientific capital. However, a capitalist (*sarma'i-dar*) does not make use of his material means, instead he entraps money and does not let others use it. ... Hence an investor is like a university professor and as respectable and dear to us as a teacher.[73]

Thus, Nematzadeh tries to leave the anti-capitalists happy with their terminology and give dignity to 'investors'. Nematzadeh is playing a game of hermeneutics, similar to that played in the industrial West over a century ago, when the term 'capitalist' had become too ideologically charged to be of any practical use. Instead, the terms 'entrepreneurs', 'industrialists' and 'producer' found widespread usage. 'Capitalist', which is frequently used with a non-complimentary adjective, is left for the speech of the left. Nematzadeh proposes the term 'entrepreneur' (*kar-afarin* – literally meaning 'creator of work') and even suggests a National Entrepreneur Appreciation Day.

The game of words aside, promoting economic liberalism entails providing security and high profit potentials for capital. This requires the state's commitment to pursuing, consistently and unequivocally, a policy to protect the domain and freedom of activity of capital by its own withdrawal from the market, both as a producer and a regulator. It also requires the state to reformulate the rules of the market to facilitate capital accumulation. The constitutional limitation on the domain of activity of the private sector (Article 44) and the Labour Law of 1990 are the main areas of legal contention. I have already referred to the constitutional limitation on the activity of capital. A revision in the constitution would be the purist solution. But that may prove too embarrassing for the leaders of the IRI. Instead, it is expected that these constitutional limitations would be gradually ignored, and as private capital finds these areas of large investment attractive, it would also find the gates for entering them sufficiently open. The labour law is a more difficult challenge for the IRI because it has direct implications for Iranian workers. The Labour Law of 1990, which reflects some of the early post-revolutionary sentiments about capital–labour relations, was rejected as un-Islamic several times and was never sanctioned by the Council of Guardians. It was finally enacted with the approval of the newly formed Council of Expediency. A revision of this law is one of the most serious demands of 'entrepreneurs'. But such a revision would be a formal repudiation of the populist position of the IRI and would entail a direct face down with Iranian labour.

The presence of the 'revolutionary foundations' and their huge conglomerates is another major obstacle of the IRI in promoting economic liberalism. While the 'revolutionary foundations' have been a source of monopolistic rent and the mainspring of much 'primitive accumulation' for a privileged few, they are a cause for concern, caution and even hostility for the majority of players in the market. The 'revolutionary foundations' are too powerful for any competitor to withstand. The issue is complicated further by the formal and informal political and economic ties between the 'revolutionary foundations' and the Islamic Revolutionary Corps and the other 'revolutionary institutions', which together serve as the coercive force of the IRI.

The economic dilemma of the IRI has been rendered even more complicated by the intensification of the cultural confrontation in Iranian society and, subsequently, the recent realignment of the forces within the regime. After two decades of cultural oppression, the IRI has not been able to compel the population to submit to its traditionalist Islamic norms of personal and public conduct and to accept its idealized traditional Islamic cultural mores. The landslide victory of Mohammad Khatami in the May 1997 presidential election was a definite achievement for the Iranian people in expressing their opposition to the imposition of the traditionalist cultural norms. Khatami, however, came to the forefront of the battle for the leadership of the IRI by the alliance of two hitherto opposing factions within the regime, namely a liberal coalition promoting economic liberalism and the hard-core remainders of the populist-statist tendency. These two factions are known in Iranian politics as the 'modern right' and 'modern left', respectively. The 'modernity' label comes from the perception that they take a more moderate position on the imposition of the traditional Islamic values than the hardliners, who are also distinguished as the 'traditional right' and 'traditional left'.

The cultural confrontation aside, Khatami must chart the course of economic development of the IRI. The sharp decline in oil prices in 1998 has brought urgency to the issue. The 1998 budget's forecast for oil prices was $16 a barrel. This was revised to $12 in May 1998.[74] In June 1998, however, Iranian crude oil was traded at $9.50 per barrel.[75] An oil income of no more than $10–$12 billion can be projected for 1998, when the annual import bill would be about $14 billion, with an outstanding foreign debt of $9–$12 billion. Prices have begun rising sharply since the spring of 1998 as foreign exchange has become more scarce and a decline in the flow of imports is expected. The unemployment rate was estimated by the officials of the IRI in April 1998 at somewhere between 9 and 12 per cent.[76] Whatever the true rate of unemployment may be, it is on the rise. In May 1998, *Payam-e Emruz* declared the conditions of industries as 'shocking' and listed 400 factories that have just closed and warned that 'several hundred are at the verge of closure.'[77] Khatami, who took a year to address the economic question, noted in May 1998 that 'the sickness of our economy is related to our poor economic structure.'[78] In August 1998 Khatami unveiled his economic policy plan, expressed as a series of 'concerns'.[79] He elaborated on the issue in November 1998, when presenting the Budget Bill 1378 (for 1999/2000) to the Majles. Khatami's plan is an eclectic composition of the views of the two factions supporting him. On the one hand, he stresses that the key to the economic recovery of Iran is the mobilization of domestic capital and attraction of foreign investment, which may be possible, he notes, only if security of capital is guaranteed and constraints imposed on the private sector are eliminated. On the other hand, to satisfy the populist-statist faction of his alliance, which finds this liberal proposition unpalatable, he makes a pledge that his administration 'will do its best to maintain social justice and a more equitable distribution of income.'[80] Yet, the structure of the proposed budget does not indicate a major departure from the policies of the previous years. Therefore, the debate over free market and state intervention continues in the midst of a severe economic crisis, as the pinch of the decline in oil revenue becomes more apparent. In

February 1999, as the IRI was celebrating the twentieth anniversary of the revolution, the Iranian currency plunged to nearly 9,000 rials per dollar, with the anticipation of reaching the 10,000 mark.[81] The economic crisis is moving once again to the centre of the political stage, while factional disputes and political assassinations have intensified the crisis of the regime. Ironically, it turns out that Khatami, who came to the presidency with a cultural campaign, is faced with the acute dilemma of the economy. The IRI has not been able to deliver what it has promised, and this has become more apparent every day. Formal repudiation of its claims is politically painful and dangerous.

Hashemi Rafsanjani, in his eight years of presidency, zigzagged his way through the repudiation process. The popular opposition was too strong for a formal turnabout. He, and all statesmen of the IRI, are familiar with the story the disgruntled Muslims who stormed the house of Uthman (the third Rightly-Guided Caliph of Muslims) in opposition to his financial reform, demanding what they believed to be their rightful share from the public fund (*bayt al-mal*). Uthman was murdered in cold blood by the angry mob. The rule of Uthman (AD 644–56) was a period of intense internal conflict in the newly established Islamic state, as the state was being transformed from a populist, rebellious Islam to the Pax Islamicus of the Umayyads (661–750) and the Abbasids (750–1258). This transformation began with Umar (the second Rightly-Guided Caliph, 634–44). Uthman, Abu Dharr,[82] Imam Ali (the fourth Rightly-Guided Caliph, murdered in 661) and Imam Hossein[83] were all, in different ways, the casualties of this transformation.[84] So far, the statesmen of the IRI have avoided Uthman's fate, but they have also failed to define the economic future of the Islamic Republic, much less to construct their promised Pax Islamicus.

Notes

1   I wish to express my gratitude to the R. C. Good Fellowship and the Faculty Development programmes of Denison University supporting these projects. I am thankful to Bahram Tavakolian and Parvin Alizadeh for their comments. I am also in debt to M. T. for valuable help. The opinions and the remaining errors are all mine.
2   See Sohrab Behdad, 'The Post-Revolutionary Economic Crisis' in Saeed Rahnema and Sohrab Behdad (eds), *Iran After the Revolution:*

The Crisis of an Islamic State, London: I. B. Tauris, 1995; and S. Behdad, 'Disputed Utopia: Islamic Economics in Revolutionary Iran', *Comparative Studies in Society and History*, 36/4, 1994.

3   Behdad, 'The Post-Revolutionary Economic Crisis'. See also Ali Rahnema and Farhad Nomani, *The Secular Miracle*, London: Zed Press, 1990.

4   Assef Bayat, *Workers and Revolution in Iran*, London: Zed Press, 1987.

5   Muhammad Baqir Sadr explains this distinction. See Behdad, 'Disputed Utopia', p. 790.

6   Behdad, 'The Post-Revolutionary Economic Crisis', p. 101.

7   See Fatemeh Moghadam, 'Property Relations in Iran 1800–1979', in S. Rahnema and S. Behdad, *Iran After the Revolution*, Chapter 3.

8   *The Constitution of Islamic Republic of Iran*, translated by Hamid Algar, Berkeley: Mizan Press, 1980, pp. 19, 21.

9   [Ruhollah Khomeini], *Payam-e Enqelab, Majmu'eh-e Payamha va Bayanat-e Emam Khomeini*, vol. III, (Fall/Winter 1979/80), p. 126, Tehran: Payam-e Azadi, 1982.

10 Ibid.

11 Bank-e Markazi, *Barresi-ye Tahavvolat Eqtesadi-ye Ba'd az Enqelab*, Tehran: Bank-e Markazi, n.d. (1984), p. 181.

12 On foreign exchange revenues being the determinant of demand for imports see Adnan Mazarei, 'Imports under a Foreign Exchange Constraint: The Case of the Islamic Republic of Iran', Middle Eastern Department, International Monetary Fund, *Working Paper*, WP/95/97, October 1995.

13 Bank-e Markazi, *Natayej-e Barresi-ye Kargaha-ye Bozorg-e San'ati-ye Keshvar, 1370*, Tehran: Bank-e Markazi, 1993, p. 17.

14 See John Weeks, *Limits to Capitalist Development; The Industrialization of Peru, 1950–1980*, Boulder, CO: Westview Press, 1985, p. 67.

15 For a more detailed study see Sohrab Behdad, 'Production and Employment in Iran: Involution and de-Industrialization Theses.' Thierry Colville (ed.), *The Economy of Islamic Iran: Between State and Market*, Louvain: Peeters for Institute Français de Recherche en Iran, 1994, which is the source for the following analysis.

16 Markaz-e Amar-e Iran (MAI), *Amar-e Kargaha-ye Kuchak-e San'ati Shahri, Sal-e 1355*, Tehran: Markaz-e Amar-e Iran, 1981, p. 10.

17 The source of statistics are MAI, *Amar-e Kargaha-ye Bozorg-e San'ati-ye Keshvar, Sal-e 1355*, Tehran: MAI, 1981; MAI, *Amar-e Kargaha-ye San'ati-ye Keshvar, Sal-e 1366, Dara-ye Panjah Nafar Kargar va Bishtar*, Tehran: MAI, 1990; MAI, *Amar-e Kargaha-ye San'ati-ye*

Keshvar, Sal-e 1366, Tehran: MAI, 1990; and Bank-e Markazi, *Natayej-e Barresi-ye Kargaha-ye Bozorg-e San'ati Keshvar, 1359*, Tehran: Bank-e Markazi, 1981.

18 MAI, *Sarshomari-ye Omumi-ye Nofus va Maskan, 1355*, Tehran: MAI, 1980; MAI, *Sarshomari-ye Omumi-ye Nofus va Maskan. 1365*, Tehran: MAI, 1988.

19 See Behdad 'Post-Revolutionary Economic Crisis', pp. 114–15.

20 *Payam-e Emruz*, 4, February/March 1994, p. 23 and *Payam-e Emruz*, 21 (December/January 1997/98), p. 75. See also Peter Waldman, 'Clergy Capitalism', *The Wall Street Journal*, 5 May 1992, which puts the budget of the Foundation for the Oppressed at $10 billion.

21 The Martyr's Foundation puts the number of martyrs of the 1979 revolution and the 1980–88 Iran–Iraq war at 213,000. 'More Than 200,000 Deaths since 1979 Revolution', Agence France Press, 13 March 1998, from www.iranian.com.

22 Bank-e Markazi, *Gozaresh-e Eqtesadi va Taraznameh*, various issues.

23 *Kayhan Hava'i* , 14 August 1991.

24 For a study of the First Five-Year Plan see M. R. Ghasimi, 'Iranian Economy after the Revolution: An Economic Appraisal of the Five Year Plan', *International Journal of Middle East Studies*, 24/4, 1992.

25 Plan and Budget Organization, *Peyvast: Qanun-e Barnameh-ye Avval Towse'eh-ye Eqtesadi, Ejtema'i va Farhangi-ye Jomhuri-ye Eslami-ye Iran, (1368–72)*, Tehran: Plan and Budget Organization, 1988, p. II–8.

26 *IMF Survey*, 30 July 1990, p. 228.

27 See *MEED*, 20 May 1994.

28 Bank-e Markazi, *Gozaresh-e Eqtesadi, 1365*, p. 164 and *Gozaresh-e Eqtesadi, 1369*, pp. 178, 181.

29 Wolfgang Lautenschlager, 'The Effects of an Overvalued Exchange Rate on the Iranian Economy, 1979–84', *International Journal of Middle East Studies*, 18/1, 1986.

30 Ibid., p. 43.

31 Ibid., p. 50.

32 Sohrab Behdad, 'Foreign Exchange Gap, Structural Constraints and the Political Economy of Exchange Rate Determination in Iran', *International Journal of Middle East Studies*, 20/ 1, 1988, p. 1.

33 *Kayhan*, 25 April 1992.

34 *MEED*, 24 February 1995. Meanwhile the textile factories in Iran were reported to be operating at less than 60 per cent capacity in February 1995 because they could not import all their needed material. Reported by www.irna.com (Islamic Republic News Agency -IRNA), Tehran, 27 February 1995.

35 Vahid Nowshirvani points out that a major part of this increase in exports is due to the increase in the legal export of Persian rugs, which were mostly exported illegally before, as the illegal foreign exchange market was much more lucrative. Therefore, a substantial part of the increase in exports between 1990–1993 is expected to be a one shot affair. See Vahid Nowshirvani, 'Sarnevesht-e Barnameh-ye Ta'dil-e Eqtesadi', *Iran Nameh*, XIII/1–2, 1995.

36 *Kayhan* , 25 April 1992.

37 M. Hashem Pesaran, 'The Iranian Foreign Exchange Policy and the Black Market for Dollars', *International Journal of Middle East Studies*, 24/1, 1992.

38 For data on import dependence of various manufacturing activities see Behdad, 'Political Economy of Exchange Rate Determination in Iran', p. 11.

39 See Hossein Farzin, 'The Political Economy of Foreign Exchange Reform', in Rahnema and Behdad, *Iran After the Revolution*, p. 191, for the average monthly rate of IR/US$ exchange between June 1992 and February 1994.

40 *MEED* , 24 April 1998, p. 21

41 See 'Key Features of the Current Exchange System', in Bank-e Markazi, *Economic Trends*, no. 9, 2nd quarter, 1997) p. 14. See also IMF, *Exchange Arrangements and Exchange Restriction, Annual Report 1997*, Washington, DC: IMF, 1997, pp. 411–15.

42 Bank-e Markazi, 'Key Features', p. 14.

43 Ibid.

44 Ministry of Commerce has three lists for imports, 'authorized', 'conditional', and 'prohibited'. See ibid.

45 *MEED*, 13 February 1998, p. 21.

46 *Iran Times*, 27 March 1998.

47 *MEED*, 24 April 1998, p. 21.

48 Ibid., 8 May 1998, p. 22.

49 Ibid., 13 November 1998, p. 16.

50 This is true if the demand for the subsidized product or service is inelastic.

51 *Iran Times*, 6 May 1998.

52 Ibid.

53 *Iran Times*, 21 October 1994.

54 *Ettela'at*, 10 November 1994.

55 *Ettela'at*, 12 November 1994.

56 *Iran Times*, 11 November 1994 and 18 November 1994.

57 *MEED*, 13 March 1998, p. 3. For a study of domestic pricing of energy products in Iran see Djavad Salehi-Isfahani, 'The Oil Sector

after the Revolution', in Rahnema and Behdad, *Iran After the Revolution*, Chapter 6.

58 See, for example, 'Tehran Mercedes Workers End Protest', C-reuter@clarinet.com (27 July 1995), reporting on the strike of the state-run Khavar Truck Company. The strike ended after management agreed to the workers' demands over wages and benefits.

59 Bank-e Markazi, *Natayej-e Barresi-ye Kargaha-ye Bozorg-e San'ati-ye Keshvar, 1375,* December/January 1997/1998, p. 17.

60 MAI, *Sarshomari-ye Omumi-ye Nofus va Maskan, 1375,* Tehran, 1997, p. 191.

61 Sazman-e Sana'i-ye Melli-ye Iran, Sherkat-e Sarma'igozari, *Gozaresh-e Tahqiqati,* No. 24, September/October 1992, pp. 24–6.

62 *The Constitution of the Islamic Republic of Iran*, p. 45.

63 *MEED*, 27 March 1998.

64 See the text of a speech by the Chairman of the Foundation for Oppressed in *Payam-e Emruz*, No. 21, December/January 1997/1998, pp. 75–6.

65 *Payam-e Emruz*, No. 21, December/January 1997/1998, pp. 76–7.

66 The companies involved were the Asalem Lumber and Nazpush Textiles. See 'Iran Reverses Two Privatizations after Protests', C-reuter@clarinet.com, Reuter, 14 August 1995.

67 *Iran Times*, 5 August 1994.

68 'Iran: IMF Points to Lost Opportunity', *MEED* , 30 January 1998, p. 18.

69 In all cases data referring to government, public or state ownership include the enterprises under the ownership of 'revolutionary foundation', i.e. 'public' enterprises.

70 MAI, *Sarshomari-ye Omumi 1355*; MAI, *Sarshomari-ye Omumi, 1365*; MAI, *Sarshomari-ye Omumi, 1375.*

71 Behdad, 'A Disputed Utopia'.

72 Ibid.

73 *Payam-e Emruz*, 14 September/October 1996, p. 23.

74 *MEED*, 1 May 1998, p. 19.

75 Barry May, 'Khatami Mulls Sweeping Economic Review', Reuters www.infoseek.com, 16 June 1998.

76 *MEED*, 1 May 1998, p. 19.

77 'Doshvariha-ye Eqtesad: Besyar Beham Pichideh, Moqe'iyat-e San'at: Besyar Tekan Dahandeh', and '400 Karkhaneh Ta'til Shod; Chand Sad Karkhaneh dar Astaneh-ye Ta'til', *Payam-e Emruz*, 23 May 1998, p. 116–19.

78 'Iranian President Interviewed on the Economy', FBIS, 15 May 1998 (also available at www.columbia.edu/sec-cgi-bin/gulf).

79 *Ettela'at*, 4 August 1998. See also *Iran Times*, 21 August–30 October 1998.
80 *Hamshahri*, 30 November 1998, electronic edition, www.neda.net/hamshahri.
81 'Iran Rial Near Free Fall', Reuter, 1 February 1999 from infoseek.go.com/Center/News.
82 The egalitarian Companion of Mohammad, who opposed the accumulation of wealth by the powerful rulers in the Islamic state and was banished to exile by Uthman, where he died in AD 652.
83 The Third Imam of the Shi'is, murdered in Karbala in 680 by Yazid, the son of Mo'awiya, the founder of the Umayyad dynasty.
84 See S. Behdad, 'Islam, Revivalism and Public Policy', in S. Behdad and F. Nomani (eds), *Islam and Public Policy*, Greenwich: JAI Press, 1997, pp. 3–8.

Part Two
Factors Influencing Economic Performance

4

Agents or Obstacles? Parastatal Foundations and Challenges for Iranian Development

Suzanne Maloney

More than two decades have passed since a mass political movement espousing the triumph of sacral authority over secular toppled a dictator, a state, and a set of assumptions about religion, modernity, and political development. The establishment of the Islamic Republic of Iran dramatically altered the political landscape of the Middle East, and the resilience of the clerical regime in Iran has proven to be one of the most surprising elements in a political metamorphosis replete with drama and diversity. Clerical government is an anomaly, both for Iran historically and for the community of nations in the modern era. There is no direct historical precedent for the leadership of the *ulama*, who have exhibited overall a notable ambivalence toward political activity. Indeed, the philosophical foundation of the Islamic Republic rests on a doctrinal reinterpretation of religious dogma, which continues to be contested by some of the leading Iranian *ulama*.

In his earliest discussions on the nature of an Islamic state, Ayatollah Ruhollah Khomeini prophesied that Islam had provided all of the answers and that an 'entire system of government' had been bequeathed in whole and perfect form by scripture.[1] After the monarchy fell, the task of constructing a successor government proved to be much more complicated than these facile predictions. The post-revolutionary panoply of theocratic, leftist and liberal groups faced the task of reinventing the state and adapting its relationship to a transformed social order – while consolidating authority over the nation and the extensive residual infrastructure of the monarchy in an environment of fierce contention among the revolutionary coalition itself.

This process of institution building embodies the fruition of revolution itself,[2] and the result – a modern, 'Islamic' state – is as innovative and compelling as the ideology and tactics which swept the ulama to power. Most inquiries into post-revolutionary Iran tend to reconcile the evolution of the Islamic Republic with the predicted pattern of post-revolutionary centralization. While conceding the novelty of its theocratic apparatus and nominally religious ideology, analyses almost across the board have interpreted Iranian political development as an unexceptional example of the inexorability of post-revolutionary state consolidation of power. The steady expansion of the state bureaucracy, the intrusion of government into hitherto private realms of behaviour, and the aggressive monopolization of power by the ulama at the expense of potential rivals and alternative perspectives support this view. The creation of parallel structures of revolutionary legitimacy and authority contribute to the consolidation process by harnessing the 'popular energy' of a society mobilized by revolution.[3] Analogies are drawn between the Islamic Republic and other authoritarian states forged through revolution, particularly the Soviet Union.[4]

This analysis of the process of state building in the Islamic Republic represents an oversimplified description of the dynamic, and provides a misleading characterization of the Islamic state. The depiction of Islamic Iran as a relentlessly centralizing state not only exaggerates the capabilities of the Iranian regime, but disregards an important and by no means isolated consequence of the revolution: the diminution of actual state capabilities by the corresponding rejuvenation and accretion of non-state actors. Contrary to the prevailing assessment, the revolution that ousted the shah and established clerical authority in Iran did not produce an unequivocally stronger and more centralized state entity. Rather, the revolution reflected centripetal tendencies which, in the reconstitution of authority under the rubric of the Islamic Republic, were only in part captured by the state itself. The contention for political dominance among social groups previously excluded or alienated from the regime enhanced the power of traditional repositories of authority which lay outside the state, especially the informal religious and merchant networks that played such a pivotal role in the revolution itself.

The past two decades of clerical rule have witnessed the transformation of these networks into modern institutions exercising profound influence over Iran's politics and economy, whose emergence has circumscribed the ability of the formal state structure to impose its will. Yet, paradoxically, these same institutions have thereby contributed to the durability of the Islamic state by institutionalizing a check to the authority of the central government. Indeed, rather than resembling the omnipresent state of the USSR, the Islamic Republic appears more analogous to post-Soviet Russia, where the crumbling of an entrenched system of power and the concomitant rise of new political and financial elites has empowered a sweeping array of puissant clientelist networks.[5]

These developments clearly have salience beyond abstract theorization; the structure of the Iranian state poses profound consequences for its ability to devise and implement policy. Particularly, the impact of state structure on the Islamic Republic's programme of economic development bears examination for a variety of reasons. The state shoulders the ominous legacy of its predecessor, the Pahlavi monarchy – which piloted the Iranian economy through an era of dramatic statistical growth, but failed to generate a solid base for industrialization or, most pointedly, to ensure its own survival. Such history suggests the urgency of the issue of state structure for the Islamic Republic: the revolutionary government needed to do more than simply defend the nation's borders and establish its own sovereignty. Today, one of the key criteria of modernity is the incorporation of the promotion of social and economic development within the rubric of the state's essential mission. This role has proven nettlesome for Middle Eastern states with patrimonial roots and distributive economies to assume, and has been characterized by the primacy of *control* of the organization of power, punctuated by intermittent and often intemperate attempts at wholesale overhaul. The issue of state-directed socio-economic progress is particularly salient in Iran, where post-revolutionary reform could be expected to serve both the *ideal* of social justice – a prominent theme of all modern revolutions – as well as the more profane *reality* of dismantling the power structure of the *ancien regime*. The mechanisms which the Islamic Republic has initiated in order to generate and distribute resources provide some insight into the way in which the state has adapted to the imperatives of governing.

This article examines the emergence of a key new institution – a network of parastatal foundations in the Islamic Republic of Iran, and in particular the largest and most influential example of these revolutionary organizations – in order to explore the relationship between state structure and socio-economic development. The foundations (or *bonyad*s) exercise profound influence over the Iranian economy as the beneficiaries of billions of dollars in assets seized from the former royal family and other exiled elites or nationalized in the course of the revolution. In conjunction with this financial muscle has come political influence; by virtue of intricate personal and institutional ties with the government, the *bonyad*s have become pivotal actors in the enduring rivalry among the ideologically oriented factions within the clerical establishment. More broadly, the evolution of the *bonyad*s as a semi-autonomous centre of power redistributes the relationship among the various social groups (especially the *bazaaris*, or traditional merchants) whose support is key to the government's survival.

Consequently, the *bonyad*s furnish a highly appropriate framework for the analysis of the post-revolutionary Iranian order, for they are neither wholly of the state, nor wholly distinct from it. Their narrative epitomizes the structural and ideological transformation of the Islamic state – from the incipient expansion of state apparatus and institutionalization of the ideological objectives of the revolution, to the drive for post-war reconstruction, economic competitiveness and organizational integration. Furthermore, their strategic mission as agents of economic development and income redistribution endows these foundations with the mantle of social justice – a potent theme in the developing world in general and an even more integral component of political legitimacy in Islamic Iran. The *bonyad*s are commented upon frequently, and yet they have not received extensive study in the Western academic or policy community largely because their accounts are closed and information about their activities is limited. However, anecdotal information culled from the Iranian and Western media provides an intriguing account of the surfeit of resources and power invested in this network and the institutional challenges faced by advocates of economic reform.

1. A Historical Overview of Charitable Foundations

Charitable foundations (or *vaqf*) have played a significant role in the development of economies and the accumulation of landed property in Islamic societies for a millennium, serving as mechanisms for untaxed savings and investment, as well as providing for the financial independence of the religious hierarchy from the auspices of the state. In Safavid Iran, the emerging conceptualization of property rights and the religiosity of the ruling dynasty popularized these religious foundations, and since that time the relative security of *vaqf* endowments in Iran provided the clergy with 'economic independence' from the state and thus enabled them to remain aloof from politics, unlike their counterparts in the Arab world.[6] However, for the same reasons, *vaqf* assets have also engaged various governments in clashes for influence with the clergy, as was certainly the case in pre-revolutionary Iran, where both Pahlavi shahs attempted to control or restrict *vaqf* properties, provoking deep resentment among traditional sectors of the population and necessitating closer cooperation between the *ulama* and the merchant communities.[7]

Religious endowments continue to command vast amounts of resources in the Islamic Republic; the Bonyad-e Astan-e Qods, which is based at the shrine of Imam Reza at Mashhad, owns property throughout the country and is assured a steady stream of revenue from the charitable alms of pilgrims. Its annual budget is said to be in the range of $2 billion.[8] Also notable amongst the religious endowments is the Bonyad-e Panzdah-e Khordad (15 Khordad Foundation), which commemorates the 1963 protests against the shah's development programme which cemented Khomeini's figurehead status among the opposition to the Pahlavi state. This foundation gained international notoriety in 1989, with a pledge of a $2 million bounty to anyone who would implement Khomeini's *fatwa* condemning author Salman Rushdie to death for apostasy. This organization exemplifies the ambiguous relationship between the various *bonyad*s and the formal state structure. The Bonyad-e Panzdah-e Khordad was closely associated with Khomeini and its director continues to be appointed by the *faqih*, the spiritual leader of the Iranian state; yet, its administrative and financial autonomy from the regime has enabled the government to claim that the foundation is not a public entity, and thus distance the government on the public stage from efforts to implement the Rushdie death sentence.[9]

However, while a few individual religious endowments have grown since the revolution, the Islamic Republic has invested far greater assets in *bonyad*s which are not associated with religious endowments. These *bonyad*s can be differentiated, on the basis of the primary sources of their funding, between those which are state-sponsored or supported (public) and those which utilize private funds for non-profit political or cultural purposes (private).[10] However, it is fair to say that these distinctions cannot be strictly applied, as nearly all of the *bonyad*s (including the religious endowments) benefit from some measure of government support, whether in the form of direct subsidies or special prerogatives. Additionally, some of those typically cited as public organizations in fact receive less direct funding and are subject to virtually no governmental oversight. The legal status of the foundations has been described as public, non-governmental organizations,[11] a somewhat paradoxical classification, but an accurate reflection of the bifurcated nature of authority in the Islamic Republic.

The best description for this heterogeneous group of organizations might be parastatal or quasi-public. Emblematic in both name and stated mission of the redistributive and idealized character of the Islamic Revolution, the *bonyad*s exemplify one of the core ideological innovations of the revolution's architect, Ayatollah Ruhollah Khomeini – the amalgamation of traditional religious imagery and modern organizational forms through a populist, class-rooted appeal that deliberately targeted a broad array of socio-economic groups. Hence, organizations which operate in the name of the 'deprived segments' of the population have, in practice, developed into conglomerates oriented toward capital accumulation, with their proclaimed ideological objectives distinctly subordinate, though never fully subsumed.

The Islamic era in Iran has seen a surge in the number of public and private foundations which are professedly operated on a non-profit basis, but are unconnected to the traditional *vaqf* system of charitable endowments. The handful of *bonyad*s that existed outside the religious infrastructure prior to the revolution had been conceived by the shah as vehicles for political, personal or cultural goals – for example, the Pahlavi Foundation and the Foundation for Ferdowsi's Shahnameh, to name just a few. Not surprisingly, the close identification of these organizations with the monarchy meant that they were disbanded in the days and weeks following the shah's ousting. In their place, the Islamic Republic has spawned a wide range of *bonyad*s as part of a frenzy of institution-building in the post-revolutionary consolidation of power and authority. Several of the largest and most influential – the Bonyad-e Mostazafan va Janbazan (Foundation of the Oppressed and Self-Sacrificers) and Bonyad-e Shahid (Martyrs' Foundation) – were entrusted with protecting the victims of the revolution and the war which soon followed and, more broadly, with fulfilling the revolutionary mandate to promote a more just society.

As the most prominent of the foundations, the Bonyad-e Mostazafan will be covered in some detail below; its slightly smaller counterpart is the Bonyad-e Shahid, which was established in March 1980 to administer the needs of veterans of the revolution and their families, and since has also undertaken responsibilities for victims of the war with Iraq. Its funding derives from expropriated property accorded to it and annual government subsidies, which totalled 398.5 billion rials in 1994 and have continued to increase.[12] As of 1991/92, Shahid owned 150 different enterprises, which were active in industrial production, construction, agriculture, commerce and services; the largest of these is the Shahid Investment Company with a wide range of its own business ventures. In addition to providing financial assistance, the cultural and charitable wing of the Bonyad-e Shahid oversees the distribution of special rights to its constituency, including prioritized university admission and employment consideration, as well as other benefits including assistance with arranging marriages.[13]

Other semi-public *bonyad*s with similar responsibilities include the Bonyad-e Omur Mohajerin-e Tahmili (Foundation for the Affairs of the Imposed War Refugees), which was a largely government-funded foundation intended to resettle families uprooted by the war and help plan reconstruction of the devastated territories, and the Imam's Relief Committee, which provides medical, educational and social assistance to rural needy families. Although the IRC owns substantial property and land holdings, it too relies heavily on government subsidies (228 billion rials in 1994).[14] In addition, several of the charitable foundations which were established outside the traditional *vaqf* system focus on cultural issues, such as the cinema-oriented Farabi Foundation, the Sazman-e Tablighat-e Islami (Islamic Propaganda Organization), and the Bonyad-e Resalat (Foundation for Prophetic Mission), which publishes the influential conservative newspaper of the same name.

Reflecting the situation of institutional dualism that prevailed during the early months of post-revolutionary consolidation, the foundations, particularly during the early years of the Islamic regime, tended to replicate functions formally assigned to the central government. In some cases, they have merged with ministries or evolved into independent government agencies for reasons involving logistical efficiency, political infighting, or both. For example, the Bonyad-e Omur Mohajerin-e Tahmili has been subsumed within the Ministry of Labour, and one of the cultural foundations, the Islamic Propaganda Organization, has gradually adopted government oversight.[15] In addition, the Housing Foundation was initially established to channel residential resources to the poor, but became a vehicle for radical clerics who advocated redistributive policies and the limitation of private property. It was later transformed into a full-fledged government ministry, although the foundation itself retains an independent identity within the Ministry.[16] Another of the post-revolutionary parastatal foundations, the Jehad-e Sazandegi (Reconstruction Crusade), was tasked with the critical role of bringing the fruits of an urban revolution to a population which remained largely based in villages and rural settings. The Jehad's efforts to promote economic development in the countryside and inculcate regime ideology were gauged to be relatively successful both within Iran and by outside observers, and it was elevated to a full government ministry in 1984. The Jehad also participated in the war effort with infrastructure development and weapons production.[17]

The *bonyads*' status as ostensibly charitable groups confers both advantages and vulnerabilities upon these organizations themselves and their patron, the state. The foundations are largely unaccountable to the government (although they are directly responsible to the *faqih*, spiritual leader of the nation), exempting their profits from taxation and enabling the organizations to preclude full disclosure of their activities. These privileges tacitly sanction the *bonyads*' intervention in both the domestic and international arena on behalf of a distinct and independent agenda that, at times, contravenes that of the government itself. An examination of the largest and most powerful of the parastatal foundations demonstrates that the *bonyads* have engaged significant resources and influence and have developed into potent networks outside the state itself. This provides creative vehicles for the mobilization of capital, but also poses significant constraints for government efforts to reform and reconstruct the Iranian economy.

2. Case Study: The Bonyad-e Mostazafan va Janbazan

The case of the Foundation for the Oppressed and the Self-Sacrificers (Bonyad-e Mostazafan va Janbazan) strikingly illustrates the challenges to economic policy posed by the *bonyads*. The reach of the MJF extends throughout the economic, political and social life of the Islamic Republic. This organization reportedly controls $12 billion in assets, including an estimated 400,000 workers in thousands of enterprises and properties ranging from agriculture, trade and industry, housing development and construction, transportation (land, shipping, and aviation) and tourism.[18] Headed until recently by Mohsen Rafiqdust, a prominent political figure in the Islamic Republic since accompanying Khomeini in his triumphant return from exile in 1979, the political resources of the Bonyad-e Mostazafan are equally imposing. When Rafiqdust boasted to an American newspaper in 1995, 'we touch the lives of every Iranian,'[19] he was hardly exaggerating.

The Bonyad-e Mostazafan was established on 5 March 1979, through a decree issued by Khomeini himself in the earliest weeks following his assumption of power and the final collapse of the monarchy. The Bonyad immediately absorbed the Pahlavi Foundation, a charitable organization created by the deposed shah in 1958 with approximately $3.2 billion in assets prior to the revolution.[20] Khomeini's Revolutionary Council clearly had ambitions for the Bonyad beyond simply harbouring the spoils of victory, however; in May 1979, the Council directed the Central Bank to provide a 1,000 million rial loan to the new organization.[21] Like the shah, who used the camouflage of charity as both a political tool and an 'economic weapon,'[22] the new regime quickly vested the MJF with extraordinary resources and political consequence; in addition to the Pahlavi Foundation holdings, the assets of the country's 51 largest industrialists were also nationalized over the course of the early months of the revolutionary government, and many of these were transferred to the control of the MJF.[23]

The evolution of the MJF corresponds to the dynamics of political contention in post-revolutionary Iran. Its early expansion represented the extent to which the former elites had become fully deprived of any popular support, as public clamour for expropriation actually in some cases pre-empted action by the central government. Through the creation of an institution into which resources of the deposed power clique could be channelled, the new government strove to restore order to the nation's economic life and to outmanoeuvre the leftist elements of the initial coalition government.[24] The establishment of the MJF also heralded the inauguration of a wholesale organizational and ideological transformation of the state, orchestrated by the Revolutionary Council under Khomeini's leadership as the clerical faction gradually subsumed genuine authority and outflanked the moderate and leftists within the Provisional Government.

Along with the Mostazafan, the Revolutionary Council quickly formalized several of the vehicles of mass mobilization during the uprising, most notably the Pasdaran or Revolutionary Guard Corps, and created new organs for consolidating its authority and achieving its vision of an Islamic social order, including the local Islamic committees, the Islamic Revolutionary Guard Corps (IRGC), and the (since disbanded) Islamic Republican Party. In some cases, these institutions cooperated with similarly tasked government bodies; in other cases, they competed and often superseded them.[25] During the early months of the revolutionary government, the MJF strengthened the dichotomy between rival centres of power and authority in the Islamic Republic, contributing to the classic post-revolutionary scenario of dual (or, arguably, multiple) sovereignty and the eventual domination of radical factions over the moderates.

After sweeping to power on the strength of rhetoric extolling the need for social justice, one of the primary objectives of Khomeini and, more broadly, the clerical faction which emerged as the centre of gravity in the Islamic Republic, was the reorientation of the economy. Thus, the creation of new vehicles of authority and influence and the redistribution of elite resources was accompanied by a dramatic programme of nationalization of major sectors of the economy, including all private banks, insurance companies, all heavy industries (which included the mining and metals industries as well as plane, ship and automobile manufacture plants), and all factories and organizations in debt.[26]

The state assumed direct ownership and control of these assets in many cases, through the National Iranian Industries Organization or the Industrial Development and Renovation Organization, and, by one analyst's calculation, absorbed direct command of 80 to 85 per cent of Iran's major production units.[27]

Still, as the pace and scope of nationalizations expanded, so did the Bonyad, as the centrepiece of the Islamic Republic's commitment to social justice and a more equitable distribution of the national wealth. Intended to embody one of the key themes of Khomeini's ideological and programmatic framework for the post-Pahlavi era – the victory of the *mostazafin* (oppressed) over their oppressors as portrayed in deliberately populist rhetoric[28] – the MJF quickly evolved into the largest non-state actor in the economy, second only to the National Iranian Oil Company in size. Over time, while other institutions have succumbed to pressure for greater efficiency and transparency as a result of the government's fitful efforts to reconstruct and modernize the economy, the MJF has not been substantially altered by the vicissitudes of changing ideological and political currents in the Islamic Republic. In fact, the Bonyad, like certain other revolutionary organizations such as the IRGC, was strengthened as a result of the war with Iraq, which, in forcing the consolidation of clerical authority, thereby accelerated and intensified the Islamization of society and the jurisdiction of trusted vehicles of power.[29] Its mission (and its title) was actually expanded in 1989 to include responsibility for those wounded in the war with Iraq – hence, the *janbazan* or ones who sacrifice themselves.

The Bonyad's structure divides its charitable activities from productive enterprises; this latter division itself consists of seven functionally oriented 'economic organizations', responsible for agriculture, commerce, construction and development, mining, tourism and recreation, transportation, and industry. Its accounts are not publicly released, and press reports vary somewhat in enumerating and appraising its assets. A conservative estimate would number its subsidiaries as at least 800 (although figures as large as 1,500 are regularly cited), employing up to 700,000 workers (or as much as 5 per cent of the male labour force), with a total value in the $10 to $12 billion range.[30] The Bonyad's contribution to the national income is significant, although here too estimates vary (anywhere from 1.5 per cent of GDP to 8–10 per cent).[31] Assets include thousands of hectares of land confiscated after the revolution, tens of thousands of individual apartment buildings and other real estate properties, and a treasure trove of personal property, including cars, carpets, and jewels.[32] Its presence in certain industries is commanding: MJF enterprises produce as much as 20 per cent of Iranian textiles, 40 per cent of Iranian soft drinks, two-thirds of all glass products and equally significant proportions of tiles, chemicals, tires and foodstuffs.[33] In some respects, the MJF's activities are as remarkable as they are widespread: in addition to a strong presence in heavy industry and ownership of thousands of apartment buildings and small enterprises, the Mostazafan exports beer (non-alcoholic, of course) and owns a Disney-style theme park outside Tehran.[34]

The Bonyad actively engages in foreign trade, with exports in recent years claimed to be anywhere between $50 million and $100 million per year. Recently, the foundation appears to be coordinating its endeavours with the Iranian government's regional ambitions, investing heavily in projects in South and Central Asia, as well as courting its Arab neighbours, such as Kuwait. According to a variety of media reports, the MJF has negotiated and/or concluded investments in government and private organizations in Bosnia, Armenia, Turkmenistan, Kazakhstan, China, Pakistan, India, Bangladesh and Pakistan; in the latter alone, foundation chairman Rafiqdust claims to have invested $200 million in development projects.[35] In the West, MJF subsidiaries trade crude oil on the world market through a UK subsidiary, import Japanese cars, operate joint venture shipping companies in Italy and England, and own German holding companies.[36] The foundation is also stewarding a revival of the tourist industry in Iran; through a network which features most of the largest hotels and a tourist airline, the MJF anticipates boosting hard-currency earnings from foreign visitors to the billion-dollar range by the turn of the century.[37] Most recently, the MJF has leapt into Iran's revitalized financial services sector, and its bulk and privileged position rank the foundation as one of the few non-state entities with the capital to compete in the recently liberalized market for banking and investment services.[38] To prove that point, a mammoth building complex under construction by the Bonyad in north Tehran – intended to house a financial centre to rival Wall Street and the City – will symbolize its market dominance.[39]

Such a far-flung investment portfolio reaps substantial rewards; the profits of the MJF are estimated at $170 million in the year which, by the Iranian calendar, ended in March 1996, and $430 million between 1990 and 1995.[40] Rafiqdust justifies the extraordinary profitability of the MJF in an increasingly strained economy by virtue of its advancement of the social justice mandated by the revolution – the foundation 'earns in the economic field and spends in the social field.'[41] Forced by strong domestic criticism in the face of a faltering economy to defend the organization, Rafiqdust contends that the MJF assists hundreds of thousands Iranian needy and disabled and that a significant proportion of the foundation's work is carried out by the disabled.[42] These statistics, too, cannot be independently obtained.

Despite the historical defence of the *vaqf* by the ulama, the MJF – which is the largest charitable organization created after the revolution – was not attached to any religious institution. This highlights the extent to which the Islamic state in Iran was deliberately construed to supersede prevailing religious institutions, rather than to empower them, a distinction noted by Afsaneh Najmabadi and Sami Zubaida in considering taxation in the Islamic Republic.[43] The decision to amass the treasures of the vilified monarchy within an institution essentially unconnected to the clerical hierarchy demonstrates an awareness by policymakers in the early days of the Islamic Republic of the potential threat from the traditional religious networks, and of the potential utility to the regime of a semi-governmental financial powerhouse. The Bonyad-e Mostazafan, like many of the other *nahadha-ye enqelabi* (revolutionary organizations), was born of the intersection of charismatic patriarchal authority and the environment of contention among diverse social groups and underwritten by the Islamic Republic's fusion of the monarchy's distributive function with the revolution's populist rhetoric.

However, given the typical centrality of the allocative state, it is equally striking to observe the extent to which the MJF (and its peers) are disengaged, at least on a formal level, from the state and from the official networks of policy-making. 'With no governmental discretion over expenses, no shareholders, no public account, and no clear legal status,'[44] the Bonyad-e Mostazafan operates, for all intents and purposes, outside the scope of both the traditional religious power structure and the government. The Bonyad has the discretion to operate solely on the basis of its own charter, which states that 'The foundation is a legal entity with financial, administrative, and employment independence, and its affairs shall be administered exclusively under the provisions of its charter and its internal regulations.'[45] The state has no direct involvement in MJF decision-making regarding either its philanthropic or productive activities, although it should be noted that a certain degree of leverage exists in the relationship between the Iranian consultative assembly, the Majles – which, despite heavy-handed ideological vetting of candidates, manifests a wide range of political debate – and the Bonyad, as well as the other foundations. Legislation frequently proscribes roles for the charitable divisions of the MJF (and the Bonyad-e Shahid), which apparently serve as official vetting agencies for benefit claims for veterans of the revolution and the war. This certainly invites the possibility of further parliamentary intrusion into the internal affairs of the foundations. More significantly, though, the Majles has a great deal of potential influence over the *bonyads*' purse strings, through budget decisions on annual subsidies and tax legislation (which has seen both the recent addition of the MJF to the tax rolls and its apparently wholesale exemption from those same taxes).

Although the MJF operates largely on the basis of self-regulation, there are very loose lines of accountability to the government. The *faqih* is empowered to appoint and remove the MJF director and, more latterly, board of directors – a 1995 modification of the governing structure of the foundation which was perceived as an attempt to provide a check to the powerful Rafiqdust.[46] In addition, the Iranian parliament has the authority to conduct its own investigations through its Article 90 Committee, although such scrutiny requires the permission of the *faqih*. However, it would appear that, to date, this jurisdiction serves more as a safety valve for public frustration over the MJF than as an actual restraint on its practices; on the several occasions that such inquiries have been undertaken, they have produced more in the way of reproaches than actual reform (see below). While the legal autonomy of the MJF and other revolutionary organizations was initially considered somewhat dubious outside Iran,[47] more recent interactions with the world economic community have endorsed their rather ambiguous and questionable role as quasi-governmental charities. A 1995 IMF study of the Iranian economy cited the division between the productive and charitable divisions of the MJF and other *bonyads* in designating them purely private organizations for the purposes of its analysis.[48]

Despite this finding, and despite the Bonyad-e Mostazafan's minimal formal links with the Iranian government, it enjoys great influence with the senior leadership by virtue of its prominent place within bureaucratic and traditional networks. Its close relationship with the Iranian security apparatus and its institutional authority were confirmed by the appointment of Mohsen Rafiqdust to lead the foundation in 1989; his credentials as the former commander of the country's unconventional military wing, the Revolutionary Guard, were irrefutably *maktabi* (or, in the Iranian context, radical). Under Rafiqdust's leadership, these organizational connections are alleged to have facilitated substantial cooperation between the two organizations in weapons procurement and production; for example, the Bonyad's heavy presence in legitimate mining and chemicals production allegedly camouflage IRGC chemical weaponry plants.[49] In addition, German intelligence sources contend that the MJF has utilized a network of sham enterprises to acquire inputs for the Revolutionary Guard's defence industry, including its biological, chemical and nuclear weapons as well as its missile development.[50] In addition, the foundation apparently undertakes international endeavours that transgress the traditional definition of trade – the MJF is commonly cited as a generous supporter and active political patron of Lebanese terrorist organization, Hezbollah.[51]

In addition to synthesizing a close relationship with the security bureaucracy of the regime, the MJF also emerged at the centre of most of the fundamental socio-economic and ideological debates that consumed Iranian politics: the clashes over the state intervention in the economy, the nationalization of foreign trade, the legitimacy of private property in Islam and the cultural revolution to propagate Islamic values. In many ways, these disputes represented the struggle among various social groups for domination of the post-revolutionary government, where debates couched in theological terms corresponded to the divergent interests of the groups grappling for authority in the aftermath of the deposition of the old elites. In this contest, the Bonyad became identified in Iran with the *bazaari*s, or merchants, who populate the traditional marketplace. This partially reflects the social origins of Rafiqdust and other key figures within the MJF.[52] On a more fundamental level, however, it represents the articulation of the synergy between the structure, activities, methods of operation, and interests of the bazaar with those of the *bonyad*s.[53]

Specifically, the *bonyad*s have absorbed the traditional networks of political and economic influence that permeated the bazaar and that have made the merchant community such a potent actor in Iranian political history, particularly in the shaping of the state over the course of the past century. The marketplace traditionally served as the core of Iranian social and economic life,[54] where a symbiotic relationship among the merchants and the clergy was reinforced through marriage, support of religious foundations and other financial connections, as well as a shared cultural outlook.[55] This relationship generated political solidarity when the interests of either group appeared threatened, and in the Tobacco Revolt, the Constitutional Revolution, and the 1963 unrest that culminated in Khomeini's exile, the bazaar bolstered clerical opposition to state policies through financial support. In 1978–79, the economic, political and cultural threat posed to traditional merchants by the shah's modernization programmes ultimately produced another successful alliance between the bazaaris and the ulama which proved to be the key factor in the success of the anti-shah movement.[56] Under the Islamic Republic, the bazaaris emerged from the protracted political contest over the permissibility of private property as a favoured economic stratum, as a result of revolutionary credentials and continued affiliations with the clerical elite. In addition, state control over the industrial sector meant that 'the commercial bourgeoisie became the most active faction of the ruling class.'[57] This, of course, represents another potent link between the bazaar and the *bonyad*s: they are 'the only winners' in the Islamic Republic's lacklustre economic history.[58]

Today, the MJF continues to occupy the forefront of political debate in Iran; however, that debate has shifted from the shaping of a socio-economic order to the quest for efficiency. To the extent that the *bonyad*s are distinct from the public sector, it may be argued that they are less encumbered by political considerations and that management of the enterprises they control will tend to be characterized by a greater degree of autonomy, and thus competitiveness, than those which are strictly state-owned. Moreover, the robustness of these foundations over the past two decades demonstrates their utility as mechanisms for capital accumulation and reinvestment. In this respect, the connection between the *bonyad*s and the bazaar community, both actual and perceived, has provided institutional incentives and facilitation for the engagement of the Iranian commercial bourgeoisie in Iran's industrial sector – a connection which the Iranian economy has traditionally lacked, to its detriment and that of the bazaar as well. Finally, the *bonyad*s' active involvement in the market for privatized state assets (as discussed below) may enable them to play a useful role in mediating between the public and private sectors during the necessary adjustment to a smaller state role in the economy. On a smaller scale, state-owned banks have fulfilled this function in Tunisia and Egypt.[59]

The *bonyad*s' role as agents of development and change certainly bears further investigation. However, it is the potential of these parastatal foundations – both as a result of their sheer size within the economy and political perks – for exacerbating the distortions that plague the Iranian economy that generates concern both in Iranian political and financial circles as well as externally. The MJF and the other foundations are loath to relinquish the prerogatives – both political and economic – that their size and proximity to power confer. Insulated by its bonds with influential social groups and powerful bureaucratic constituencies, the Bonyad-e Mostazafan in particular utilizes the favourable environment to evade excessive oversight and to maximize its own rewards. One analyst has described the MJF as 'a giant monopoly with vast control over the Iranian economy' and the *bonyad*s, as a group, as 'a major source of distortion and non-transparency in resource allocation and a major financial drag on the Iranian economy.'[60]

Such criticisms are hardly new for the Bonyad-e Mostazafan. The MJF has been dogged since its inception by allegations of corruption and abuses of power, allegations which strike at the core of the state's Islamic legitimacy and thus threaten to sully the regime itself, despite the government's lack of any day-to-day authority over the organization. Initially at least such charges inhered in its function: the MJF's role as the beneficiary of expropriated resources exposed it to all the criticism and suspicion of the targets of government seizure.[61] Within a year of its establishment, 800 complaints were submitted to a parliamentary investigatory committee initiated by then-president Abol Hassan Bani-Sadr. Nonetheless, the early political utility of the MJF to more radical elements within the clerical faction preserved its autonomy and squelched the investigation. Changes were initiated, however; one of the MJF's first directors, Mohandes Khamushi, was sacked over misuses of funds after Khomeini himself implied, in a play on his own rhetoric, that the institution had begun to serve the greedy rather than the needy (the *mostakbarin* rather than the *mostazafin*).[62] Later, the leadership of the foundation was conferred upon Mohsen Rafiqdust, who was given a mandate to rid the foundation of any fraud or excess.[63]

Rafiqdust's leadership of the MJF has produced a steady increase in its earnings, but has in fact entrenched the popular image of the organization as exploitative and praetorian. Protests are reported to have erupted in Shiraz in 1992 over MJF mis-management.[64] More recently, the MJF withstood a parliamentary investigation in 1995–96, which concluded that the foundation had engaged in influence peddling.[65] Perhaps the severest blow to the prestige and stability of the foundation came in the form of the conviction of Rafiqdust's brother in the embezzlement scandal that came to be known as Iran's 'trial of the century'. The embezzle-ment of $450 million from Bank Saaderat did not involve Rafiqdust or the foundation explicitly; however, the conviction of Morteza Rafiqdust and seven others unleashed an unprecedented level of criticism against the MJF and its leadership.[66] The scandal captured popular imagination, re-igniting the rhetoric of the radicals and threatening to taint the Rafsanjani-era economic liberalization with the stigma of personal enrichment and oppression – themes markedly reminiscent of the opposition move-ment under the monarchy.[67] Rafiqdust has received the continuing endorsement of the leadership, however, although Khamene'i's 1995 renewal of his post is qualified by the mandate of 'carrying out the necessary reforms and improving the capabilities and cohesion of the foundation,' as well as by the addition of a board of trustees to oversee the MJF.[68] However, the political power of the Bonyad-e Mostazafan has enabled it to elude any real structural modifications, and its pattern of support and interconnecting interests with both the current regime and key social and political constituencies in Iran indicates that the *bonyad* possesses the institutional fortitude to resist externally imposed controls.

Assessing the impact of the *bonyads* on the economy requires consideration of both the immediate and tertiary costs and benefits. First, the organizations command a significant and politically sacrosanct segment of public expenditure. Despite an intense effort to reduce the government budget as part of structural adjustment, the *bonyad*s and the state sector comprise two-thirds of annual government expenditure. Expenditures on 'social justice' – which include the *bonyad*s as well as state welfare organizations and activities – have increased steadily, and are projected to rise again in the current budget. Such increases reportedly come at the expense of budget cuts to the Ministry of Energy and various provincial disbursements.[69] In addition, the MJF has enjoyed a tax-exempt status as a charitable organization since its inception; although the Majles terminated that privilege, at least on paper, in 1992, the MJF continues to enjoy a virtually wholesale tax immunity. The sum – certainly in the multi-million dollar range – that the government might otherwise accrue if they were private businesses represents forfeited revenues.[70]

But beyond their direct costs, the *bonyad*s' political and economic activity engender a wide range of distortions for Iranian development efforts. The MJF benefits from preferential access to foreign exchange, enabling the MJF and other *bonyad*s to muscle out the small businessman, while political clout enabled the foundations to compensate for the briefly liberalized exchange rate with additional credit from the state-controlled banking sector.[71] Further, the *bonyad*s are not subject to the bulk of regulations which govern the activities of state-owned enterprises, which preclude intrusive government audits and other restrictions on its management, such as employment regulation. The MJF, for example, thus enjoys an almost unconstrained capacity for intervention in the Iranian economy (and political competition) which has led observers to characterize it as 'a state within a state.'[72] The scant oversight also lends some credence to suggestions that the MJF is an active participant in Iran's underground economy, reportedly selling everything from foreign currency to pharmaceuticals to contraband American cigarettes on the black market for a profit of ten-fold or more.[73]

The nature and scope of the *bonyad*s pose additional impediments for efforts to promote competition and economic efficiency in Iran. The MJF's vast scope and political sway facilitates market dominance, and its relationships both with the other *bonyad*s and with state-owned enterprises provide preferential access to contracts and opportunities. The extent to which the *bonyad*s as a group coordinate their activities cannot be assessed; however, the pattern of cooperative activities and transfer of resources between the various foundations (and the government itself) suggests that these organizations, individually and as a very loosely associated group, exert a meaningful level of market control. This aggregation of industrial activity within the *bonyad*s during the initial period of post-revolutionary consolidation and during the war with Iraq certainly presented some economies of scale which imparted a certain rational justification to their structure. However, at some juncture, Iranian development must address the extent to which these foundations – and in particular the Bonyad-e Mostazafan – are heavily integrated, both vertically and horizontally, in certain key industries. The MJF's presence in the transportation sector – where it controls car production, shipping and domestic aviation, and engineers the largest road and rail projects – undoubtedly deters competition and creates barriers for entry of new private sector actors in these markets.

The cross-sectoral scope and political influence of the Bonyad-e Mostazafan enables it to engage in tactics which redefine the concept of unfair trade practices, which impair opportunities for growth by subverting competition and certainly amplify external concerns that Iran provides a hostile climate for foreign investment. One notable example is a vicious campaign waged for control of the domestic soft-drink market, which the MJF has dominated since the revolution. In an effort to outflank the competition from Coca-Cola products under a 1993 franchising agreement with a local partner, Rafiqdust himself disparaged the agreement as an attempt by the West to corrupt Iranian culture and issued this challenge: 'God willing, we will soon drive all foreign Coca-Cola plants out of Iran.' The outburst provoked parliamentary and newspaper debates, and reported labour unrest and supply disruptions. The episode illustrated to other potential investors that the *bonyad*s were a force to be reckoned with; for example, when Pepsi-Cola (which bore not simply identification with the US, but a historical association with a well-known royalist and Baha'i) returned to the Iranian market the following year, the company affiliated itself with a subsidiary of the Astan-e Qods Foundation, based at the Mashhad shrine of Imam Reza.[74]

In addition, the lack of transparency or accountability that surround the MJF and other *bonyad*s helps foster the sizeable 'grey zone' of economic activity that exists on the fringes of legal enterprise in Iran. Since the crackdowns on corruption which quickly followed the early reform efforts under Rafsanjani, rent-seeking behaviour among government enterprises has become more resourceful. In recent years, the proliferation of private companies attached to government ministries – which utilize government resources, but serve to benefit private groups or individuals – has been exacerbated by inadequate regulatory control.[75] A recent case involves the investigation into a string of government-owned, profit-making dummy corporations set up to perform sub-contracting services for the Construction Crusade ministry. Since government ministries were prohibited from creating such companies, the scheme was facilitated by the 'gift' of three corporations from the MJF in 1987. These three holding companies encompassed 53 productive units, employing 23,000 workers and making an estimated 20 billion tumans in annual profits – and, after a somewhat acrimonious debate, were eventually accorded status as non-governmental, public institutions themselves. In this way, government resources were effectively transferred outside the purview of the state, enriching well-placed individuals along the way and contributing to the escalation of prices through non-competitive bidding.[76]

There are some indications that the *bonyad*s have rationalized as they have matured; the MJF has undertaken a major campaign to divest, at least partially, its small affiliates by selling shares on the Tehran Stock Exchange in an effort to both gradually trim its subordinate ventures as well as stimulate the private sector.[77] They have been major players in the rejuvenation of the Tehran Stock Exchange, and along with the state-run commercial banks, have served as the main customers in the privatization of large state enterprises on the Exchange.[78] The *bonyad*s may well be the only organizations in Iran capable of absorbing the increasingly privatized assets of the state sector; they occupy the enviable position of being capital-rich in a prevailing environment which is distinctly not. The privatization effort to date has stumbled as a result of the perception and reality that such transfers purely benefited the privileged segments of society. As one newspaper commented: 'in the name of privatization, a number of healthy public industries and enterprises were transferred to hand-picked persons at peanuts prices. It was not privatization, it was auctioning of national assets.'[79]

Ironically, however, when the sell-off of state enterprises recommenced in 1995, the very first offering on the stock exchange saw a successful bid by the Shahid Investment Company, a subsidiary of the Bonyad-e Shahid, for a controlling share in Iran Metal Industries from the Industrial Development and Renovation Organization. To further call into question the efficiency of the transaction, it should be noted that the government also allocated funding to Shahid for such purchases.[80] Meanwhile, the owner of a textile mill aptly summarized the dilemma for the private sector: 'The government is fully determined to privatize, but there are big problems. Private-sector investors are not so big as to be able to buy such big factories, and financial institutions are not prepared to help private buyouts.'[81] Clearly, then, the *bonyad*s threaten the effectiveness of government divestment policies, potentially resulting in a recycling of capital from public to semi-public control, with the stock exchange serving as 'an instrument for exchanging ownership from one group of public sector to another group.'[82]

By posing such impediments to reform, the net effect of the parastatal foundations on Iran's structural adjustment programmes can only be surmised as negative. However, the productive dynamism that these enterprises create, and the possible synergy between public and private enterprise that these organizations pose for socio-economic development should not be ruled out. Self-interested pressure on the government by the *bonyad*s for greater privatization has helped to provide the momentum for broad privatization measures and the liberalization of the economy.[83] In addition, the *bonyad*s have offered enthusiastic support for the government's gradual shift to an export-led growth strategy, and their orientation toward foreign trade (particularly within the emerging markets of the region) will, despite its political dimensions, certainly facilitate a more outward focus for the economy as a whole. The MJF has also worked cooperatively on certain issues with the government to manage the economy, and it is standard practice for the Bonyad-e Mostazafan to dramatically increase basic food imports to mitigate the impact of a government subsidy reduction.[84] This sort of crisis management contributes to short-term stability and could help to preclude the sort of urban unrest which has waylaid structural adjustment programmes elsewhere in the region. Nonetheless, Iranian economists caution that in the long run, 'an organization that does not see it necessary to abide by conventional systems will have to adjust or default.'[85]

3. The 'Message of 2nd Khordad' and its Implications for the Bonyads

For several years now, the Iranian media has been littered with references to the 'message of 2nd Khordad' – i.e., 23 May, the date of the 1997 presidential elections which produced a stunning victory for the reputed moderate Mohammad Khatami. The phrase is used both as a sort of rallying cry for the acceleration of political and economic reform (along the lines of President Clinton's unofficial slogan during the 1992 campaign, 'it's the economy, stupid') and a potent admonition of the tenor of popular opinion to the groups and individuals who opposed Khatami. Interestingly, however, Khatami's popularity can largely be traced to his identification with cultural liberalization, while his erstwhile opponent, Majles speaker Ali Akbar Nateq-Nuri, had prominently featured economic reform in his election programme as part of his close affiliation with the bazaar. Khatami's mandate on economic issues, then, is somewhat tenuous. The sensational arrest and release of Gholamhossein Karbaschi, the mayor of Tehran whose ambitious urban development programmes had earned him the enmity of the traditional commercial sector, represents a temporary victory for the technocrats over the bazaar. However, in the fluid factional contention that persists in Iran, public outrage over corruption and the sanctity of the revolutionary ideals of social justice could easily shift the momentum in the other direction.

What are the implications of this new era in Iranian politics for the *bonyads*? Certainly the replacement of Bonyad-e Mostazafan director Mohsen Rafiqdust in July 1999 represents a telling indication of things to come. His replacement, former minister of defence Mohammad Foruzandeh, has pledged to work more cooperatively with the formal government. Rafiqdust was closely associated with the faction backing Nateq-Nuri, who adopts a harder-line approach especially on cultural and economic issues. In recent months, pressure has come from the Majles and from the newspapers, which serve as bully pulpits for the various political factions within the government, to impose greater scrutiny on the Bonyad-e Mostazafan and the other foundations. One publication audaciously questioned the subsidies to the prosperous Bonyad-e Astan-e Qods – one of the oldest religious endowments at Iran's holiest Shi'a shrine – suggesting that transfers should in fact occur in reverse. In a thinly veiled jab at the MJF and the other large parastatal foundations, the magazine continued: 'Nongovern-mental foundations which receive limitless and unaccountable government funds, and which are not answerable to the government or the nation, are among the most difficult economic, political, cultural, and even foreign policy (!) problems of the country.'[86]

Should the political and economic pressure on the regime grow too intense, the *bonyad*s might prove easy scapegoats for econ-omic woes and tempting targets of revenue and hard currency for a cash-strapped government. Critics of the *bonyad*s have advo-cated divesting the organizations of productive assets, arguing that the status quo enables political considerations to prevail over economic signals. With the profits from such sales, the *bonyad*s themselves could focus on what is their professed first priority – charity and social progress.[87] However, it remains questionable that the country possesses either the means or the mechanism for such a massive transfer of resources. In fact, a simpler and perhaps more feasible step in the direction of rationalizing the *bonyad*s would be the release of the income statements and balance sheets of the *bonyad*s. This is an idea which is slowly gaining currency in Iran.[88]

Although political jousting over the precedence of efficiency versus social justice continues in Iran today, the debate over the appropriate path for the country's economic future has largely been pre-empted by the urgency of the need for improved economic efficiency. Soon, the post-revolutionary Iranian baby boom will reach maturity, spilling another 800,000 job-seekers onto the streets each year in a country which currently generates approximately 300,000 new employment opportunities annually.[89] This scenario portends a serious crisis of legitimacy for Tehran, whose commitment to the highly utopian ideals of the revolution remains a critical component of its popular legitimacy, even as its implementation is increasingly criticized. The *bonyad*s occupy a complicated position in the evolution of the Islamic Republic in the post-Khomeini era; as political gate-keepers, they may provide alternative vehicles for popular participation and social action, but also appear to replicate the narrow base of interest vested in the regime that doomed the shah. As regards their economic influence, the *bonyad*s may, by promoting the rationalization of the state's role in the economy, paradoxically but deliberately position themselves and the small groups of individuals who control their activities as the true repository of authority in Iran. Both of these factors mean that the *bonyads* have profound implications for the future of the Iranian political process, and for the tenor and conduct of regional relations.

Notes

1 Ayatollah Ruhollah Khomeini, *Hokumat-e Islami* (Islamic Government), as translated in Hamid Algar, *Islam and Revolution: Writings and Declarations of Imam Khomeini*, Berkeley: Mizan Press, 1981, p. 137.

2 Samuel Huntington, *Political Order in Changing Societies*, New Haven: Yale University Press, 1968, p. 266; Theda Skocpol, *States and Social Revolutions: A Comparative Analysis of France, Russia, and China*, Cambridge: Cambridge University Press, 1979, p. 163.

3 Farideh Farhi, *States and Urban-Based Revolutions: Iran and Nicaragua*, Urbana: University of Illinois Press, 1990, p. 10.

4 Theda Skocpol, 'Rentier State and Shi'a Islam in the Iranian Revolution', *Theory and Society*, Volume 11, 1982, pp. 278–9; Tim McDaniel, *Autocracy, Modernization, and Revolution in Russia and Iran*, Princeton: Princeton University Press, 1991.

5 Tatiana Vorozheikina, 'Clientelism and the Process of Political Democratization in Russia', in Luis Roniger and Ayse Gunes-Ayata, (eds), *Democracy, Clientelism and Civil Society*, Boulder: Lynne Reinner Publishers, 1994.

6 Nikki R. Keddie, 'Can Revolutions be Predicted?' in Nikki R. Keddie, ed., *Debating Revolutions*, New York: New York University Press, 1995, p. 12.

7 Cyrus Vakili-Zad, 'Continuity and Change: The Structure of Power in Iran', in Bina and Zanganeh (1992), p. 22. For a detailed overview of the history of *vaqf* in Iran, see Fatemeh E. Moghadam, 'Property Rights and Islamic Revolution in Iran', in Haleh Esfandiari and A. L. Udovitch (eds), *The Economic Dimensions of Middle Eastern History*, Princeton: The Darwin Press, 1990, pp. 148–54.

8 Hooshang Amirahmadi, 'Bunyad', in John L. Esposito, ed., *Encyclopedia of the Modern Islamic World*, 1995, vol. 1, pp. 234–5.

9 Christophe de Roquefeuil, 'Affaire Rushdie: les durs du regime iranien font monter la pression', *Agence France Press*, 13 February 1997; 'President Rafsanjani on his Future, Rushdie, Foreign Ties, other Issues', Vision of the Islamic Republic Network 1, 12 February 1997. From BBC *Summary of World Broadcasts*, 17 February 1997.

10 Amirahmadi, in Esposito (ed.), 1995, pp. 234–7; Farhad Kazemi, 'Civil Society and Iranian Politics', in Augustus Richard Norton, *Civil*

Society in the Middle East, vol. 2, New York: E. J. Brill, 1996, pp. 141–7.

11 The charter of the Bonyad-e Shahid (Martyrs' Foundation), for example, describes it as 'a public and non-governmental institution' with 'legal status and financial and administrative independence.' From 'Majles: 11 Nov. Session', *Resalat,* 12 November 1997, pp. 12–13, in FBIS-NES-98–051, 20 February 1998.

12 'Details of Subsidies Amounting to More than 6,088bn Rials', IRNA, 24 May 1994, as translated in *BBC Summary of World Broadcasts,* 31 May 1994; 'President Hashemi-Rafsanjani Presents 1376 Budget Bill to Majles', *Ettela'at,* 24 November 1996, pp. 2–3, in FBIS-NES-96–232, 24 November 1996.

13 'Bonyad-e Shahid', Ehsan Yarshater (ed.), *Encyclopaedia Iranica,* Costa Mesa: Mazda, pp. 360–1; Amirahmadi, in Esposito, (ed.), 1995, pp. 236–7; Iran Research Group, *Iran Yearbook 1989–1990,* Bonn: MB Medien & Bucher Verlagsgesellschaft mbH, 1989, pp. 10/45–6.

14 'Details of Subsidies Amounting to more than 6,088bn Rials', *IRNA,* 24 May 1994. See also Asghar Schirazi, *Islamic Development Policy The Agrarian Question in Iran,* Boulder: Lynne Rienner Publishers, 1993, pp. 163–4.

15 Amirahmadi, in Esposito, ed., 1995, p. 235; 'Majles Session: 30 Apr 96', *Resalat,* 1 May 1996, pp. 5, 13, in FBIS-NES-96–139–S, 1 May 1996.

16 Shaul Bakhash, *The Reign of the Ayatollahs: Iran and the Islamic Revolution,* New York: Basic Books, Inc., Publishers, 1986, pp. 186–9; Jahangir Amuzegar, *Iran's Economy Under the Islamic Republic,* London: I.B.Tauris & Co Ltd, 1993, pp. 101–2.

17 For a detailed review of the evolution of the Jehad, see Schirazi (1993).

18 Kazemi (1996), p. 146.

19 Colin Barraclough, 'Iranian Poverty Fund Bankrolls Fun Parks and Much More', *The Christian Science Monitor,* 1 February 1995, p. 9.

20 Dilip Hiro, *Iran Under the Ayatollahs,* New York: Routledge, 1985, pp. 131–2.

21 Ali Rashidi, 'De-Privatization Process and the Iranian Economy after the Revolution of 1979', in Thierry Colville (ed.), *The Economy of Islamic Iran: Between State and Market,* Louvain: Peeters for Institut Français de Recherche en Iran, 1994, p. 47.

22 Hiro (1985), pp. 131–2.

23 Anoushirvan Ehteshami, *After Khomeini: The Iranian Second Republic,* Routledge, 1995; see pp. 83–8 for a description of the major industrial families under the shah and the process of nationalization.

24 Vahid Nowshirvani and Patrick Clawson, 'The State and Social Equity in Postrevolutionary Iran', in Myron Weiner and Ali Banuazizi (eds), *The Politics of Social Transformation in Afghanistan, Iran, and Pakistan*, Syracuse: Syracuse University Press, 1994, p. 255; Ehteshami (1995), p. 86.

25 Amirahmadi provides an economical overview of the conflict among 'parallel organizations' in Hooshang Amirahmadi, 'Economic Costs of the War and the Reconstruction in Iran', in Cyrus Bina and Hamid Zaganeh, (eds), *Modern Capitalism and Islamic Ideology in Iran*, London: Macmillan, 1992, pp. 274.

26 Mansour Moaddel, *Class, Politics, and Ideology in the Iranian Revolution*, New York: Columbia University Press, 1993, pp. 252–3.

27 Ehteshami (1995), p. 86.

28 Ervand Abrahamian, *Khomeinsim: Essays on the Islamic Republic*, Berkeley: University of California Press, 1993, p. 16.

29 W. Thom Workman, *The Social Origins of the Iran–Iraq War*, Boulder: Lynn Rienner Publishers, 1994, pp. 128–30.

30 These figures are widely quoted in various articles in the Western media, for example: 'State Foundations Dominate Economy', *The Financial Times*, 17 July 1997, p. 4; 'Dual Control', *The Economist*, 18 January 1997, p. 7; in 1994, a Majles deputy cited a government audit which estimated that approximately one-third of the more than 2,200 public organizations were affiliated with the MJF. 'RESALAT Reports on Majles Sessions – 3 July', *Resalat*, 4 July 1994, pp. 5, 15, in FBIS-NES-94–152–S.

31 Lower estimate from International Monetary Fund, *Islamic Republic of Iran – Recent Economic Developments*, IMF Staff Country Report no. 95/121. Washington, DC: December 1995, p. 46; upper estimate from Iran Research Group, 1989, p. 10/43.

32 Amuzegar (1993), pp. 100–1.

33 Shahrzad Moshaver, 'Mostazafan & Janbazan Foundation under Majlis Scrutiny', *Payam Emruz*, February and March 1995, no. 4, pp. 22–3; 'Rafiqdust Details Mosta'zafan Foundation Activities', *Kayhan*, International Edition, 19 November 1994, p. 8.

34 *MEED*, 28 October 1994, p. 30; 'For the Oppressed', *The Economist*, 25 September 1993, p. 58.

35 See 'Iranian Official: Iran Ready To Help Bosnian Reconstruction', *IRNA*, 12 Oct. 1997, in FBIS-NES-97–285; 'Officials Discuss Development of Trade, Industrial Ties', *IRNA*, 7 June 1997, in FBIS-NES-97–159; 'Iran: Turkmenistan in Asbestos for Tiles Agreement', *MEED*, 29 August 1994; 'Joint Road Transport Company with Kazakhstan', Infoprod Research, 24 July 1997; 'Beijing for Further

Expansion of Ties with Tehran', *IRNA*, 6 January 1997, as transcribed in FBIS-NES-97-0041 'MJF Bulks Up Bon Air With Russian Aircraft', *Iran News*, 3 October 1996, pp. 2–3, in FBIS-NES-96–197; 'Indian Company Calls for Cooperation with Iran', *Compass Newswire*, 13 September 1996. 'Dhaka Tehran Ties', *The Morning Sun*, 23 July 1995, p. 4, as transcribed in FBIS-NES-95–145; 'Iran: Kuwaiti Visit Reviews Cooperation With Iranian Foundation', *IRNA*, 8 October 1997, in FBIS-NES-97–282.

36 Hossein Farzin, 'The Political Economy of Foreign Exchange Reform' in S. Rahnema and S. Behdad (eds), *Iran After the Revolution: Crisis of an Islamic State*, London: I.B.Tauris & Co Ltd., 1995, p. 181; 'Japanese Automakers Resuming Exports to Iran', *Comline Daily News Transportation*, 18 June 1992; 'Coint Leases Odino Valperga Italeuropa Ahead of Acquisition', *Il Sole,* 19 August 1993; 'Bright Lights of London Bring Major Reefer Trade Players in from the Cold', *Lloyds List*, 13 December 1996; Thomas Scheurer, 'Pious Regards from an Ice-Cold Warrier', (sic) in Munich *Focus*, 10 October 1994, pp. 99–101, in FBIS-WEU-94–198.

37 'Rafiqdust Details Mosta'zafan Foundation Activities', *Kayhan International*, 19 November 1994, p. 8, in FBIS-NES-95–003; 'Book Early to Avoid the Rush', *The Economist*, 20 January 1996, p. 45; 'Iran Softening its Global Image to Bring Foreign Cash', *South China Morning Post*, 24 August 1997, p. 5.

38 'Iran', *Euromoney*, January/February 1997; 'Bonyad-e Mostazafan's Activities Detailed – Financial Establishments', *Resalat*, 2 September 1995, p. 15, in FBIS-NES-95–242, 2 September 1995.

39 'The Foundation of the Oppressed and Tehran's Biggest Financial Center', *Payam-e Emruz*, No. 22, 21 March, 22 April, 1998, p. 7, in FBIS-NES-98–098, 8 April 1998.

40 'Iran's Caspian Sea Highway Project Inaugurated, Ecologists Upset', *Deutsche Presse-Agentur*, 9 December 1996; Reuters World Service, 4 January 1995.

41 Alberto Negri, 'All the (Former) Martyrs' Power', *Il Sole*, 20 July 1995, p. 7, in FBIS-NES-95–145.

42 'Most Figures in Majles Committee Report on the MJF are Incorrect', *Iran News*, 12 June 1996, p. 1, in FBIS-NES-96–121, 12 June 1996.

43 Afsaneh Najmabadi, 'Depoliticization of a Rentier State: The Case of Pahlavi Iran', Chapter 10, in Hazem Beblawi and Giacomo Luciani (eds), *The Rentier State*, New York: 1987, pp. 226–7; Sami Zubaida, *Islam, The People and The State*, London: Routledge, 1988, pp. 175–6.

44 Farzin (1995), p. 183.

45 Text from the charter of the MJF was quoted, in English, in Shahrzad Moshaver, 'Mostazafan & Janbazan Foundation under Majlis Scrutiny', *Payam Emruz*, February & March 1995, no. 4, pp. 22–3.
46 'Iran Foundation Chief Reappointed with Less Powers', *Reuters World Service*, 22 July 1995.
47 The status of the *bonyad*s raised some questions at the Iran-U.S. Claims Tribunal over whether they should be considered entities controlled by the Islamic government. See 'The Hague: First Anniversary But Nobody's Dancing', *Middle East Executive Reports*, January, 1983, p. 11.
48 IMF, 1995.
49 Mohammad Mohaddessin, *Islamic Fundamentalism: The New Global Threat*, Washington, DC: Seven Locks Press, 1993, p. 133.
50 Karl Guenther Barth and Joerg Schmitt, 'Hot Goods for the Mullahs', Stern, 11 September 1997, pp. 182–4; 'Iran trying to use German technology to make arms, Bonn warns', *Deutsche Presse-Agentur*, 15 December 1994.
51 Kenneth Katzman, *The Warriors of Islam: Iran's Revolutionary Guard*, Boulder: Westview Press, 1993, p. 33.
52 Moaddel (1993), pp. 149–50; Robert D. Kaplan, 'A Bazaari's World', *The Atlantic*, March 1996, pp. 28–31.
53 It should be noted, however, that the bazaar is neither homogeneous nor static, and that in some cases – notably, the liberalization of the exchange rate – the interests of some segments of the bazaar diverge from those of the *bonyad*s.
54 'In the traditional economy the bazaar was more than a market-place; it was the granary, the workshop, the bank and the religious centre for the whole society. It was there that landowners sold their crops, craftsmen manufactured their wares, traders marketed their goods, those in need of money raised loans, and it was there that businessmen built and financed mosques and schools.' Ervand Abrahamian, 'The Crowd in Iranian Politics, 1905–53', in Haleh Afshar (ed.), *Iran: A Revolution in Turmoil*, Basingstoke: Macmillan, 1985, p. 128. See also Mizagh Parsa, 'Mosque of Last Resort: State Reform and Social Conflict in the Early 1960s', in John Foran (ed.), *A Century of Revolution: Social Movements in Iran*, Minneapolis: University of Minnesota Press, 1994, p. 147.
55 Homa Omid, *Islam and the Post-Revolutionary State in Iran*, New York: St Martin's Press, 1994, p. 10.
56 M. Reza Behnam, *Cultural Foundations of Iranian Politics*, Salt Lake City: University of Utah Press, 1986, pp. 92–4; Guilan Denoeux, *Urban Unrest in the Middle East: Comparative Study of Informal*

Networks in Egypt, Iran, and Lebanon, Albany: State University of New York Press, 1993, pp. 135–48; Farhi (1990), pp. 119–20; McDaniel (1991), pp. 145–6. McDaniel also notes (pp. 103–4) that although the bazaar perceived itself under siege from the monarchy's Westernization programme, the movement against the shah coalesced at a time when the bazaar still retained much of its sway over the economy, thus maximizing the impact of its resources.

57 Ehteshami (1995), p. 90.
58 Colin Barraclough, 'Despite Tradition of Trade, Iran Has Few Entrepreneurs', *The Christian Science Monitor*, 9 April 1997, p. 8.
59 Iliya Harik, 'Privatization: The Issue, the Prospects, and the Fears', in Iliya Harik and Denis J. Sullivan, eds, *Privatization and Liberalization in the Middle East*, Bloomington: Indiana University Press, 1992, p. 11.
60 Farzin (1995), pp. 183–4.
61 It bears noting that, although nearly two decades have passed, outrage over the confiscations remains: a recent newspaper carried a letter from a distraught homeowner threatening suicide as a result of MJF attempts to claim his home. 'Iran News Reviews Iranian Press, Television', *Iran News*, 5 January 1998, p. 3, FBIS-NES-98–012.
62 Moaddel (1993), pp. 249–50.
63 Katzman, (1993), p. 41.
64 David Menashri, *Revolution at a Crossroads: Iran's Domestic Politics and Regional Ambitions*, Washington: The Washington Institute for Near East Policy, 1997, p. 55.
65 'Iranian Foundation Head Denies Accusations of Corruption', *The New York Times*, 8 January 1995, p. 8; 'Iran: Committees in Fourth Majlis Strongly Criticise Bank-e Markazi and Bonyad-e Mostazafan & Janbazan', *MEED*, 3 June 1996; 'Iran Probe Blasts Central Bank for Mismanagement', *Reuters Financial Service*, 26 May 1996.
66 Con Coughlin, 'Banking Fraud Overstretches Mullah's Credit', *The Sunday Telegraph*, 6 August 1995; 'Brother of Powerful Iranian in Fraud Case', *Reuters*, 29 June 1995; 'Iran: Bank Fraudster Hanged', *MEED*, 1 December 1995, p. 14.
67 Ahmad Ghoreishi and Dariush Zahedi, 'Prospects for Regime Change in Iran', *Middle East Policy*, vol. V, no. 1, January 1997, pp. 87–8; notable is the castigation of both the embezzlement *and* the handling of the case by the government from Ayatollah Ali Akbar Meshkini, head of the Assembly of Experts (which selects the *faqih*). Meshkini voiced frustration that has been echoed in the popular press with the impression of favouritism in the prosecution of the case, saying in a sermon that 'When people of low rank commit a crime or an offence,

they are immediately pursued, imprisoned, locked up and ruined ... However, when we find some big shot, they merely move him from one town to another and give him another post, maybe even higher than his previous post.' *Reuters World Service*, 23 July 1995.

68 'Brother of Accused in Saderat Trial Reappointed as Oppressed Foundation Head', *Vision of the Islamic Republic of Iran Network 1*, 22 July 1995, in BBC, *Summary of World Broadcasts*, 24 July 1995; 'Iran Foundation Chief Reappointed with Less Powers', *Reuters World Service*, 22 July 1995.

69 'State Foundations Dominate Economy', *FT*, 17 July 1997, p.4; 'Iranian Regime Sticks to Creative Budgeting', *FT*, 30 January 1997, p. 3; IMF, 1995, Appendix V, Tables 26 and 27, pp. 75–6; 'Iranian Official on Deficit of Next Year's Budget Plan', *IRNA*, 31 January 1998, in FBIS-NES-98–031; 'Iran News Reviews Recent Developments Covered in Newspapers', *Iran News*, 28 January 1998, pp. 3, 15, in FBIS-NES-98–034, 3 February 1998.

70 IMF, 1995, p. 23.

71 Massoud Karshenas and M. Hashem Pesaran, 'Exchange Rate Unification: The Role of Markets and Planning in the Iranian Economic Reconstruction', in Colville (ed.), (1994), p. 171.

72 Scheuer, *Focus*, 1994, pp. 99–101.

73 Farzin (1995), p. 183; Sandra Mackey, *The Iranians: Persia, Islam and the Soul of a Nation*, New York: E. P. Dutton, 1996, p. 370; Scheurer, *Focus*, pp. 99–101, in FBIS-WEU-94–198.

74 Scheuer, *Focus* (1994), pp. 99–101.

75 Rahim Moqaddam, 'Interview with Mohammad Reza Bahonar, Majles Deputy from Tehran', *Keyhan*, 2 July 1997, p. 7, in FBIS-NES-97–258, 15 September 1997.

76 'Iranian Deputy on Wealth Accumulation', reprinted in *Resalat*, 27 August 1997, pp. 1, 13, (from an interview in *Sobh*), in FBIS-NES-97–261, 18 September 1997.

77 See remarks of Rafiqdust in 'MJF Bulks Up Bon Air with Russian Aircraft', *Iran News*, 3 October 1996, pp. 2–3, as transcribed in FBIS-NES-96–197; also see the comments of MJF Vice Chairman Mohammad Saeidi Kia in 'Iran', *Euromoney*, January/February 1997.

78 IMF, 1995, p.16.

79 'Privatization, Export of Non-Oil Goods Vital to Rescue our Economy', *Tehran Times*, 28 January 1998, pp. 4, 15, in FBIS-NES-98–034, 'Iran: Paper on Privatization, Need to Boost Non-Oil Exports', 3 February 1998.

80 'Privatization Back on Track', *Middle East Economic Digest*, 4 August 1995, p. 20; 'Deprived Areas To Receive Funds', *Resalat*, 24 January 1996, pp. 5, 12, in FBIS-NES-96–139–S.

81 *MEED*, 19 February 1993, p. 12.

82 Firouzeh Khalatbari, 'The Tehran Stock Exchange and Privatization of Public Sector Enterprises in Iran: A Study of Obstacles to the Private Sector Development', in Colville (ed.), (1994), p. 200.

83 Hooshang Amirahmadi, 'An Evaluation of Iran's First Development Plan and Challenges Facing the Second Plan', *Proceedings of a One-Day Conference: Economic Development in Post-Revolutionary Iran*, The Department of Economics and Finance, School of Business Administration, 3 March 1995.

84 Rafiqdust took credit for intervening – at government request – to moderate the price of chickens, iron, tea, rice and cooking oil. 'For the Oppressed', *The Economist*, 25 September 1993, p. 58. See also Barraclough (1995), p. 9.

85 Sayed Leilaz, an economic columnist for the Iranian daily *Hamshari*, as quoted in *NYT*, 7 January 1995, p. 8.

86 *Iran-e Farda*, no. 37, 22 September–22 October, 1997, pp. 25–8, in FBIS-NES-98–049, 18 February 1998.

87 Massoud Karshenas, 'Structural Adjustment and the Iranian Economy', in Nemat Shafik, ed., *Economic Challenges Facing Middle Eastern and North African Countries: Alternative Futures*, New York: St Martin's Press, 1988, p. 220.

88 'Majles: 9 Nov 97 Session', *Resalat*, 10 November 1997, pp. 5, 13, in FBIS-NES-98–051, 20 February 1998; 'Expansion Projects, Economic, Social Information', *Salam*, 22 September 1995, p. 9, in FBIS-NES-95–233.

89 'Faction Infighting for Economic Control', *Keyhan*, 23 May 1996, p. 4, in FBIS-NES-96–144; 'Foremost Economic Issues', *Salam*, 28 October 1997, pp. 4, 11, FBIS-NES-97–352, 18 December 1997.

5

Population Dynamics in Post-Revolutionary Iran: A Re-examination of Evidence[1]

Hassan Hakimian

1. Introduction

Evidence on population growth in Iran after the 1979 revolution points to deep-seated and radical changes in the pace and nature of the country's demographic transition. In less than two decades, as indicated by two general population censuses, Iran witnessed, first, a steep and unprecedented rise in its population growth rate in the 1980s followed by a sharp slow-down in the 1990s. The developments of both periods come as sharp contrast to the gradual nature and early stages of demographic transition believed to have started in Iran in the 1970s (Aghajanian, 1991).[2]

According to the first census conducted under the Islamic Republic in 1986, population growth climbed to 3.91 per cent per annum in the intercensal period 1976–86. This contrasts sharply with the results of the latest census conducted in 1996, which indicate a drop in growth rates to less than 2 per cent for the subsequent intercensal period (1986–96; for the five-year period 1991–96 the rate is even lower at 1.47 per cent). Such a drastic change in the population growth tempo, and the short period of time over which it seems to have occurred, have generated some scepticism about the reliability and precision of the census data.

The 1986 census, for instance, was undertaken under difficult conditions when Iran was affected by war and internal strife. This has led some observers to view its results with particular caution (Pakdaman, 1987).

Despite open doubts about the evidence, there has been no systematic study or evaluation of the quality of data generated by these two censuses. This chapter is thus concerned with a critical appraisal of the consistency and reliability of the quantitative evidence on Iran's demographic development since 1979.

A re-evaluation exercise of this type is considered worthwhile for at least three reasons. First, it is necessary for achieving a consensus view on the *scale* and *nature* of demographic developments in Iran after the revolution. Second, it is a pre-requisite for an evaluation of the *causes* and *consequences* of these changes. And last, but not least, it has wider implications for population and development debates beyond Iran. Iran's experience of rapid and radical two-way change in population growth has been combined with equally far-reaching and shifting changes in government's population policy. Any lessons drawn from her experience can contribute positively to debates on the role of population policy, as well as, more generally, to the determinants of demographic transition and fertility change in developing countries.

The chapter is organized as follows. Section two reviews first the evidence on Iran's population dynamics since the late 1970s. This is followed by a scrutiny of this evidence in section three, and in particular an examination of doubts and controversies regarding the two censuses of 1986 and 1996. Mortality and fertility trends are critically examined in section four, where a number of checks are carried out (such as an analysis of intercensal survival ratios and incremental growth) in order to verify the reliability and consistency of the evidence. Section five summarizes the findings and offers some conclusions.

2. Population Boom and Bust: The Evidence

Iran's principal sources of demographic data are the National Censuses of Population and Housing conducted by the Statistical Centre of Iran (SCI). There have been five censuses to date in ten-yearly intervals since 1956. Two of these were held after the revolution: the first in 1986, at the time of war with Iraq; the second, more recently, in November 1996. Partly as a reaction to the 1986 census results, and partly to assess the effects of the war, an interim census-survey was introduced in 1991, for the first time after a five-year period. This was followed by smaller annual surveys for the purposes of monitoring population trends and characteristics in the first half of the 1990s.

Other than SCI, two other institutions generate data relating to population: The Civil Registration Organization (CRO) and the Ministry of Health and Medical Education (MOHME). The former, established in the 1920s, specializes in the collection of vital statistics, while the Ministry of Health's concern with demography relates to the evaluation of its primary health care network since the late 1980s and other specific health projects in the country (Shadpour: 1994).[3]

Given wide differences in the objectives and methodologies of data collection by these three institutions, however, their findings are far from consistent. The CRO's registration of vital events, for instance, suffers from incomplete coverage, particularly in respect of deaths. Under-coverage is thought to be most serious in rural areas and among women (UNFPA, 1995: 25). MOHME's surveys, on the other hand, produce rare insights into fertility, mortality and women's reproductive health practices and knowledge in rural areas particularly for recent years (see Shadpour, 1994: 43–8, for a description of the Health Information System). They are, however, less authoritative in their coverage of urban areas.[4]

The multiplicity of information sources on population can create obvious difficulties and drawbacks for researchers, but it can also be used advantageously by them to examine data accuracy and consistency from more than one source.[5] In view of the systematicity and scale of SCI's data collection, this section concentrates mainly on census data to summarize Iran's demographic development in the 1980s and 1990s. Other sources will be drawn upon where necessary, to reflect on these and to assist us with evaluating them.

Figure 1 gives an overview of the population growth trend in Iran in the last three decades. The drastic nature of developments in the early 1980s can be seen from the fact that average annual population growth climbed to nearly 4 per cent in the intercensal period 1976–86 and was followed by an equally striking drop thereafter. The scale and speed of the subsequent fall in growth rate (to 1.96 per cent on a comparable basis between 1986 and

1996, or 1.47 per cent per annum on a five-yearly intercensal period for 1991–96) is matched by the speed with which growth escalated in the early 1980s. As stated before, the abrupt nature of these changes, namely, the steep rise and the subsequent slow-down in population tempo have led to some doubts about the accuracy and precision of the census data.

Figure 1: Iran – Intercensal Population Growth Rates, 1966–96

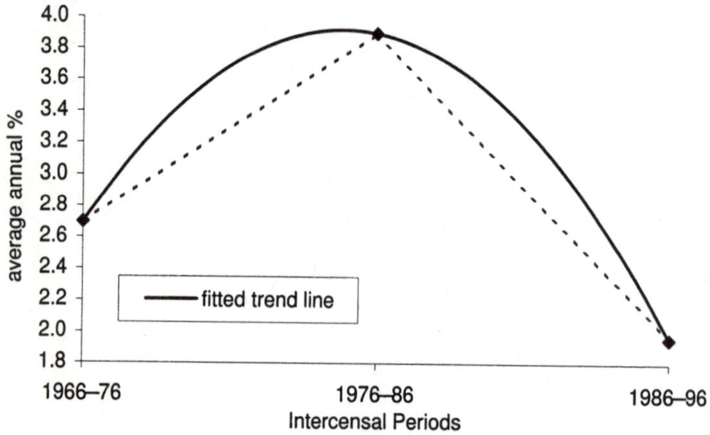

Source: Based on SCI census data.

Table 1, also compiled from the census data, complements the above growth data with a broader perspective on demographic change before and after the revolution. In almost every respect, the 1980s appear to stand out for the rapid escalation of population dynamics, and the 1990s for the noticeable reversal of this trend.

It can be seen that Iran's population expanded by 50 per cent in the ten years to 1986, when it approached 50 million people. In incremental terms, this meant a staggering (net) addition of about 16 million youngsters boosting Iran's population, which stood at just under 34 million three years before the revolution. Other indicators too give an idea of the extent of the set-back to demographic transition in the 1980s: fertility (measured by child-woman ratio, CWR) rose 17 per cent over the previous intercensal period, reaching almost 860; while average net annual incremental growth rose two-fold, reaching about 1.6 million persons per annum.

Population Dynamics in Post-Revolutionary Iran

The scale and speed of the ensuing downswing seems to have been as unusual as the upswing preceding it. Combined evidence from the census survey of 1991 and the 1996 census confirms a slow-down was already under way by the early 1990s and has continued since. Average annual population growth rate, for instance, fell to an all time low of 1.5 per cent over the 1991–96 period; fertility (CWR) declined by a third (to about 420); and net annual population increments fell back to below one million again (see Table 1). Only a few years after population dynamics had escalated in Iran, the trend was reversed and a significant slow-down was firmly established by the mid-1990s.

Table 1: Summary Demographic Data: Iran, 1976–96

	1976	1986	1991	1996
Total Population (million)	33.709	49.445	55.837	60.055
Average Annual Growth Rate (%)[a]	2.71	3.91	2.46	1.47
Net Average Annual Increment (million)[a]	0.79	1.57	1.28	0.84
Sex Ratio[b]	106	105	106	103
Percentage Urban	47	54.3	57	61.3
0–4 Age Group as % of Total	16.1	18.3	14.6	10.3
Child-Woman Ratio (CWR)[c]	732.5	857.9	667.9	420.4

a Intercensal periods, ten-yearly for 1976 and 1986, and five-yearly for 1991 and 1996.
b Male per 100 female.
c Children aged 0–4 per thousand women of reproductive age (15–49).

Sources: SCI, various census publications.

Figure 2 places Iran's demographic experience in a comparative regional context. It compares the trend for Iran's crude birth rate with the Middle East and North Africa (MENA) region as a whole as well as with Egypt and Turkey – both with comparable population sizes to Iran. In general, Iran stands out for a higher crude birth rate trend line by MENA's standards since the 1970s. The upward trend in the 1980s also appears to be unique in Iran. Although, with the recent drop in fertility in the 1990s, the gap has been narrowing, it appears that both Turkey and Egypt are more firmly established along their demographic transition paths.

Figure 2: Comparative Trends in Crude Birth Rate, 1972–95

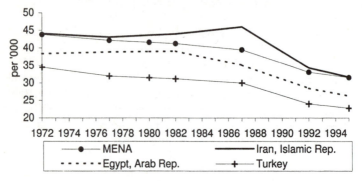

Source: Based on World Bank (1997).

Table 2 sheds further light on Iran's mortality and fertility trends in a similar comparative context. This demonstrates that, compared to Turkey and Egypt, for instance, swings in Iran's population growth have been achieved mainly by a differential fertility pattern, and, to a more limited extent, by a declining mortality rate (including infant mortality). Although generally in line with Middle Eastern norms in the 1970s and 1980s, Iran's crude death rate had, by the 1990s, fallen below that of both the MENA region and lower middle-income countries. Infant mortality, too, reflected this trend. It continued to decline continuously, falling below that of both Turkey and Egypt by the mid-1990s (reaching 45 per thousand in 1995 from 112 per thousand in 1977).[6]

As mentioned before, fertility differentials appear to be the main factor behind the perceived pattern of population growth surge and decline in Iran. The total fertility rate (TFR) in Iran has been consistently higher than in Egypt and Turkey. Although in average terms it appears to have followed a similar trend compared with the MENA region, it should be remembered that the latter embraces countries with some of the highest population growth rates in the world.[7]

Table 2 also shows the pervasive effect of the 'Islamic baby boom' on fertility trends. Iran's earlier trend of declining TFR was arrested during the 1980s. By 1987, it had risen to 6.3 (children per woman of productive age), clearly indicating that Iran's demographic transition had stalled (Aghajanian, 1991). By the 1990s, however, the fall had resumed again.

Table 2: Iran's Demographic Transition in Comparative Context, 1970–95

	1970	1972	1977	1980	1982	1987	1992	1995
Death Rate[a]								
Iran	15.5	14.5	11.9	11.4	11.0	9.7	6.4	5.9
Turkey	12.4	11.6	10.2	9.7	9.4	8.4	7.0	6.7
Egypt	17.1	16.3	14.2	13.3	12.7	10.8	8.6	8.1
Middle East and North Africa	16.4	15.5	12.6	11.8	11.1	9.4	7.5	6.9
Lower Middle Income Countries	13.7	13.0	11.1	10.3	9.7	8.8	8.1	8.1
Infant Mortality[b]								
Iran	131.2	122	112	91.6	78	59	50	45.2
Turkey	144	138	120	109.2	102	81	53	47.6
Egypt	158	150	131	119.6	112	79	63	55.6
Total Fertility Rate[c]								
Iran	6.7	6.5	6.1	6.1	6.2	6.3	5.0	4.5
Turkey	5.3	5.0	4.5	4.3	4.1	3.8	2.9	2.7
Egypt	5.9	5.5	5.3	5.1	5.1	4.3	3.8	3.4
Middle East and North Africa	6.8	6.6	6.2	6.1	6.0	5.5	4.7	4.2
Lower Middle Income Countries	4.5	5.0	4.5	3.7	3.7	3.4	2.9	3.0

a Crude death rate, per 1,000 people.
b Below one-year mortality rate, per 1,000 live births.
c TFR: the total number of children a woman is likely to have during the whole span of her productive age (15–49) assuming she experiences age specific fertility rates observed in a particular period.

Source: World Bank (1997).

3. Scrutinizing the Evidence

The evidence examined above makes it clear that Iran's demographic development followed an unusual pattern after the late 1970s. Data generated by the last two censuses suggest a sea-change in the country's demographic behaviour with two contradictory phases emerging in the 1980s and 1990s. The last section examined the scale of these apparent changes both over time and in a comparative context.

A more substantive examination of the determinants of fertility change in Iran (both proximate determinants of fertility and its socio-economic causes) is beyond the scope of this chapter, which has more modest aims. This section is concerned with the quality of the evidence behind these changes and is, therefore, devoted to a critical interrogation of the data from Iran's last two censuses. Hopefully, such a clarification of the quantitative evidence can contribute to fuller discussions of these developments.

3.1 The 1986 Census

As we have seen, the 1986 census was the primary source of information about the substantial upswing in population growth in the first decade after the revolution. Being the first census undertaken by the Islamic government, it was of special interest in shedding light on the extent and direction of demographic change under the new regime. It was also received more controversially given radical changes in official policy and attitude towards population that came with the new regime.

Few areas, perhaps, reflected the values of the incoming Islamic government as strongly as its pro-natalist stance towards family planning and population control. In a sharp reversal of past policy, changes were introduced both in the regulatory environment and in the socio-economic sphere to promote women's traditional role in the family and in the economy. The minimum age of marriage was, for instance, lowered to 9 for girls (and 14 for men); family planning clinics were shut down; early marriage was promoted and birth control was discouraged. Women's contribution was increasingly sought in the domestic arena and in 'raising generations of good Muslims' (see Aghajanian, 1991: 705).

In this climate, official reactions to the census results were initially positive. A new total figure of 50 million Iranians in 1986, although a clear shock to most observers, was hailed by high level government officials as a major success for the Islamic regime.[8] Before too long, however, realism set in and a more critical understanding of the possible consequences of demographic transformation on such a scale led the way for a swift reversal of official population policy in the second half of the 1980s. This in turn led to the adoption of an active population control policy after 1988 including the distribution and promotion of contraceptives by MOHME, and, more recently, limiting official benefits to three children only (UNFPA, 1995: 14 and 20–3; Mehryar, 1995; see also Bulatao and Richardson, 1994: 21–4 for a discussion of more recent policy).

Scrutinizing the findings of the census is important not only for evaluating the impact of the government's pro-natalist policies in the 1980s, but also for its implications for developments thereafter. Undoubtedly, this census set a benchmark against which subsequent developments are judged (such as the apparently drastic decline in population growth in the 1990s). Ascertaining its reliability is thus directly relevant to the study of Iran's post-revolutionary demographic transformation in general. Below, we examine some of the doubts that have been expressed about its results and findings.

Pakdaman questioned the accuracy and consistency of the 1986 census soon after its preliminary results were published (Pakdaman, 1987). In his view, a number of considerations pointed to the strong possibility of over-enumeration resulting in inflated population statistics in Iran in this period. Some of these doubts are rooted in the design and conduct of the census (such as administrative capacity and implementation difficulties), others emanate from a more in-depth study of its findings scrutinized against earlier population projections and surveys.

In contrast to earlier censuses, the 1986 census adopted a new norm for enumeration based on an individual's 'normal place of residence'. Accordingly, all those considered 'ordinarily resident' in a household were included regardless of their current whereabouts (e.g., even if they were 'temporarily absent' from the place of enumeration).[9] But as Pakdaman observes, this introduces great difficulties in a country with substantial populations in flux due to the war with Iraq and refugees from neighbouring countries (Afghanistan and Iraq). This is further complicated by a substantial number of Iranians who emigrated abroad after the revolution (Section 4 below discusses the difficulties of estimating actual numbers involved). Since many left for political reasons and for fear of persecution, information about their whereabouts would be considered sensitive. It is not clear, for instance, how this may have affected the attitude or behaviour of respondents when dealing with questions about their household or family members abroad.

Moreover, some areas of the country (notably, Kurdistan) were affected by internal strife. Again, it is not clear how the census and its results may have been affected by a low degree of local cooperation with government officials in such regions.

While these and other similar considerations raise questions about the reliability and accuracy of the census data, they do not necessarily generate *prima facie* evidence for the direction of any likely bias. For instance, lack of local cooperation may arguably result in under-reporting. By contrast, dealing with war refugees may lead to double-counting. Similarly, the operation of an extensive rationing system, introduced to deal with basic food shortages and rocketing prices during the war, may have also encouraged over-reporting.[10]

Population growth on the scale indicated by the census is also surprising in the face of a possible rise in mortality and deterioration in health and medical standards due to the war. Although there are no reliable estimates of the war dead, and the official statistics on mortality seem to indicate only a modest slow-down in its downward trend during the 1980s (see Table 2 above), the direct impact is, nevertheless, likely to have been significant. Arguably, general health and medical standards may also have suffered indirectly by a host of other factors such as out-migration of medical personnel, university closures affecting training of personnel, and resources being siphoned off to sustain the war effort during much of the 1980s (Pakdaman, 1987: 55; Aghajanian, 1991: 709–10). We will come back to this point in Section 4.1 below when discussing survival ratios.

The short-term and transient nature of the baby boom itself raises further doubts over its actual or real extent and scale. As stated earlier, evidence for a substantial slow-down in population growth was found only five years later, i.e. in the 1991 census-survey, which was specially instigated to monitor population trends. This declining trend has since been confirmed by a number of surveys including the latest census in 1996. The speed with which the boom 'occurred' as well as its subsequent 'disappearance' raise questions about how real it was in the first instance, and whether it might not have been more than a 'statistical bubble'. Again, this issue is examined in section 4.2 below.

Last, but not least, comparisons with earlier population projections have provided further grounds for scepticism. Pakdaman examines different trajectories of Iran's population from 1981 through 2001 under four different scenarios. These projections are based on vital statistics estimated by a joint UN and SCI study pertaining to the years 1973–76 (SCI, 1978). This is generally considered one of the most authoritative and reliable population sources in Iran prior to the revolution. The scenarios make different assumptions about expected fertility and mortality trends in

Iran and have indicative value only. The assumptions and the trajectory results are summarized in Table 3. Another two columns give the deviation of the 1986 and 1996 projections from the actual or reported census results.

Table 3: Population Projections for Iran, Alternative Scenarios, 1981–2001 (in thousands)
(implicit intercensal annual growth rates are given in brackets)

Scenarios	1981	1986	1986 Deviation from actual	1991	1996	1996 Deviation from actual	2001
A	39,669 (3.31)	47,116 (3.50)	-2,329	56,280 (3.62)	67,269 (3.63)	+7,214	80,449 (3.64)
B	39,318 (3.13)	45,936 (3.16)	-3,509	53,642 (3.15)	62,386 (3.07)	+2,331	72,312 (3.00)
C	38,968 (2.94)	44,804 (2.83)	-4,641	51,200 (2.70)	58,030 (2.53)	-2,025	65,322 (2.40)
D	39,402 (3.17)	46,262 (3.26)	-3,183	54,237 (3.23)	63,677 (3.26)	+3,622	74,510 (3.19)

Scenarios: A: Constant fertility; declining mortality.
B: Fertility and mortality declining by 1 per cent per annum.
C: Mortality as in B, but fertility declining by 2 per cent per annum.
D: Constant fertility and mortality.

Source: Based on Pakdaman (1987: 49).

Scenarios B and C assume that demographic transition, which appeared to have started in the 1970s, would continue unabated albeit with different tempos (C shows a faster fall in fertility). A and D take a more conservative view by allowing fertility to remain constant. Reflecting the pre-revolutionary expectations of continuity in demographic transition, neither of the four scenarios allows for a rise in fertility (as the 1980s' evidence seems to suggest). With these assumptions in mind, Pakdaman considers scenarios A and C as 'maximalist' and 'minimalist' projections of Iran's future population respectively (1987: 48–9).

It is clear from Table 3 that under all four situations, the 1986 projections fall short of the reported census count (of 49,445,000 – see Table 1 above). Discrepancies are in the region of 2.3–4.6 million people (or a margin of about 5–10 per cent). This, plus the fact that even the maximalist projection (A) proves to be conservative, fuel scepticism about the credibility of the 1986 census results.

3.2 The 1996 Census

Ironically, if the 1986 census met with suspicions of over-enumeration, the latest census, held in November 1996, has aroused misgivings about possible *under*-estimation of the total count of population in Iran. This census has not yet received detailed critical attention. However, judging by early and informal reactions to it, it is clear that its total figure of just over 60 million people for 1996 (see Table 1 above) is regarded by some as an under-estimation of the 'true' total population figure.

Again, evidence for this comes from different sources including large discrepancies with earlier population projections and the structure and conduct of the census itself.

Referring back to Table 3, for instance, it is clear that three of the four projections discussed in the last section over-shoot the official figure within a range of 2.3–7.2 million people. Only projection C (the 'minimalist' scenario) produces an underestimation (by just over 2 million). Similarly, there are gross discrepancies in the population projections of the World Bank and UN for Iran for the 1990s. The World Bank's estimate of Iran's population in 1995 (i.e. a year *before* the census) was over 65 million (World Bank, 1997). On this basis, and using demographic parameters for the early 1990s, a population of 60 million is thought to have been surpassed between 1992 and 1993. Similarly, there is a sharp contrast with the UN's Population Division pre-census estimate of Iran's population at nearly 70 million in 1996 (UN, 1995). It is, of course, possible that these projections, and similar expectations about the data for the 1990s, were raised by the 1986 baseline evidence. The possibility of inaccuracy in the 1996 census cannot be ruled out either, especially in the light of anecdotal evidence suggesting a degree of 'under-coverage' in this census.

In 1996, enumeration was conducted for the first time with reference to the respondents' (and their household members') birth certificates.[11] Whilst this is likely to have improved precision in some respects (for instance, in recording birth details and age calculations), it is likely to have increased inaccuracy in other respects. First, by adding another layer of administration, it is likely to have reduced coverage. A greater degree of cooperation and assumption of responsibility by respondent heads of households may be required to compensate for this. Second, birth registrations are much less complete and reliable in rural areas (especially amongst the older generations). Third, fears and inhibitions relating to military service among young male deserters may encourage 'drop out' from the population count.

Equally uncharacteristically, the 1996 census was combined with a desire to collect other 'institutional' data simultaneously. For instance, Iran's Post Office seized upon the opportunity to collect, update and construct a comprehensive coding system for the entire country. A short section was thus added to the census questionnaire for this purpose. This placed a greater burden on the enumerators and required a greater degree of openness by respondents over their identity and place of residence – neither of which could have helped with data collection or its accuracy.[12]

Anecdotal evidence regarding inaccuracies in population head-counts is not unusual. What is perhaps more remarkable in this context is the consistency with which a measure of *under-enumeration* has been alleged.[13] Unfortunately, in the absence of a standard post-enumeration quality check survey, it is very difficult to establish with any accuracy whether, and to what extent, the incidence of under-reporting was in fact real in the last census.

4. A Critical Appraisal

This section re-visits the quantitative evidence on population growth in Iran and interrogates it in the light of doubts articulated above. Evidence is re-examined and checked for internal consistency and reliability regarding the main determinants of population growth: net natural growth and (net) immigration. Net natural growth is further studied by an examination of survival ratios and incremental growth. The former reflects the apparent mortality rates of a base-period (existing) population and the latter represents net new additions within a specific intercensal period.

In focusing on these two demographic factors, the section has two main objectives: to re-evaluate the quantitative evidence on the population trends in the 1980s and 1990s, and to verify the significance of variations in fertility in explaining the contrasting patterns of growth perceived over these two periods.

4.1 Survival Ratio Analysis

Table 4 provides an analysis of 'survival ratios' for different age groups over three intercensal periods between 1966 and 1996. These ratios indicate for all those in a given age-cohort the probability of survival to, and inclusion in, the next census (normally a ten-year period).[14] They are thus expected to take a value below one – if we abstract from net international immigration. Inversely affected by age-specific mortality rates, survival ratios also vary across different age groups and over time.

Table 4 reports these ratios for three consecutive periods of 1966–76, 1976–86 and 1986–96. The 'total' figures refer to the probability of the whole population in a *base* year (i.e. in the previous census) surviving to the next census and being enumerated by it. Thus the total for 1976–86 indicates the chance of survival for the 1976 population by 1986. It therefore excludes all those in the 0–9 age group in 1986 (that is, those added to the population in the intervening period).

Table 4: Survival Ratios for Intercensal Periods, 1966–96

| Age cohort at: | | 1966–76 | 1976–86 | 1986–96 |
Base census	Next census			
0–4	10–14	0.944	1.087	1.004
5–9	15–19	0.851	0.984	0.945
10–14	20–24	0.901	0.975	*0.885*
15–19	25–29	0.968	1.014	*0.907*
20–24	30–34	0.991	1.049	*0.949*
25–29	35–39	0.957	1.003	0.978
30–34	40–44	0.969	0.970	0.960
35–39	45–49	0.951	0.975	0.951
40–44	50–54	0.977	*0.958*	*0.924*
45–49	55–59	0.812	0.963	0.862
50–54	60–64	0.761	0.891	0.865
55+	65+	0.559	0.607	0.645
Total		0.892	0.975	0.918

Source: Computed from census data (SCI: various issues).

As can be seen, the table seems to suggest a certain degree of anomaly for ratios in the 1976–86 period. First, the total ratio (97.5 per cent) appears artificially high and out of line with other intercensal periods (in the range of 89 to 92 per cent). Second, these anomalies seem to affect mostly the younger age groups. To highlight this, ratios close to one and exceeding it are emboldened in the table – as are those appearing unduly high (e.g., the 45–49 cohort for 1976–86). Moreover, expecting a downward trend for general (and age-specific) mortality rates over time, falls in survival ratios below those of the 1966–76 period are also treated as anomalous, and are underlined in the table for ease of reference. Several instances can be seen in the 1986–96 column.

The pattern emerging in Table 4 – abnormally high ratios for 1976–86 and inordinately low figures for 1986–96 – appears to confirm suspicions of over- and under-enumeration in the 1986 and 1996 censuses respectively. To verify this, we now turn to the main factors affecting survival ratios: net immigration and changes in mortality rates over time.

As mentioned earlier in section 3, international migration to and from Iran is of particular interest in the period 1976–86. This concerns mainly the large number of war refugees from Afghanistan, and to a smaller extent Iraq, and the exodus of unknown numbers of Iranians abroad for political and economic reasons after the revolution. In the absence of data, unfortunately, it is not possible to assess the impact of these movements on Iran's population growth with any credible degree of accuracy. Annex Table 1 has been compiled to show, purely for demonstrative purposes, the wide range, and conflicting nature of some of these estimates. For instance, whereas external estimates of Afghan refugees in Iran generally exceed 2 million, Iran's official count of the Afghanis in 1986 is no more than three-quarters of a million. Even when all foreign nationals resident in Iran are included, they add up to a total of less than a million according to the 1986 census.

Similarly, there are no reliable estimates of the number of Iranians in the diaspora. The same table shows only a selection of disparate and sporadic data on some Iranian communities abroad (chiefly in the US, Turkey and a handful of European countries).[15] As stated above, these estimates are neither complete nor consistent with one another whether in terms of their coverage or timing of the count (some refer to 'exiles' and 'refugees', others to the

Iranian population more generally); yet they serve to demonstrate a very general idea about the likely scale of numbers involved.

As mentioned before, there is uncertainty as to how Iran's emigrants were treated in the 1986 enumeration (see section 3.1 above). If they were included in the population headcount, then the census figures merely need to be adjusted down for the number of war refugees from neighbouring countries (perhaps up to a million and a half or so by the mid-1980s). If they were left out, then it is plausible to assume that immigration into and out of Iran possibly moderate each other with negligible impact on the total population (this may not, of course, be true of specific age groups). Regarding 1996, however, given the length of time involved and the likely formalization of the status of Iranians abroad, it is likely that they will have been treated more explicitly as 'residents abroad' and hence excluded from enumeration. This could also be another reason for the apparently lower than expected total population count in that year (see section 3.2 above). In any case, it is doubtful if net immigration can explain the full force of changes in the perceived survival rates (or population changes for that matter) over time.

Changes in mortality rates do not seem capable of explaining the anomalous survival ratios either. Regarding the 1980s, no amount of fall in mortality should be able, *ceteris paribus*, to raise survival ratios to above 100 per cent! On the contrary, the direct and indirect impact of war, as we have seen before, is more likely to have affected these ratios adversely. Regarding the 1990s, the rise in survival ratios appears in line with expected social and economic improvements after the war. Nevertheless, a fall in survival chances of some age cohorts to levels below those of the 1970s and 1960s still appear to be counter-intuitive.

Other than emigration and mortality, another factor to consider is the possibility of inaccuracy in the 1986 data along the lines discussed in the preceding sections. To deal with this, we proceed with a number of checks against data.[16] Two scenarios are examined for the 1976–86 period in Table 5; with their implications further explored in Table 6.

The first scenario assumes stationary survival ratios in the intercensal periods 1966–76 and 1976–86 – at levels pertaining to the former period (1966–76). Although somewhat implausible, the implicit static trend of mortality rates may be attributed to the adverse impact of war. The second scenario allows for some improvements in mortality over time by adopting an average of the two periods' ratios for 1976–86. In both cases, new survival ratios are recalculated for the 1986–96 period accordingly.

Table 5: Estimated Survival Ratios for 1976–86 and 1986–96 Under Alternative Assumptions

Age cohort at:		Scenario 1*		Scenario 2*	
Base census	Next census	1976–86	1986–96	1976–86	1986–96
0–4	10–14	0.944	**1.004**	**1.016**	**1.004**
5–9	15–19	0.851	0.945	0.917	0.945
10–14	20–24	0.901	**1.018**	0.938	0.948
15–19	25–29	0.968	**1.049**	0.991	0.972
20–24	30–34	0.991	**1.026**	**1.020**	<u>0.986</u>
25–29	35–39	0.957	**1.025**	0.980	**1.002**
30–34	40–44	0.969	**1.016**	0.969	0.988
35–39	45–49	0.951	**0.996**	0.963	0.973
40–44	50–54	0.977	0.925	0.968	<u>0.925</u>
45–49	55–59	0.812	0.884	0.888	0.873
50–54	60–64	0.761	0.848	0.826	0.856
55+	65+	0.559	0.736	0.583	0.687
Total		0.892	0.972	0.934	0.945

* Scenario 1 assumes constant age-specific survival ratios for 1976–86 at 1966–76 levels. Scenario 2 averages out the recorded survival ratios for these two intercensal periods and applies them to 1976–86. In both cases, new ratios are recalculated for 1986–96 accordingly.

Source: Computed from census data (SCI: various issues).

It can be seen that Scenario 1 does not purge the 1986–96 data of the anomalous ratios, i.e., those close to or greater than one (these are again emboldened in the Table for ease of reference). The new total, too, appears to be artificially high, suggesting 97.2 per cent of the 1986 population were expected to be alive and enumerated by 1996. This is perhaps not surprising in view of the much lower survival ratios for the 1960s and 1970s adopted for the 1980s by this methodology.

By contrast, Scenario 2 performs much better: indicating total survival ratios of 93.4 per cent and 94.5 per cent respectively for 1976–86 and 1986–96, and largely eliminating the anomalous survival ratios for specific-age cohorts in both periods. However, the ratios for the 20–24 and 40–44 age cohorts (underlined in the table) are still below the ratios for a comparable period a decade earlier (1966–76). This may be due to under-enumeration in 1996.

The general possibility of under-enumeration in the 1996 census, however, appears somewhat weakened in the light of the preceding analysis except for a few cohorts as mentioned above. It appears that the corrections to 1986 data, under Scenario 2, appear capable of rectifying the anomalies overall. Judged by survival rates at least, the evidence for alleged under-enumeration in 1996 appears to remain circumstantial. As suggested before, it is possible that this arises from raised expectations about population growth and size (in turn fuelled by over-enumeration in 1986) and a more explicit exclusion of Iranians settled abroad from this census.

Table 6 takes the analysis further by examining the implications of the above scenarios for estimates of total population. It re-estimates the 1986 population according to each of these possibilities and compares the results with those of the census. As expected, both scenarios indicate over-reporting for 1986. For Scenario 1, this reaches 2.7 million or 5.5 per cent of the reported count, and in the case of Scenario 2, it is estimated at 1.3 million or just over 2.7 per cent of the total reported enumeration. The latter also comes closest to Scenario A of population projections examined earlier in Table 3 (though still wide by about a million). This has to do with the fact that in both cases, the main spur to growth comes from falling mortality (even though this assumption is somewhat moderated under Scenario 2 through averaging), while fertility changes are kept out of the picture. This is what the next section turns to.

Table 6: 1986 Population Under Alternative Survival Ratio Hypotheses

	Total population 1986 ('000)	Over-enumeration ('000)	Over-enumeration (%)	Average annual growth rate 1976–86 (%)
Scenario 1*	46,718	+2,727	+5.51	3.32
Scenario 2*	48,074	+1,371	+2.77	3.61
Census count	49,445	–	–	3.91

* For a specification of these scenarios, see Table 5 above.

4.2 Incremental Growth

The discussion in the last section focused on the survival rates of different age cohorts, from one census period to another. An examination of these rates was useful for assessing the impact of mortality on the population of a baseline census until the next. It also proved useful in giving insights into data consistency and reliability. The analysis, however, left out of the picture the below-ten age group, or the *net* incremental natural additions to the population in a typically ten-year intercensal period. In this section, therefore, we focus on the 0–9 years age cohort in order to examine the significance of increased births and fertility for population growth.[17]

The questions we specifically address are: to what extent are the observed population trends explained by the new births momentum, and if so, how reliable is the evidence? We may recall that, from evidence examined earlier, the 1980s in particular saw a major baby boom with net incremental additions to population climbing to an average of about 1.6 million per annum (or a total of 16 million people). By the first half of the 1990s, however, these figures were back at pre-boom levels indicating a drastic fall of about half (see Table 1). In view of the scale and speed of the fall, how sustainable is the evidence pointing to the baby boom in those years?

The most direct evidence of population increase is found in CRO's annual register of births. Figure 3 depicts the data for the period 1972–94. Despite the well-known weaknesses of the vital registrations system in Iran (see section 2 above), these data are, nevertheless, useful in giving an indication of the trend and variations in officially-registered births over time.

The data here seem to indicate a rather unique and rapid jump in births registrations in the late 1970s and early 1980s. The boom seems to have started in the first two years of the revolution, when birth registrations reportedly shot up by 24 per cent and 45 per cent in respectively 1979 and 1980 (allowing for the conception period, this suggests that the initial momentum may have actually surged over the tumultuous period leading to the change of the regime, i.e. in 1978). Annual increments climbed to almost 2.5 million for the first time in 1980 and 1981, almost double the average for the years immediately preceding the revolution. After that absolute population increments remained high until 1986 when they began to fall sharply. By the mid-1990s, they had regained the levels of the mid-1970s.

Reservations about the quality of these data are well-founded in view of their almost certain incomplete coverage. Late registration of births, as well as administrative delays in the compilation and assembly of data at provincial levels, too, make the precision of the data for specific years unreliable. Another complication arises from the possibility of false documents being issued in response to the rationing system, which linked benefits directly to household size (see section 3.1 above).

Figure 3: Annual Registered Births, 1972–94

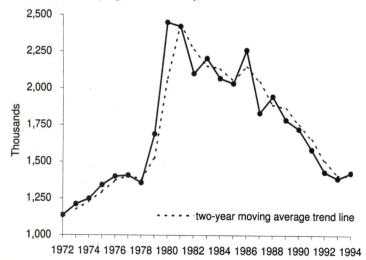

Source: Based on data from the Civil Registration Organization (CRO), compiled from SCI (*Salnameh*, various issues).

Nevertheless, it is unlikely that these concerns may have distorted the observed *trend*. For instance, the main take-off in birth registrations (1978 onwards) preceded the war and the introduction of the rationing system in the first half of the 1980s. It also appears counter-intuitive that this take-off should coincide with the period of revolutionary turmoil, when strikes, departmental closures and general lack of administrative cooperation may have arguably dampened – not increased – registrations. Thus even with due qualifications, it appears plausible that a significant rise in fertility *did* take place in the revolution's heyday and was the main spur to increased population growth in the fist half of the 1980s.

Further confirmation of this trend comes from an analysis of the age profile of the 1986 and 1996 populations. This is based on a translation of single file age data from each census into corresponding or reference years of birth. Figure 4 plots the survivors of those born in each reference year who are enumerated by each of these censuses as a proportion of the corresponding census total. The similar shapes of the two curves seem to indicate similarity in the age structure of the populations enumerated by both censuses. The vertical gap between the two curves reflects mortality differentials (and possible net foreign immigration) for single file age groups. Overall, both figures exhibit similar trends and appear to confirm a clear proportionate rise in the number of those born between 1978 and 1984.

The fact that both censuses seem to reinforce this message, combined with the CRO trend above, seems sufficient evidence to suggest that a real population boom did take place possibly some time between 1979–84.[18] The same evidence also seems to suggest that there has been a substantial proportionate decline in net additions to the population since 1986.

Figure 4: Population by Birth Year as a Percentage of Total Enumerations in 1986 and 1996

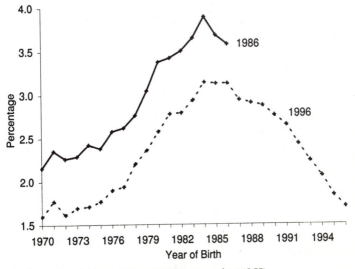

Source: Computed from 1986 and 1996 census data (SCI).

5. Summary and Conclusions

This chapter has addressed two principal questions:

1. To what extent is the quantitative evidence on Iran's post-revolutionary population dynamics reliable and indicative of the true demographic developments in the country since the advent of the new regime in 1979?
2. To what extent was the rapid rise and fall in the population growth tempo brought about by a pattern of boom and bust in fertility behaviour?

The following points summarize our findings:

- There is some evidence of over-enumeration in the 1986 census results. This is found from an analysis of survival ratios, which points to the possibility of about 2.7 per cent over-enumeration (about 1.3 million). Allowing for a similar possibility among the 0–9 age group (i.e., those born in the period 1976–86) could push up this figure, as would the exclusion of about one million enumerated foreign nationals from the headcount. One important implication of this finding is that it modifies the perceived intercensal population growth rate from 3.9 per cent downwards – to about 3.5 per cent (still quite high by Iran's and other developing country standards).
- Evidence on alleged *under*-coverage in the 1996 census is not corroborated by analysis in this paper and thus remains circumstantial pending further research. The modification of the preceding census also implies that the slow-down phase to 1996 was more moderate than apparent, but real enough, nevertheless.
- Changes in fertility behaviour have been principally responsible for the observed (and modified) pattern of growth. In fact, moderating the 1986 results is not incompatible with the fact that changes were driven mainly by a significant 'Islamic' baby boom in the early years of the revolution (and a slow-down afterwards).
- The timing of the boom is interesting in that it seems to have been initiated in 1978 (at the peak of revolutionary fervour and well before the war-time rationing system was in place) and continued over most of the early phase of the revolutionary period from 1979 to 1984. This pattern was reversed in the

late 1980s and early 1990s with sharp falls in fertility reported widely in various surveys and in the 1996 census.

There is no doubt that fertility changes of the order discussed above are related to interesting and radical changes in population policy and socio-economic conditions in Iran in the period under study. This chapter and its narrow focus on quantitative evidence will hopefully contribute to a fuller discussion of these issues in the future.

Annex Table 1: Estimates of International Migration To and From Iran in the 1980s and 1990s

	Estimates	Description	Source
Immigrants from:			
Afghanistan Iraq	1,900,000 95,000	Refugees and asylum- seekers (end 1993)	US Committee for Refugees, 1994; quoted in Loescher and Loescher (1994: 75)
Afghanistan	1.9–3.6 million	Refugees (1980s)	UNHCR; quoted in UNFPA (1995: 13)
Afghanistan Iraq	755,257 84,109	Enumerated in Iran (1986)	Iran's 1986 census
Emigrants to:			
USA	240,000– 335,000*	General population	1986 US Immigration and Naturalization Service; quoted in Fathi (1991: 120)
Turkey	300,000– 1,500,00	General population	Unofficial UNHCR estimate (Ankara); quoted in Bauer (1991: 96)
France	20,158**	Total population including 4,700 refugees in December 1987	Office Français de Protection des Refugies et Apartides; quoted in Nassehy-Behnam (1991: 104)
Germany	10,000	Asylum applicants in Berlin, by the end of 1986	Office of the Asylum Matters Section Landeseinwohneramt Berlin; quoted in Bauer (1991: 96)
Holland	6,000	Asylum applicants in 1994	Netherlands Ministry of Justice.

Notes: * Half are believed to be living in California, mainly in Los Angeles City.
** Some 9,095 of these are believed to reside in Paris.

Notes

1 An earlier version of this paper was presented at the *Middle East Economic Association's* Annual Conference in Chicago, 3–5 January 1998. I would like to thank the participants for their comments. The research and preparation of the paper benefited from advice and discussion with various researchers and scholars during a field visit to Iran in 1997. Among them are: Dr A. H. Mehryar of the Institute for Research on Planning and Development (IRPD), several members of staff at the Ministry of Health and Medical Education, the Statistical Centre of Iran and UNFPA offices in Tehran. The paper was inspired by discussions with Nasser Pakdaman, and received helpful comments from Sohrab Behdad, Parvin Alizadeh and Akbar Aghajanian. Their contribution is gratefully acknowledged without implicating any of them in the remaining errors and shortcomings of the paper.

2 Demographic transition refers to a combined process of declining death and birth rates over the development cycle. This was first observed in today's industrial countries and now increasingly – albeit unevenly – in developing countries. In pre-Revolutionary Iran, the results of a comprehensive population and fertility survey conducted jointly by the UN and The Statistical Centre of Iran provided early evidence on the beginnings of a fall in fertility in the 1970s (SCI, 1978).

3 Other smaller establishments also generate a variety of demographic data. These are: university departments (such as the Schools of Public Health and Social Sciences at Tehran University and the Department of Demography at Shiraz University); Iran Statistics Institute; the Population and Manpower Bureau in the Planning and Budget Organization; and the Department of Demographic and Planning Research at the Ministry of Housing and Urban Development (UNFPA, 1995: 27).

4 According to UNFPA, coordinating the various demographic data collection initiatives in the country remains as yet an unfulfilled task (1995: 23–6 and 56–8).

5 For a good discussion of the problems associated with direct and indirect methods of collecting data on infant mortality in developing countries, see UN (1992). This work shows, *inter alia*, that there is no single, superior method of collecting demographic data in most countries and various data sources need to be carefully scrutinized for their reliability.

6 As we shall see below, the mortality data, particularly for the war years in the 1980s, are disputed. The general picture here, however, is one of disparities widening after the early 1990s.

7   Bahrain, Jordan, Kuwait, Libya, Qatar, Saudi Arabia and UAE were amongst the seventeen developing countries with fastest population growth rates in the 1980s (World Bank, 1997).

8   Commending the results of the census, the then prime minister, Hossein Moussavi, hailed the addition of 'some eleven million people since the revolution' as a major boost to Iran's Islamic population. In his view, this was a source of 'major developments' in the region and in the Islamic world more generally (*Kayhan*, 7 Aban 1365 quoted in Pakdaman, 1987: 41). For a general discussion of the government's pro-natalist policies in these years, see Aghajanian (1991) and Mehryar (1995). Aghajanian (1989) provides an overview of the pre-revolutionary population and family planning policies in Iran.

9   More specifically, the categories used were: present, temporarily absent, POW, disappeared (in the war), overseas, and 'others'. The definition excluded foreign personnel and their families in Iran, but it included Iran's diplomatic personnel and their families abroad (see SCI: 1986).

10 As the benefits were directly related to family size, this may have encouraged over-reporting in some cases. Even more likely, perhaps, rationing may have encouraged a rise in actual family size. This is further discussed in section 4.2 below.

11 Other features of the census were: the questionnaire was shortened to about half its normal length (i.e., two pages); and the fertility and mortality sections, included for all households in 1986, were excluded from the general questionnaire and were applied to a sample of 5 per cent only.

12 This tendency was exacerbated, when at early stages of enumeration, the Taxation Office of the Ministry of Finance reportedly tried to use the occasion to collect data for updating its records. Such was the adverse impact of this on the respondents' attitude to enumeration that the practice was soon stopped with the census office strenuously denying in the mass media that the two efforts were related (based on informal discussions and information from personnel at the Statistical Centre of Iran).

13 Even in casual conversations, many known 'missed' cases are intimated. According to unconfirmed reports, the final figure of 60 million was a result of 'rounding up' an actual census count of about 57 million. While anecdotal evidence of this type has to be received with caution and care, its scale and consistency can, nevertheless, give some insight into the circumstances in which enumeration took place.

14 Survival ratios refer to the proportion of a given age cohort in base year that are alive and enumerated in a future census. If the intercensal

period is defined by (n) years, the ratio in question refers to the ratio of those in (X+n) cohort enumerated in period (t+n) to those in cohort (X) enumerated in period (t).

15 Figures for Pakistan, another large concentration area for Iranian emigrants, were not available.

16 The possibility of under-enumeration in the 1976 census cannot be ruled out, either. However, for reasons elaborated on in section 2, the reliability of the 1986 census is considered more circumspect. After all, this was the first census conducted by the new administration under difficult conditions; whereas its predecessor (in 1976) was the third successive census conducted by the *ancien regime*. SCI, too, is likely to have suffered from loss of staff and technical expertise after the revolution.

17 This age group, too, is influenced by mortality and net international immigration. For simplicity, however, here we focus on births and fertility data only.

18 Mehryar and Tabibian (1997: 5) who conduct a similar analysis report that the rural population in fact continued to rise until 1986.

6

The Effect of Non-Economic Factors in the Process of Production in Iran

Seyed Morteza Afghah[1]

The causes of the backwardness of developing societies are an issue that has long been at the core of many social scientists' studies. Many scientific works have tackled the issue with the hope of suggesting ways to eradicate backwardness among Third World countries. Economists, among others, have concentrated mostly on economic factors; i.e. labour, capital and natural resources, as the main elements necessary for economic development. A few works, however, have dealt with the effect of non-economic factors in economic development taking a quantitative approach (see for instance: Adelman and Morris, 1967).

For Iran in particular, where this research has been carried out, the existing works have merely raised the importance of non-economic factors in economic development rather than setting out to use conventional quantitative or qualitative approaches to examine their effect. This research attempts to fill the gap by examining the effect of non-economic factors in the process of production in Iran.

As the survey has been implemented in Iran, a general familiarity with the country's post-revolutionary economic situation is useful.[1] It is also worth referring briefly to the attitude of Islam towards material life. This is essential since Iranians have a profound faith in Islam – especially after the Islamic Revolution in 1979 when an Islamic system has ruled all aspects of life in the country.

Based on the existing resources,[2] Islam is not merely a spiritual religion, nor is it a completely secular philosophy. Though a hereafter-oriented religion, salvation in the life hereafter is conditioned on a moderate enjoyment of material life. Poverty, for instance, the main issue in all underdeveloped societies, is a condition whose existence in Muslim societies is severely disapproved of by Islam and this has obliged an Islamic government to seek to eradicate it from society. Such a view of poverty is mostly due to the fact that it is a serious obstacle to Muslims in pursuing their religious tasks (see *Qur'an*, 2: 268).[3] This must favour development.

In general, Islam seems to be a religion that cannot be seen solely as an obstacle to development, but also has the potential to encourage Muslim societies to develop their socio-cultural as well as their economic and political conditions. What is likely to be responsible for the backwardness of Muslim societies is, first, a misunderstanding among Muslims of the Islamic instructions, and second, a lack of commitment to the instructions as a whole; that is to say a tendency to pick and choose among them determined by tastes that may have become rooted in a specific historical background and culture.

1. Post-Revolutionary Socio-Economic Conditions

The revolution of 1979 brought about many socio-cultural changes in society. Besides the spread of a desire for the predominance of religious values across the country, the will to remove poverty and spread social justice were important slogans during the revolutionary period. This was supposed to be possible partly through fighting capitalists and capitalism. As a result, investors were treated as people who exploit the masses and usurp the result of their employees' work, leading to windfall wealth. Thus, any desire for investment in a society in which profit-seeking is an 'anti-value' was viewed as sterile.

The spread of such a negative view of capitalists was rooted in the unfortunate history of many local capitalists. In fact, one should say, wealthy people in developing countries have not played the same positive role as investors have played – or play –

in the economic development of developed societies (Todaro, 1994, 159).

However, whatever the reason(s) for this anti-capitalist feeling in Iran, its consequence for production has been negative. This socio-cultural environment, which persisted through the post-revolutionary years, had serious economic consequences. The most conspicuous effect appeared when, ten years after the revolution and one year after the termination of the war between Iraq and Iran, Mr Rafsanjani started his presidential term with an emphasis on privatization. He mobilized everything in this cause and tried to justify the need for it to assist economic growth in the country. However, despite some successes, there was in practice much resistance to the policy, even among intermediate government staff. Such a feeling seems to have become a culture and changing it will need much time.

The scale of government and the involvement of government in many economic activities, directly and indirectly, is another feature of the post-revolutionary period. In ideal conditions, the interference of a wise, national efficient government in guiding the process of development is justified in all countries, but chiefly in developing countries and especially during the early years of progress. The recent *World Development Report* (1997) has also emphasized such a view.

However, while an efficient government can reinforce and guide the process of development, the interference of an inefficient government in economic activities can slow down or stop the production process. In Iran, especially after the revolution, many of the new managers and officials were young and lacked appropriate experience. They were also heavily engaged in activities related to the war. Both these issues created many problems in government activities. Inefficiencies are also due to many external and internal socio-political and economic problems, though there have been considerable attempts to reduce the impact of these.

However, the existence of this problem, whatever the reasons for it, created many obstacles in the way of producers. In fact, economic activities are connected in many ways to government, especially in Iran. Government in Iran has the monopoly of supplying foreign exchange at the official rate.[4] Thus, many economic activities which use foreign exchange for their external purchases inevitably have economic relationships with government offices.

Because the banking system is public, obtaining bank loans is another area of dependence on government. Furthermore, to establish an economic activity one needs to have authorizations from a variety of government offices. Some productive activities, for example food and hygienic products, need licenses not only for their operations, but also to supply their products to the market. Having control over production, distribution and the prices of some goods essential in the daily consumption of people is another government–private sector relationship. However, over the last decade, many attempts have been made to change conditions in favour of production. This survey tries to examine the success or failure of such efforts.

2. Methodology

As mentioned above, the objective of this paper is to examine the effect of non-economic factors in production. To do this, the researcher preferred to use primary material as other possible approaches had limitations so far as both the reliability and the availability of data were concerned. Thus, two complementary activities were carried out simultaneously. First, 800 question-naires were distributed by mail to productive project managers and some industrial policy-makers. Second, some 30 in-depth interviews with policy makers and big firm managers – mostly of government firms – were carried out. Both these activities were aimed at finding the main obstacles to production by asking those who were involved in production. Production was the most feasible indicator that could be examined in this research as an acceptable index for GNP.

The questionnaire was divided into several parts. The first inquired about some general characteristics of the firms, e.g. number of workers, kind of production, etc.; the second part contained the main questions. While representing economic and non-economic elements,[5] this part comprised 10 questions on what were considered to be the main obstacles to the process of production in any firm.

The ten factors suggested in the questionnaire as the main obstacles to production were: shortage of capital (Shortcap), dependency on the government sector (Depgov), the banking system (Bank), labour issues (Lablaw), lack of foreign exchange (Foriex), lack of demand (Lackdem), dependency on other firms

(Otherfir), existence of a society unsympathetic to production (Nonprocul), the non-production orientation of some officials (Nonprorie) and instability in government regulations concerned with production (Changlaw).

The last two factors deserve more explanation. The first, the existence of a society unsympathetic to production, refers to a condition in which productive firms operate in a society which is not practically concerned with economic progress, although it is concerned with economic progress to the extent that socio-cultural values are secured. In other words, in such a society socio-cultural, traditional, customary and religious issues take precedence over economic activities and, in effect, over securing economic growth. The existence of such a culture influences all aspects of social, economic and political life. Policies, regulations, laws, behaviour, practical actions and, in general, the orientation of the society are an echo of the preference and priority for non-economic factors over economic ones.

The second factor refers to the existence of an excessive concern among some officials over non-productive and socio-cultural issues, for example political interests and relations, self-interest or nepotism, at the expense of productive ones. This in fact is an outcome of the existence of the non-productive culture in the society dealt with in the previous question. But it is restricted to officials and is, therefore, narrower in character and range than the previous issue which points to the existence of a whole society unsympathetic to production.

The final part of the questionnaire was devoted to the level of each firm's production. As many managers were reluctant to state their actual production, they were asked about the 'percentage of optimum production capacity being used'. Due to numerous difficulties, many of which were suggested in the questionnaire, firms in Iran have normally been producing below their nominal production capacities. This was, therefore, supposed to be the best quantitative criterion to evaluate the success or failure of the firms in contributing to their own economic growth and, thus, national growth.

3. The Results of the Survey

3.1 General Characteristics of the Firms
From about 800 mailed questionnaires, 144 of the managers (18%) responded. In addition, 33 face-to-face in-depth interviews

were conducted. A preliminary review of the results shows that the survey embraced a variety of firms in terms of the number of workers, the amount of investment, kinds of production, etc. According to the data collected, the oldest firm was established in 1938 while the newest was established in 1994. The distribution, however, shows that more than 50 per cent of the firms were established after 1983 (median = 1983) (Table 1).

Table 1: Date of Establishment

Date	Years*	%*	No.	%	Cumulative per cent
Before 1963	25	42.4	13	10.2	10.2
1964–1973	10	16.9	19	15.0	25.2
1974–1979	6	10.2	17	13.4	38.6
1980–1987	8	13.6	42	33.1	71.7
1988–1997	10	16.9	36	28.4	100.0
Missing	–	–	17	Missing	
Total	59	100.0	144		

* These refer to the years and their related per cents that a category covers.

A review of the ownership of the participant firms shows that about 94 (65%) of the firms were private, 25 (17%) were under government control, while 19 (13%) were semi-government and only 4 (2.8%) were co-operatives (Table 2).

Table 2: Ownership

Ownership	No.	%	Cumulative per cent
Private	94	65.3	65.3
Government	25	17.4	83.1
Semi-government	19	13.2	96.3
Co-operative	4	2.8	99.1
Missing	2	1.4	100.0
Total	144		

3.2 Number and Characteristics of Workers

The total number of workers in the firms in the survey was 36,631, of whom all except 3,062 were men. Two firms did not report their employment. These firms had labour forces of varying size. The average number of employees was 257 and the median shows that 50 per cent of the firms had under 87 workers. The smallest number of workers in a firm was 8, while the largest was 2,332.

Table 3 illustrates the composition of the workers in the firms under study. Based on this table, of the total number of workers 2,697 (7.4%) were graduates and 8,458 (23.1%) had diplomas. These two groups of workers were mostly in managerial and administrative jobs. The rest were manual workers among whom 9,211 (25.1%) were skilled, 8,346 (22.8%) were semi-skilled, and 7,919 (21.6%) were unskilled (Table 3).

Table 3: Distribution of Workers by Skill and by Sex

Skill	Graduate			Diploma			Skilled		
Sex	F	M	T	F	M	T	F	M	T
No. of workers	372	2325	2697	1013	7445	8458	612	8599	9211
Percentage			7.4			23.1			25.1

Table 3: (Continued)

Semi-skilled			Unskilled			Total		
F	M	T	F	M	T	F	M	GT
729	7617	8346	336	7583	7919	3062	32569	36631
		22.8			21.6			100

F = Female; M = Male; T = Total; GT = Grand Total.

3.3 Types of Production

About three-quarters of the firms in this research produced consumer goods and the rest (one quarter) produced either intermediate or investment goods sold to other businesses; i.e. 27 per cent intermediate goods and 21 per cent investment goods. Some produced more than one type of good (Table 4).

Table 4: Broad Types of Production

Types of production	Number	Percentage
Consumer Goods	104	72.2
Intermediate	39	27.1
Investment	30	20.8

3.3. Per Cent of Optimum Production Capacity Used (Proper)
Based on this data, average production is about 50 per cent of optimum capacity; 8 (5.6%) firms produce less than a quarter of their capacity. The highest percentage was 90 and the lowest 15.[6] Only 31 firms (22%) produced more than 66 per cent of their capacity. It is clear, therefore, that some inquiry into the causes of this malfunction is justified. This survey is confined to external causes and does not attempt to examine internal, technical and managerial factors (Table 5).

Table 5: Optimum Production Capacity Used

Capacity %	No.	%	Cum %
10–25	8	5.6	5.6
26–50	65	45.1	50.7
51–65	40	27.8	78.8
More than 66	31	21.5	100.0
Total	144	100	

By way of comparison, a report from the Wolverhampton Business School[7] (1988) relating to manufacturing firms in the West Midlands in the UK indicates that over 80 per cent of 'Chemical,' 'Metal' and 'other manufacturers' were working at over 70 per cent capacity (the traditional norm for manufacturing). As is obvious, manufacturers in Iran have produced far less than this. This comparison reveals that, while in Iran nearly 80 per cent of manufacturing firms produced less than 65 per cent of their optimum capacity, in the UK more than 80 per cent of manufacturers produced over 70 per cent.

4. Analysis of the Results

In this section, the results of the descriptive analysis of the ten main variables are provided. The frequency of different choices,[8] along with related percentages, are mostly highlighted. The order in which these 10 variables are presented is based on the degree of their importance as reflected by respondents; e.g. the variable which has the highest frequency in the choice 'very important' is presented first and other variables are put forward in turn, based on this criterion. Furthermore, to make the analysis easier, the three top choices, i.e. 'very important', 'quite important' and 'important' as a whole are considered as 'important' and the bottom two choices, i.e. 'fairly unimportant' and 'not important' are also combined as 'not important'. These two broad categories, therefore, have been dealt with for each of the ten variables. The interviews and additional points written into the mail questionnaires by respondents concerned with each of the ten variables are also analysed based on a qualitative approach, and their results are included, where appropriate, as supplementary points.

4.1 Frequent Changes in Laws and Regulations (Changlaw)

It was considered that frequent changes in laws and regulations were likely to be an important hindrance to production – preventing firms reaching their optimum production. In relation to the questionnaire survey, about 47 per cent of respondents emphasized this problem as 'very important', that is the highest number compared with the other factors. If the other important choices, i.e. 'quite important' and 'important', are added to this option, it shows that about 94 per cent of managers highlighted this issue as a serious obstacle to their production (Table 6).

This issue was also strongly emphasized by most of the interviewees as a serious obstacle in Iran. However, instability in legal conditions has, in the view of many managers, several dimensions. Some complained about the lack of a comprehensive policy for economic activities, especially for industrial activities. Most of the managers interviewed emphasized that such instabilities are due to lack of a fixed plan or policy. In other words, they believed the reason for much of this kind of disorder is the lack of a stable macro-plan for production. This leads to the introduction of a variety of regulations. A general manager stated that 'the changes in laws and policies are so fast that one can call them "weekly" or even "daily" changes.' The central bank, for instance, said one interviewee, 'released several directives in less than one year.' This bank has the key role in providing foreign exchange at the official rate so vital for many producers in Iran.

Table 6: Obstacles to Production: Frequent Changes in Laws and Regulations (Changlaw)

Value Label	Value	No.	%	Cum%
Very important	5	65	47.1	47.1
Quite important	4	38	27.5	74.6
Important	3	26	18.8	93.5
Fairly unimportant	2	4	2.9	96.4
Not important	1	5	3.6	100.0
Missing	-1	6	Missing	
Total		144	100.0 (138)	

Another problem is the personal interpretation by officials of such new laws. Many respondents added that these changes were so frequent that related staff and officials could not understand them, giving rise to different interpretations by different government officers. Another problem, highlighted by many managers, was the lack of harmony or co-ordination between related government offices. This, in turn, has led to chaos and disorder thus causing confusion and delay among investors and managers.

As mentioned below, changes in policies and regulations in the banking system were another issue to the fore. Instability in the regulations in the banking system, some respondents argued, causes the confidence of investors to suffer so much that they feel that they cannot rely on banking sources at any stage in the processing of their applications.

Many respondents complained that such disorders mainly affect industrial production, while trade and commerce, which are of lesser importance to the economy, do not suffer as much. It is important to indicate that, due to the high inflation rate during the last decade, brokers' activities are spreading. The trade and commerce sector, mentioned above, mainly includes activities that are not under government control and are thus immune to many of the problems highlighted by production managers.

4.2 The Existence of a Society Unsympathetic to Production (Nonprocul)

The result of this question is interesting. Fifty-nine firms (42%) indicated this item as a 'very important' obstacle to their production (Table 7). If the three first ranks of importance are considered, exactly 90 per cent of managers highlighted this issue as an important one. This means that, for respondents, the need to work in a non-productive culture has the second highest degree of importance. Only four respondents out of 144 failed to respond to this question, an indication that it is a very common and much felt obstacle to production (Table 7). These results are also strongly confirmed by information extracted from the qualitative analysis.

Table 7: Obstacles to Production: The Existence of a Non-Productive Culture (Nonprocul)

Value Label	Value	No.	%	Cum%
Very important	5	59	42.1	42.1
Quite important	4	42	30.0	72.1
Important	3	25	17.9	90.0
Fairly unimportant	2	7	5.0	95.0
Not important	1	7	5.0	100.0
Missing	-1	4	Missing	
Total		144	100 (140)	

One of the most common ideas suggested both in many interviews and in mail questionnaires was society's negative view of investors. Several respondents made similar statements to the effect that, because of some Marxist slogans bandied about during the revolutionary period, 'people see us as thieves'. This anti-capitalist feeling is still an active orientation among many ordinary people and officials. A manager who was interviewed explained his experience during a negotiation meeting with some government officers. There was a dispute with officials over the price for his firm's production. Because the firm needed the support of the government office in question,' he had to persuade them into an agreed price. 'When we offered a price,' the manager stated, 'the government officer rejected it because they believed my profit would be high, based on what they calculated immediately in that meeting, and they told me "you should not gain such a high amount of profit."' Reflecting a less strong view towards investors, some respondents stated that investors and producers have been confused with brokers.

In addition to a negative view of investors, many firms complained about the attention paid to consumers (by government and society), sometimes even at the expense of production. This is, as many managers believed, through controlling prices at a fixed level. Such a policy means less profit for firms and therefore no incentive for investors to increase their investment, leading them in the end to give up productive activity. Complaints that such policies created indifference and made them reluctant to increase their production through more projects were even made by many managers of state enterprises.

While Changlaw focused on changes in the law, the emphasis here is on sheer regulation and bureaucracy. A manager complained, for instance, that to establish an industrial firm, one has to get the agreement of several government offices. In addition to many delays due to obstructive bureaucracy in government offices, sometimes conflicts, arguments and different interpretations of the regulations by staff in different offices caused even more delay in pursuing the necessary affairs.

For example, there was a dispute between two government organizations; both believed that they had to give the deed of land needed to establish an industrial firm. According to an interviewee, there were many investors waiting for the agreement. It took about one year for the problem between the two offices to be solved. The interviewee told us that during this period investors could not proceed with their affairs, i.e. applying for bank loans, getting authority from other government offices etc., because they had to show proof that they possessed landed property.

Many similar problems were reported in other interviews. A dairy factory manager, for instance, explained that his company needed more electric power to meet local demand. While it had secured the necessary capital and other prerequisites, a serious argument between the electricity company and railway company caused more than six months delay in taking the necessary steps.

Another interesting case was reported by a manager who was producing hygienic tools for hospitals. He reported, 'we need no capital, experts or foreign exchange, we have already secured all production factors and the firm is producing at an optimum capacity. The problem is with a government office that is responsible for giving a licence for selling hygienic goods.' He presented evidence showing that they had applied for the licence more than a year earlier but, at the time of the interview, had not received any reply. He claimed that he had already obtained all the necessary proofs that their products were based on the 'national standard' – a known official authority for producers.

And, finally, a respondent asked 'how can we be optimistic about progress in production if policy makers are not really concerned with production?' In such a socio-political situation, one would be naive to think that there is any interest among local investors in contributing to the progress of production, let alone foreign investors.[10]

A fourth dimension of the non-productive culture pointed to by some managers was the neglect of religious concerns. One manager wondered why Iranian society paid so little attention to values such as discipline, hard work, securing society's livelihood, the removal of poverty and the development of science – all essential for economic growth and development and highly valued by Islam. While in theory policy makers emphasized these positive beliefs, in practice considerable disorder, laziness at work, breaking of promises and other actions which are the opposite to such beliefs could be observed.

Many respondents referred to the economic consequences of the existence of such a socio-cultural and historical environment. Some believed that, because of such tough limitations on productive activities, rich people are more interested in investing in brokerage, or in trade and commercial activities.

As a result, one can conclude that the orientation of the society is generally anti-production. This is because the investor is hated, seeking profit is disapproved of, production is not valued by many officials, and so on. A manager argued that, 'while seeking profit is a God-granted motive, such a valuable motive is killed in the society, both directly and indirectly.' This happens directly in many cases where some intermediate officials do not perform affairs related to investors because the latter are hated, and indirectly by putting considerable obstacles in the way of those seeking to establish a firm or continue existing activities.

4.3 Shortage of Capital (Shortcap)
The third most important of the possible obstacles to the progress of production was shortage of capital. Table 8 shows that 57 firms

(40%) indicated that this factor was 'very important'. The results, too, show that about 82 per cent of respondents highlighted this factor as an important element in their production process.

An important feature of this variable is that it has the minimum number of missing values (non-responses). This could be due to the fact that this is the first choice offered in the questionnaire. Or perhaps it is due to the fact that it is a known, easily recognized and important current issue among respondent firms.

Table 8: Obstacles to Production: Shortage of Capital (Shortcap)

Degree of importance	Value	No.	%	Cum%
Very important	5	57	40.4	40.4
Quite important	4	30	21.3	61.7
Important	3	28	19.9	81.6
Fairly unimportant	2	16	11.3	92.9
Not important	1	10	7.1	100.0
Missing	-1	3	Missing	
Total		144	100.0	

Based on the qualitative analysis, although many respondents highlighted the lack of capital (known as lack of liquidity among managers in Iran) as a serious problem for their firms, they concentrated mostly on delay in the procedures for gaining a loan from the banking system. In other words, shortage of capital is not in itself a problem, but the conditions that give rise to the problem have to be dealt with.

Many investors or managers, even those employed by government, complained about the variety of government tolls, taxes and other charges that reduced their profit and thus lay behind the lack of capital for further investment from their own sources. An interviewee, for instance, argued that 'there are several taxes, tolls and government charges, collected only from producers and not from brokers'. Others also referred to such government charges as the reason for their lack of capital for further investment. The percentage (90%) of those who indicated this as a critical reason (in subsequent questions concerned with Shortcap) for their shortage of actual capital reveals that it is a serious problem for productive activities.

One manager explained that, 'while many other firms obtain part of their necessary liquidity (capital) through "selling short" to the private sector, we cannot access such a source because government is the only customer for our goods. This is the most important obstacle for us in obtaining the necessary capital, because obtaining payment for goods from government is so difficult and involves many delays.' He also argued that sometimes the government firm concerned ran out of money or, in cases where this was not the problem, the bureaucracy in the government offices created lots of delays.

Another manager similarly explained that 'we have a problem with government for six months in every year. Over the last three months of the financial year, government offices are usually out of money while they receive their budget three months after the start of the next financial year.' Thus, a manager stated, 'to obtain the money that government firms owe, many notices, huge documentation and lots of managerial and staff time are necessary so that the government repays its debts.'

However, while shortage of capital is the third most important factor for the firms, the results obtained from analysing interviews and considering the responses to additional points in the questionnaires, show that most of the problem arises from the banking system or the existence of bureaucracy in government offices. Shortage of capital among many private firms is connected to government in two ways: first, government is a very big customer for many local producers; second, government in the shape of the Central Bank exclusively provides the foreign exchange necessary at the official rate. As a result, the government system in the economy is the main culprit in creating delays in the circulation of existing capital in society.

In general, many believed that, despite the existing shortage, capital was a very important factor in their production; available capital is, moreover, wasted for the many socio-cultural reasons suggested in other parts of the questionnaire. In other words, not only are firms facing an actual shortage of capital, but also their limited capital is widely wasted for a variety of reasons. Consequently, the capital-output ratio[11] is increased and this ultimately leads to a general reduction in production.

4.4 Labour Law (Lablaw)

The ramifications of Iran's labour law have been a major issue for all economic (and probably non-economic) activities over the last two decades. Many managers complained about the limitations on their managerial authority imposed by the law. As shown in Table 9, about 90 per cent of respondents have marked the issue as 'important', 'quite important', or 'very important'. Fifty out of 144 respondents emphasized this issue as a most important problem for their activities. Significantly, there are again few missing responses (only 5).

Table 9: Obstacles to Production: Labour Law (Lablaw)

Value Label	Value	No.	%	Cum%
Very important	5	50	36.0	36.0
Quite important	4	41	29.5	65.5
Important	3	32	23.0	88.5
Fairly unimportant	2	11	7.9	96.4
Not important	1	5	3.6	100.0
Missing	-1	5	Missing	
Total		144	100.0 (139)	

The results of qualitative analysis also show a high concern among respondents about labour issues, especially the effects of the labour law. Many additional points, besides crossing the boxes related to labour law in the mail questionnaire, echo the high importance of this issue to the firms. Many respondents believed that the labour law is concerned only with labour at the expense of work and production. Others indicated that this law protects labour while the employer is not protected by any parallel regulations.

Many respondents described the labour law as a weapon in labour's hands against employers. This is because, as some indicated, the law sees labour and employers as enemies who are fighting against each other, rather than as parts of a single body with a common goal. This may be a reflection of the environment of the post-revolutionary period and the historical characteristics of industrial societies. Some argued that this law is only of benefit to labour in the short term, and in the long term is detrimental to workers' interests. And, finally, one respondent likened the effect of the labour law on an investor to a person whose hands and feet are tied and who is then asked to swim.

Given these features, several implications are to be expected for productive firms or for production as a whole. Many believed that the law resulted in very high labour costs which, in turn, created a situation where employers are reluctant to employ more workers. Michael Todaro (1994, 234) has referred to this issue in developing countries generally as a major reason for unemployment.

Some respondents argued that the law had indeed caused an increase in unemployment. One wrote 'we need 45 employees but we prefer to employ only 20'. Similarly, another respondent indicated that: 'the law causes chaos and disorder in the factory. I have therefore reduced my workers to the minimum level.' Or another argued that: 'if an employer has the right to employ, s/he has to have the right to discharge inefficient workers. But, because we have not the right to discharge a delinquent worker, we prefer not to employ more workers.' Many, too, added short statements such as: 'fewer workers, more production' or 'fewer workers guarantee more production' and one believed that 'fewer personnel, less trouble, but more production and more satisfaction for existing workers.'

A major consequence of this law is the reluctance of rich people and investors to invest in productive projects and their tendency to engage in brokerage activities instead. A brick plant manager told me that he had decided to sell his firm and invest in speculative activities. The reasons for his decision included huge problems with workers, the labour law, and consequent frequent interference by local labour offices in affairs related to workers. He believed that there was no sign of any government support.

Two more quotations reflect the extent to which the labour law has affected the confidence of producers. One respondent added this statement to his questionnaire: 'the effect of labour law on production is greater than the effect of an invasion of the country by a foreign enemy', and another believed that 'it is a disaster for the country and will lead to the destruction of production'. Although such statements may be interpreted as a typical capitalist exaggeration of the issue, they do, at least, reflect the deep negative impact of a law that seems to be biased towards the labour force.

4.5 The Banking System (Bank)

Fifthly, the importance of the banking system in the production process, like the shortage of capital, was emphasized by 112 (82%) respondents. In other words, more than 80 per cent of respondents believed that problems with the banking system were 'important', 'quite important' or 'very important'. The number of missing values is 8 (Table 10).

Table 10: Obstacles to Production: The Banking System (Bank)

Value Label	Value	No.	%	Cum%
Very important	5	37	27.2	27.2
Quite important	4	42	30.9	58.1
Important	3	32	23.5	81.6
Fairly unimportant	2	15	11.0	92.6
Not important	1	10	7.4	100.0
Missing	-1	8	Missing	
Total		144	100.0 (136)	

As with previous factors, the banking system and its effects on the performance of productive firms have been highlighted in most of the interviews as well as in the additional points in the questionnaires. In the meeting between the Ministry of Industry and some 30 producers, for instance, about 28 people complained of problems with the banking system. The most common issues are summarized here along with other points extracted from the interviews and questionnaires.

Many respondents argued that the banking system is commercial and service sector orientated. In other words, they believed that the banking system is far more interested in giving loans for commercial activities than to producers like themselves. This is considered to be mostly due to the fact that the commercial sector has fewer problems and thus offers a better guarantee of capital returns for banks compared with productive firms which have huge obstacles in their way. This situation, namely the better conditions for commercial activities in the country, has been dealt with in an earlier section, i.e. as part of the existence of the non-economic culture in the society.

The existence of an inefficient bureaucracy in the banking system is another issue that was highlighted by many respondents. The prevalence of such inefficiency is, probably, mostly due to the fact that the banking system has been nationalized since the revolution and banks are ruled by the government system.

Whatever the reason, the bureaucracy in the banking system impacts on production since the process of approving or rejecting an application from producers for a loan takes a long time. A respondent wrote in his questionnaire that: 'the bank told me that it would be at least one month before it could start dealing with my application.' In a more acute case, an interviewee explained: 'it took about six months for the bank to process my documents and finally reject my application.' Furthermore, the banking system asks for considerable documentation, i.e. proof of the possession of land, the agreement of the environment protection office, etc., for each loan application. It is obvious, given the existence of similar bureaucracy in other parts of the government system, that assembling such documents in itself takes undue time. Finally, from the time of applying for a loan from the banking system to the time of getting it, policies and regulations may change. Such changes sometimes affect even previously approved applications. At least two such cases were mentioned in the general meeting between the minister for industries and investors.

The existence of such a situation in the banking system, which is the only official source that grants capital to producers, has pushed investors into approaching usurers to provide their necessary capital. This, in turn, imposes an increase in production costs leading to inflation or to the bankruptcy of some newly established firms.

The above issues raised, in relationship to the banking system, lead us to the conclusion that the banking system has not been a reliable support to economic activities in Iran in the last decade.

4.6 Foreign Exchange (Foriex)

Discussion now turns to the remaining four issues that were of lesser importance to respondents. Foreign exchange, as mentioned in the methodology section, is another, if less important, issue for firms in Iran. With a moderate number of missing values (8), more than 67 per cent of respondents have indicated this factor as an important issue including 32 (23.5%) who assessed it as 'very important' (Table 11).

Table 11: Obstacles to Production: Shortage of Foreign Exchange (Foriex)

Value Label	Value	No.	%	Cum%
Very important	5	32	23.5	23.5
Quite important	4	29	21.3	44.9
Important	3	31	22.8	67.6
Fairly unimportant	2	21	15.4	83.1
Not important	1	23	16.9	100.0
Missing	-1	8	Missing	
Total		144	100.0	

Such relatively modest results for this factor were not expected, since obtaining foreign exchange is a dominant issue in many economic activities. Despite many attempts to reduce the dependence of the economy on foreign exchange, it was still expected to be one of the most common issues that firms would complain about (as they commonly do elsewhere). However, this dependency varies in different industries. Those with more complicated technologies have a stronger dependency on foreign exchange than others as they need to purchase equipment abroad.

Nevertheless, only a few respondents mentioned lack of foreign exchange as a major problem. This is not, perhaps, due to the fact that it was not a problem, but because it is part of capital that is mainly supplied by the banking system. It is, therefore, probable that the issue was included in respondents' minds (if not explicitly) in the answers to questions related to the banking system or the role of government in the economy. Some managers, for instance, complained about changes in government policies concerned with foreign exchange and others referred to the central bank as the one official supplier of foreign exchange. It may also indicate that other obstacles were considered more critical.

The firms using highly advanced technologies are more dependent on foreign exchange and thus suffer more from foreign exchange instability. However, although lack of foreign exchange has been the critical issue for many firms, the problem with instability in laws, regulations and policies and, in general, the inefficiency of government as the exclusive source of supply of foreign exchange, has reinforced the problem. This, in turn, causes many delays in completing projects or in pursuing current affairs.

4.7 Non-Production Orientation of Some Officials (Nonprorie)
This variable, as a non-economic element, was an important
barrier to production in responding firms. More than 72 per cent
of respondents referred to this item as 'very important', 'quite
important' or 'important' (Table 12).

Table 12: Obstacles to Production: Non-production Orientation
(Nonprorie)

Value Label	Value	No.	%	Cum%
Very important	5	28	20.4	20.4
Quite important	4	44	32.1	52.6
Important	3	27	19.7	72.3
Fairly unimportant	2	20	2.0	86.9
Not important	1	18	13.1	100.0
Missing	-1	7	Missing	
Total		144	100.0	

In interviews, and at additional points too, some interviewees
gave examples of government managers who behave in ways that
do not necessarily lead to better production conditions. As a
common example, reference was made to the appointment of
government officials or managers whose selection (in all economic
sectors – agriculture, industry, and services) was not necessarily
based on their ability to increase production, but on their possession of certain socio-political characteristics. This is normal in
all revolutionary governments.

Some arguments between managers in different offices, which
cause chaos and disorder in the production process, were not
based on their concerns about production, but on their own socio-
political interests, or on their self-interest. Some respondents
referred to issues such as employment based on nepotism in
government offices and political or social interests as other
examples of behaviour in this category.

In general, the existence of such an environment among officials
leads to many problems, such as inefficiency in offices and delays
in pursuing affairs related to production. Despite many attempts
during recent years to correct the situation, it seems that the
problem still has a great deal of impact on the production process.

4.8 Dependency on Government (Depgov)

Besides investing directly in many activities, government in Iran, as in many other developing countries, has wide control over private sector activities. Such controls, in fact, started under the previous regime but were reinforced after the revolution and especially as a consequence of the Iran–Iraq war.

Dependency on government is considered an important obstacle by 68 per cent of respondents. Among these, 26 (19.5%) firms referred to it as 'very important' (Table 13). However, the number of missing cases, i.e. 11, is the second highest amongst these 10 variables.

Table 13: Obstacles to Production: Dependency on Government (Depgov)

Value Label	Value	No.	%	Cum%
Very important	5	26	19.5	19.5
Quite important	4	30	22.6	42.1
Important	3	35	26.3	68.4
Fairly unimportant	2	26	19.5	88.0
Not important	1	16	12.0	100.0
Missing	-1	11	Missing	
Total		144	100.0 (134)	

Nevertheless, a review of the written comments added to mail questionnaires shows that some respondents confused 'dependency on government' with 'ownership by government'. Despite such a mistake, and the fact that the problem of dependency on government was echoed in other items, such as frequent changes in laws, the banking system, foreign exchange, non-productive culture, many of the interviewees and the additional comments in the questionnaires brought dependency directly to the fore.

A general manager in charge of a number of industrial activities, for instance, argued: 'dependency on government brings with it a transfer of inefficiency to other economic activities through a very inefficient bureaucracy and frequent changes in laws and regulations.' In another interview, a general manager of a big firm said: 'we are also suffering from the existence of government bureaucracy in an indirect way. Because the National Health

Service is government, most of our workers are not enthusiastic, energetic and lively because the government service to them is very poor and involves lots of time-wasting and bureaucracy, so that most of their time on leave is spent in pursuing administrative affairs in order to get their money from government offices. This is a really important issue in a firm with a large number of workers.' Finally, in reply to the question 'what is the main obstacle for your production?', one interviewee said: 'only government'.

As a result, it is obvious that the government in Iran has a critical role in the process of development and its inefficiency causes irretrievable losses to the economy of Iran. Problems concerned with government efficiency could also be a consequence of the chaos that followed the revolution and eight years war, as well as being due to the many pressures imposed by external forces during the last two decades. However, some recent improvements in the economy show that the government is struggling to remove these defects and is determined to reduce its inefficiency.

However, lack of demand (Lackdem) and dependency on other firms (Otherfir) were not emphasized by respondents as important factors for their production and, thus, are not explained in detail here (see Table 14 for their general outcomes).

5. General and Comparative Review of the Ten Variables (Summary of the Results)

As illustrated in Table 14, Changlaw is the most important factor, i.e. 65 (42%) of respondents refer to it as very important. Nonprocul, Shortcap, Lablaw and Bank are the next most significant factors as 59 (42%), 57 (40%), 50 (36%) and 37 (27%) of respondents, respectively, refer to them as very important. The second column, i.e., important,[12] is very similar to the first column but Lablaw moves to third and Nonprorie to sixth position while Lackdem falls to tenth.

All in all, the initial findings are strongly supportive of the view that non-economic factors have had a greater influence than economic factors on the production of firms in Iran during recent years. Factors such as Changlaw, Nonprocul, Lablaw, and Bank respectively are, among others, considered as the most important obstacles to the production of respondent firms. However, Changlaw, Nonprocul, Depgov and Lablaw are particularly emphasized as the most serious impediments to the production process. Furthermore, these four factors were the core of all discussions in the interviews as well as additional points written into the mail questionnaires.

Table 14: The Ten Variables Ranked by Importance

	No. ranking this most important		Number ranking this important		Number ranking this unimportant		Missing answers
	No.	%	No.	%	No.	%	No.
Changlaw	65	47	129	93	9	6.5	6
Nonprocul	59	42	126	90	14	10	4
Shortcap	57	40	115	81	26	18	3
Lablaw	50	36	123	88	16	11.5	5
Bank	37	27	112	82	8	6	8
Foriex	32	23.5	92	68	44	32	8
Nonprorie	28	20	99	72	38	28	7
Lackdem	29	22	70	53	62	47	12
Depgov	26	19.5	91	68	42	31.5	11
Otherfir	18	13	73	54	61	45.5	10

In Nonprocul, the problems stem from the impractical view of society and policy makers and the priority given to non-productive affairs, i.e. socio-political and cultural concerns, over productive affairs. Even those respondents who indicated capital, banks and foreign exchange as important impediments to production were mainly complaining about the bureaucracy, changes in law, and the low importance of production to staff in government offices, etc. as the factors causing the above problems. Hardly a respondent referred to a straightforward shortage of capital or foreign exchange as a problem in itself. Their complaints are mostly about the procedures by which they obtain the approved loan or the foreign exchange allocated to them.

In general, the results of this survey show that many of the factors stem from the considerable socio-cultural issues existing in Iranian society. Shortage of capital, for instance, was mostly due to problems with the banking system. This, in turn, stemmed from the fact that the orientation of the banking system seems to be to non-productive activities. Many of the problems in the banking system themselves stem from its dependency on government.

Government, too, due to the existence of the non-production environment in the society, has many problems that impose obstacles to the increase of production. The existence of such an environment also affects issues related to labour that, in turn, create considerable problems in the way of production. All are, therefore, closely interrelated.

6. Conclusion

The results prove that non-economic factors have been more influential than economic ones in the process of production in Iran. In other words, it can be concluded that non-economic factors are responsible for the many failures that have occurred in the way of economic development in Iran over the last decades.

Apart from the negative effects on the economy of the post-revolutionary socio-economic turmoil, and eight years of war between Iraq and Iran, the results support the view that a lack of practical sympathy towards economic progress among policy makers, and the existence of an anti-production government system, and a general culture that is more concerned with socio-cultural affairs than increasing production, are the main factors responsible for many productivity failures in the production projects.

Despite essential changes in the view of policy makers as a result of the election of President Rafsanjani in 1989, and his attempts to provide a more practical production-orientated atmosphere, the wide and deep spread of the socio-cultural tendency to emphasize culture and traditions hindered the occurrence of fundamental changes in existing economic conditions. The findings of the field study, again, prove that non-economic factors are still the main obstacles to production, economic growth and consequently economic development in Iran.

This seems to be a vital issue with which policy makers have to deal. Religious leaders, among others, can play a key role in changing the existing environment. While there is the necessary theoretical context in Islamic instructions, a more practical commitment to economic activities and material affairs (based on Islam) by religious leaders, who are also the political leaders at present, may give rise to a situation in which economic development can occur.

Notes

1 For more information about Iran's economy, see references in bibliography or see my PhD thesis: S. M. Afghah (1998).

2 For more information about Islam and development, see resources in the bibliography or my PhD thesis, op. cit.

3 *Nahjul Balagha, Sermons and Letters of Imam Ali Ibn Abi Talib,* translated by Askari Jafri, Eleventh Revised Edition, Islamic Seminary Publications. Also: 'And Imam Sadiq said: "There are three things which their little portion of them are still considered too much: . . . 3– Poverty.' (I have received this hadith by e-mail from the following address: ZD00007@auabdpo.dpo.uab.edu. The original source is: Kolaini, *Osul-e Kafi,* which is one of the main Shi'ite sources).

4 Foreign exchange transactions are banned in the free market in Iran, though they were allowed for a limited period in recent years. Thus, the foreign exchange rate in the black market is much higher than the official rate.

5 To avoid bias in respondents' replies, these catagories were not distinguished.

6 There was one firm producing at 90 per cent and two at 85 per cent of their optimum capacity; the rest were under 80 per cent. On the other hand, one firm was producing at 15 per cent and three at 25 per cent; the rest produced at more than 30 per cent.

7 See also a similar report in The Birmingham Post (Manning, 1.7.88) about the capacity utilization of West Midlands manufacturers.

8 There were five categories; i.e. very important, quite important, important, fairly unimportant and not important.

9 It provided the inputs for the firm at a price known as the 'government price' that was less than the so-called black market price.

10 During the last eight years, the government has invited foreign capital to invest in economic projects in Iran.

11 A ratio that shows the units of capital needed to produce a unit of output over a given period of time. See glossary section in Michael P. Todaro (1994), p. 664.

12 As the sum of the first three choices; i.e. very important, quite important, and important.

Part Three
Women's Social Participation

7

Women's Socio-Economic Participation and Iran's Changing Political Economy

Valentine M. Moghadam

How will the changing political economy in Iran and the challenges of globalization affect women's employment? To date, Iran remains an oil-based economy as yet some distance away from a restructured economy. Still, the pressures of soaring inflation, a huge foreign debt, a growing labour force, high unemployment, income disparities, and social dissatisfaction – along with an apparent commitment to economic liberalization – have led to a number of policy changes and shifting priorities with implications for women's economic and social participation.

Thus far, patterns of women's employment in Iran have been influenced by the oil-based nature of the economy; by the policy of import-substitution industrialization which has favoured capital-intensive, male-intensive industries; by cultural attitudes and gender bias which render many occupations inappropriate or off-limits to women; by women's low level of literacy, educational attainment, and skills relative to men; and by high rates of fertility. These factors affected, and indeed limited, the supply of and demand for female labour, especially in the 1980s.

The results of the 1986 census, which came to light in 1988, seem to have prompted a number of significant policy shifts on the part of the government of then President Rafsanjani and sparked debates, studies, and research projects concerning population issues, women's economic and social roles, and development strategies. Among the most startling findings of the 1986 census was the high rate of fertility and consequently of population growth, the growth in unemployment, the expansion of the self-employed category of workers as opposed to those in regular waged and salaried jobs, and the extremely small size of the female labour force. In a situation of declining oil revenues and state income, growing poverty, and indebtedness from the huge expenditures of war with Iraq, the government was faced with the compelling need to change the course of social and economic development. The Islamic Republic's First Five-Year Plan (1989–93) sought increased revenues through the rapid expansion of the oil sector and export promotion, and attempted to link Iran's economy with the global economy by reducing import controls, by attracting foreign investment, and by attempting to unify the exchange rate (Karshenas, 1995). At the same time, a concerted campaign was established to reduce the rate of population growth, and thereby alleviate pressures on the labour market and on social services. Gender advocates began to call attention to women as agents of development and urged an end to discriminatory practices in the areas of education and employment.

The first stage of economic liberalization was not successful, and it adversely affected lower-income, middle-income and fixed-income households – a very large proportion of the population. Unemployment grew in both urban and rural areas. The 1991 multi-round population census revealed a continuing growth of self-employment for men and women, limited job opportunities for women in the formal sector, and high unemployment rates among women. The underground economy and informal sector have swelled – mainly on the part of employed men taking on second and third jobs, and in some cases illegal currency exchange transactions, to augment their deteriorating wages and to bolster the household budget. Meanwhile, whether for economic need or for personal aspirations, more and more Iranian women are seeking employment – and finding that there exist extremely limited job opportunities for them. Recent legislative innovations in Iran – the equal division of marital property in the event of a wife's divorce by her husband and discussions about wages for housework – would seem to reflect these economic and labour-market realities, as well as the reigning Islamic ideology emphasizing the importance of the family and marital roles.

The Second Five-Year Plan, adopted in February 1995, and the election in 1997 of a liberal and reform-minded president, Mohammad Khatami, indicated that the state may be changing its priorities. It suggested a transition from ideological purity to economic development, from growth through oil exports to human resource development, and from inwardness to an outward orientation – with positive implications for women. However, as recently as 1999, factionalism within the government continued to thwart plans to establish a coherent and consistent economic reform programme. As a result, there has been limited progress in women's employment situation, despite women's own determination to enhance their social participation by obtaining higher education, seeking jobs, and attaining public visibility through a lively and sometimes controversial women's press. Although women's share of civil service employment has grown, women remain a small percentage of the measured labour force and a smaller proportion of the salaried work force. The 'patriarchal gender contract' – whereby men are deemed the breadwinners and women are regarded as mothers and housewives – remains intact.[1]

This chapter examines the evolution of women's social positions and labour force participation since the Iranian Revolution. A major focus in on the employment and unemployment situation during the 1990s and the challenges of the future.

Women's Socio-Economic Participation in the 1980s

The prolific literature on Iranian women that appeared during the 1980s described an exceedingly disadvantaged position for women in the years following the Islamic Revolution. The implementation of Islamic law placed women in the legal status of minors; new educational and employment policies discriminated against women and women' were all but excluded from the realm of formal politics, which had taken on a masculine and clerical cast. Nor did the political economy of the 1980s favour women's socio-economic participation.

In the 1980s, the Iranian economy was predominantly oil-based, with exports of crude petroleum or oil products accounting for most of the country's export revenues. Steel, petrochemicals, and copper remain the country's three basic industries, and these are capital-intensive, male-intensive industries. During the Iran–Iraq war of 1980–88, capital and assets were channelled towards the defence industry, which is also traditionally male-intensive. Of the modern manufacturing plants that were established under the shah's regime, those that remained in production (estimated at only 20 per cent of the total by value of output) encountered serious difficulties. At the end of 1988 it was reported that most factories were operating at less than 50 per cent of their capacity, owing to shortages of raw materials from abroad (Fischer, 1989: 440). The stated policies of the Islamic government favoured small-scale, traditional or bazaar-related enterprises; not surprisingly, self-employment grew between the 1976 and 1986 population censuses.

According to the 1986 census data, some 990,000 women (and 11 million men) were classified as employed, which was 9 per cent of the total employed population.[2] The largest number of enumerated women were in private and public services; agriculture ranked second, with about 263,000 women, and industry third, with 216,000 women employees. Clearly vast numbers of women were not being counted in the agricultural sector; the figure for men in agriculture was nearly 3 million. Only about 508,000 women were reported as employees (salaried), of which 408,000 women were in the public sector (out of a total of 3.4 million public sector employees) and 100,000 women in the private sector (out of a total of 1.8 million private sector employees).

In terms of distribution of the female labour force across occupational groups, women were found to be: (a) professional, technical and related workers (35 per cent of employed women); (b) agricultural, animal husbandry, forestry, fishing and hunting workers (26.6 per cent of employed women), and (c) production and transport workers (23.4 per cent of employed women). Women were extremely under-represented in managerial, administrative, clerical, and sales work. In a pattern typical of the Middle East, the age categories with the highest reported activity rates (albeit very low by international standards) were 15–24 and 25–29, with a marked decline in the age categories 30–40. After age 40, female activity rates are extremely low.

Compared with other developing countries, not to mention developed countries, the female share of salaried employment in Iran is extremely small. Compared with Iran's 11 per cent female share of the labour force and 9 per cent share of the salaried work force, women's labour force shares in 1990 were about 18 per cent in Turkey and Tunisia, 28 per cent in Mexico, 35–38 per cent in Cuba, Malaysia and Korea, and 47 per cent in Bulgaria (see ILO, 1994).

Characteristics of the employed female population according to the 1986 census thus included the following:

- The female share of the total labour force and of salaried employment was very small, at under 10 per cent (down from 13.8 per cent of the salaried work force in 1976);

- Most women in the work force were wage and salary workers in the government sector, mainly as teachers and health workers employed by the Ministries of Health and Education, working in the state schools and universities and in the public health centres; these women enjoyed social insurance, including pensions, health care, maternity leave, and other benefits.

- In contrast, large numbers of 'employed' women in the private sector were not receiving a wage for their work. Indeed, the proportion of women in the private sector receiving a wage or salary was only 19 per cent.

- Apart from carpet-weaving and traditional craft work, women's role in modern industrial production was limited – only 14 per cent of the manufacturing labour force, and mostly unwaged.

- An extreme form of occupational sex-segregation existed.

- Women were almost non-existent in decision-making positions.

- Women's role in agriculture was deemed marginal; the majority of rural women were designated 'housewives' in the census. There were few female agricultural extension agents; this resulted from discriminatory education and training policies that barred women from agrarian affairs and veterinary science.

- The unemployment rate of women was very high: 25.5 per cent; for the urban areas, it was 29 per cent.

The low figures for women in the work force were partly a function of educational tracking whereby women students are concentrated in the social sciences and humanities rather than distributed more evenly across the disciplines. In the 1980s, there was also a rigorous quota system and certain fields of study (veterinary science, agricultural extension, some engineering fields) were expressly off-limits to women. In the academic year 1986/87, out of 431 university fields, fully 123 did not have any women enrolled. Methodological differences between the 1976 and 1986 censuses and under-counting of women in non-regular employment may account for some of the decline in female employment, but the emergence of the Islamic discourse on women and the family certainly contributed. Priority was assigned to the reproductive role of women and to their rearing of children. Not surprisingly, and in a context of official pro-natalism, the total fertility rate remained high, estimated at 5.6–6.0. Accordingly, in 1986, 45.5 per cent of the population was under the age of 15 (Islamic Republic of Iran, 1988).

Women's Non-Agricultural Employment: Manufacturing and the Bureaucracy

The manpower and census data of the 1970s reported a majority of active women in the manufacturing sector, while agriculture and services accounted for an additional 46.2 per cent of female employment. The high rate of female employment in manufacturing was due to the inclusion of cottage industries in this sector. In fact, in 1971 more than half of the economically active women in rural areas worked in small textile workshops. More than 88 per cent of these were carpet-weaving workshops; the rest comprised such crafts as spinning, knitting, and rug weaving. The 1976 census showed that the female share of manufacturing was over 38 per cent; women earning wages and salaries in public and private-sector manufacturing made up about 20 per cent of the total (176,346 women out of 900,856 wage and salary workers in manufacturing).

In 1983 industrial statistics revealed 40,000 female wage and salary earners in urban factory employment, representing a 6 per cent female share. Clearly there had been a sharp decline in female factory employment. By the mid-1980s there was a further decline in industrial work by women, although the *Statistical Yearbook 1364* (1985–86) showed a decrease in industrial employment for both men and women, indicating the weakness of this sector of the economy. In 1986, women in the manufacturing sector represented 14.5 per cent of the total (210,787 women out of 1,451,330 manufacturing workers of all statuses), but as a percentage of the salaried employees, women's share was only 6.7 per cent. According to one account (Nassehy, 1993: 39), there were only 33,000 women textile workers in 1986.

These numbers suggest that between the census of 1976 and that of 1986, working-class women experienced the greatest job losses. After the revolution, women continued to work in the large industrial establishments, but their participation in modern sector industrial activity was almost insignificant. Moreover, their employment status was often that of a non-regular worker in the private sector rather than a salaried employee, located in the informal sector rather than the formal sector. Of the total manufacturing female labour force, fully 153,000 (71 per cent) were rural, which is indicative of the predominant role played by carpet-weaving in women's 'manufacturing' employment.[3]

Much of the job loss is explained by the events during and immediately after the Iranian revolution, when the large privately-owned firms were taken over by workers' councils, or closed down and subsequently nationalized. New recruitment policies favoured men (Moghadam, 1988: 233). Nassehy cites one source to the effect that around 98 per cent of the job losses for women occurred in the large industrial units. In the course of the decade, more women workers lost jobs. She explains that private industry stopped investing in productive enterprises and concentrated its capital in 'high-profit non-productive speculation' (Nassehy, 1993: 41). Many productive units also ceased operations due to the shortage of basic materials or stricter labour laws. The women who were laid off, including thousands of women textile workers, did not possess the skills to enter other branches of the economy.

The Iran–Iraq War of 1980–88 had contradictory effects on women's employment. On the one hand, it offered some employment opportunities for women due to the mobilization of the men at the war front. However, it did not lead to any significant increases in employment, much less to the growth of women's employment in manufacturing, because it drained so much of the country's finances and contributed to the dearth of capital investments in labour-intensive productive sectors. At least two other factors deserve mention. The decline in carpet exports as a result of new revolutionary economic policies may have resulted in a decline in female activity in carpet-weaving, which had previously formed the bulk of female 'manufacturing' employment. Rural–urban migration further led to an abandonment of carpet-weaving.⁴ These factors – along with the small size of Iran's modern manufacturing sector and the absence of foreign investment in labour-intensive, female-intensive industries such as textiles, garments, and food processing – contributed to the limited involvement of women in the manufacturing sector.

In 1986 Iranian women constituted 14.5 per cent of the total manufacturing work force. ILO data shows that women's shares are much higher in other countries: 40–45 per cent in Tunisia, Bulgaria, Malaysia, and Korea; about 25 per cent in Turkey and Mexico; and 35–40 per cent in Vietnam, China and Poland.

In contrast to the drastic change in women's industrial employment after the revolution, as reflected in the official statistics, women in the professions and especially in the state bureaucracy did not experience a significant decline in their share of employment. The most dramatic loss of occupation for middle-class and highly educated women occurred among those in the legal profession, although their numbers had been small to begin with. Women were barred from being judges, and though the law schools accepted women, there was much discouragement of their entering this field. Indeed, across the middle-class professions, all women experienced ideological pressures to conform, especially to the new cultural codes and the laws on dress and comportment. Further, their position was hardly equal to that of male employees.⁵

In 1986, female civil service employees – that is, employees of ministries and state agencies – comprised 28 per cent of the total number of government employees of 1.4 million and 41 per cent of the total employed female population. The largest numbers of female government employees were in the Ministries of Education and Health. The same was true of male state employees, and this concentration obtained in pre-revolutionary Iran as well. Women's share of total public sector employment, however, was only 14 per cent because of men's far higher participation in the steel works, oil fields, and other state-owned industrial units and enterprises such as hotels. In these public sector enterprises, women were barely represented.

Middle-class women in the professions experienced gender bias in the social insurance system, and in some agencies they received fewer benefits than the men. For example, '[The] New Year bonus was paid differently in Iran's Aeroplane Industries to men and women employees. Married women employees were given [the] single person's bonus. Also, when it comes to housing benefits, women are deprived under the pretext that one person in the family is eligible to housing rights and that is the husband' (Nassehy, 1993: 40). Socio-economic rights as well as socio-economic participation were circumscribed for women during the 1980s.

Women's Socio-Economic Participation in the 1990s

The end of the Iran–Iraq war, the death of Ayatollah Khomeini, and the unsettling results of the 1986 census prompted policy changes and a measure of social, economic, and political liberalization in the late 1980s.

The Islamic Republic's First Five-Year Plan, which went into effect on 21 March 1990, sought, *inter alia*, to decrease the size of the public sector and encourage the growth of the private sector (Ghasimi, 1992). On the premise that reintegration in the world economy was necessary and desirable, the plan called for a shift from the earlier reliance on the agricultural sector to the expansion of manufacturing for export (Karshenas and Mazarei, 1991). The Rafsanjani government extended invitations to foreign investors, along with taxation and operations incentives, and encouraged joint ventures in petroleum and petrochemicals. As the scarcity of managerial and skilled resources could impede the realization of the plan, the government encouraged expatriate entrepreneurs, technicians and engineers to return to the country. For a while, the Iranian economy experienced an impressive rate of growth – about 11 per cent in 1990 and 1991.

Beginning in 1990 Iran also borrowed heavily on international markets, increasing total foreign debt from $6.5 billion in 1989 to $22.3 billion in 1995. The bulk of this long-term debt was owed or guaranteed by the government and it swelled from a low of 4.8 per cent of GNP in 1980 to 30 per cent of GNP. The debt-to-export service ratio increased from 6.8 per cent of exports in 1980 to 21.8 per cent in 1994 (Dadkhah, 1996: 11). This created pressures on the government to implement a long-term national development strategy to curb spending (especially on imports), to focus on raising the quality of human resources, to encourage domestic savings, and to attract domestic and foreign investments in economic sectors that might increase foreign exchange earnings, such as export manufacturing and tourism. The Khatami government was expected to continue the liberalization programme and resolve economic difficulties. However, continuing political divisions have impeded the implementation of a sound and long-term economic development strategy.

Women's Unemployment: An Urban and Rural Problem
At the beginning of the decade, women's unemployment remained high, and there was a tremendous increase in the unemployment of rural women, especially in the under-30 age groups.

According to the 1991 census, the female share of the measured labour force in Iran was only 11 per cent, but the female unemployment rate was disproportionately high. The 1991 census found that 1.2 million women were employed while nearly 350,000 reported themselves unemployed and seeking employment. For men, the figures were 12.1 million employed and 1.6 million unemployed (Islamic Republic of Iran, 1372/1993: Table 8, p. 64). The unemployment rate for women was 25 per cent, compared with 9 per cent for men. Of the 334,749 urban and rural women who were unemployed in 1991 and seeking work, some 144,407 (43 per cent) were in the age category 15–19 – very likely young women from working-class or low-income families – while 111,117 (33 per cent) were in the age category 20–24.

Female unemployment is arguably more serious than male unemployment, not only because of the disproportionately high rate, but also because unemployed women are less likely than men to engage in informal-sector or underground economic activity. And to the extent that educated women are among the unemployed, this suggests a serious waste of human capital. The increase in the numbers of unemployed women, including rural women, is reflected in Table 1.

The unemployment situation is certainly a function of the declining economic fortunes of the state, which includes lower oil revenues, lack of foreign and domestic investments and low economic growth. But it is also linked to the rather high total fertility rate of 6.0 per cent during the early 1990s, only half a percentage point lower than the rate during 1970–75 (UN, 1995). The population growth rate of 2.71 during 1990–95, while considerably lower than that of the 1980s, remained unsustainable, given the country's economic stagnation and unemployment problems. Table 2 provides data on economic activity, status of employment and unemployment in Iran in 1991.

Table 1: Total Number of Rural and Urban Iranian Women Seeking Employment in 1986 and 1991, and Breakdown of Under-30 Age Groups

Age Group	1986		1991	
	Rural	Urban	Rural	Urban
Total	77,367	199,593	142,557	192,192
15–19	40,049	71,728	73,959	70,448
20–24	18,446	77,065	38,498	72,619
25–29	5,419	26,242	11,074	25,260

Source: Islamic Republic of Iran, 1995a, Table 4.

Table 2: Population, Economic Activity, Employment Status, and Unemployment, 1991

Description	Male	Female
1. Population and economic activity		
Population 10 years of age and over (total)	19,997,274	18,657,775
Active population	13,107,062	1,629,642
Employed population	11,865,389	1,231,223
Urban areas		
Population 10 years and over	11,664,532	10,818,805
Active population	7,530,080	958,542
Employed population	6,856,868	752,010
Rural areas		
Population 10 years and over	8,208,764	7,725,409
Active population	5,488,869	661,536
Employed population	4,930,587	474,003
2. Employment status		
Total	11,865,389	1,231,226
Employer	386,194	9,647
Own-account worker	5,196,554	256,498
Private sector wage and salary earner	2,229,045	118,759
Public sector wage and salary earner	3,731,704	613,884
Unpaid family worker	189,593	147,440
Not reported	132,299	84,998
3. Unemployment rate	9.47%	24.45%
Urban	8.94%	21.55%
Rural	10.17%	28.35%

Source: Statistical Centre of Iran, 1991, *Population Census*.

Valentine M. Moghadam

These tables do not capture women's economic activity in the informal sector. Studies are needed to determine the type and extent of informal-sector activities, which have expanded, and women's roles within this sector. In May 1994, during research travel in Iran, I observed women selling chewing gum in the streets of Tehran and soft drinks to tourists in Persepolis. Given the limited nature of employment opportunities for women, home-based work is possibly expanding. In the urban areas much tailoring, knitting, hairdressing and other personal services are done at home, while in the rural areas the production of handicrafts and rugs is also carried out largely at home. Of course, even before the revolution many of the hair and beauty services for women were carried out informally, partly to avoid payment of taxes. But after the revolution hair salons and beauty shops closed down, as these were regarded by puritans within the ruling group as evidence of Pahlavi-style conspicuous consumption or as Islamically inappropriate, especially where the hair stylists were men. As recently as 1994, the hotels had barber shops for men but no hair salons for women. Hence the apparent proliferation of home-based hair and beauty services for women in the contemporary Islamic Republic.

Policy Changes and Shifting Priorities: Implications for Women
As I have argued in previous studies (Moghadam 1988, 1993), the impact of the Islamic Republic's preoccupation with cultural and ideological issues, while considerable, was sometimes attenuated by economic imperatives and socio-demographic needs. Moreover, in response to pressures from 'Islamic feminists' – advocates for women in the bureaucracy and in the women's press – the government revised some policies and initiatives pertaining to women and work. After the late 1980s, some restrictions on women's educational achievement – such as limiting female enrolment in a number of fields of study – were removed. This was important given the gender gaps in education and literacy and the limited educational attainment of the population. In the early 1990s, the mean years of schooling of the adult population (aged 25 years and older) were only 4.6 for men and 3.1 for women (UNESCO, 1994). Adult illiteracy rates were 35.5 per cent for men and 56.7 per cent for women. For the younger population, however, education became more accessible, although a gender gap remains. The number of female students per 100,000 inhabitants increased four-fold between 1980 and 1992, from 192 to 764. Consequently,

244

'school life expectancy' is increasing for girls, though more so for boys. In 1992 it was estimated that Iranian boys would complete 9.9 years of education and Iranian girls 7.6 years (UNESCO, 1995).

In 1987 the High Council of the Cultural Revolution set up the Women's Social and Cultural Council, charged with studying the legal, social, and economic problems of women, and in 1992 it adopted a set of employment policies for women. This new directive, while reiterating the importance of family roles and continuing to rule out certain occupations and professions as Islamically inappropriate, encouraged the integration of women in the labour force and attention to their interests and needs

The state's pro-natalist policy was replaced by a policy to stabilize the population through family planning. As part of this effort, the 1367/1988 law on maternity leave stipulated three months' paid leave for the first and second child, one month for the third and none for subsequent childbirths. In July 1991 the government approved a proposal by the Ministry of Health whereby any family benefits end with the third child. Family planning clinics throughout the country distribute contraceptives and family planning advice, frequently free of charge. In Tehran in May 1994, the streets were filled with signs promoting fewer children, linking small families to a higher quality of life and healthier children.[6]

During the 1990s the field of law became more open to women. In April 1993 there were 2,661 registered lawyers in Iran, including 185 women (Lawyers Committee for Human Rights, 1993: 44). The law of 1371/1992 allows for the employment of 'women legal consultants' in the Special Civil Courts (Islamic Republic of Iran, 1994, 1995a).

Women's share of government employment grew during the 1990s – although this is perhaps as much a reflection of the deterioration of government wages and the increasing partici-pation of men in the private sector as it is an indicator of progress in the advancement of women. The number of public-service employees was nearly 2 million in 1994, of which 603,000, or about 31 per cent, were women. Again, the Ministries of Education and Health employed most of these women (43.8 per cent and 40 per cent respectively), and nearly 34 per cent of them had university degrees. Women were under-represented in the private sector. Whereas a total of 3.5 million persons were employed in the private sector and covered by the Social Security Organization in 1994, only 237,000, or 6.7 per cent, were women (Islamic Republic of Iran, 1995a: 45–6).

The 1990s also saw a new, if belated, attention to women in the agricultural sector. This is best described in Iran's National Report to the Fourth World Conference on Women (Islamic Republic of Iran, 1995a: 37):

> In Iran, women's share of agricultural labour is stated to be at 40 per cent. This figure does not take into account their activities at the household level, including vegetable gardening, flower production, etc., which supplement the family income. In fact, some informal statistics refer to women's share in cultivation to the extent of 70 per cent in rice, 90 per cent in summer crops and vegetables, 50 per cent in cotton and oil crops, and 30 per cent in fruit harvesting.
>
> Other rural women's activities that are economically important include handicraft production and carpet weaving. Women account for 70 per cent of the nation's handicraft production, and about 88 per cent of embroidery and carpet production in the country. Actually, the economic importance of rural women can be seen in the fact that agricultural products and rural handicrafts constitute 62 per cent of the total non-oil exports of Iran.
>
> In 1993, the Rural Women's Development Office was established in the Ministry of Agriculture to coordinate and implement projects for the advancement of rural women. With the help of 160 women extension agents, the Rural Women's Development Office is actively coordinating requirements of rural women in areas of agricultural extension and education by organizing separate classes and courses in the various fields of agriculture, nutrition, and environmental hygiene. This Office has recently undertaken the task of organizing rural female youth clubs to occupy the free time of young female villagers in useful training, sports and other meaningful activities.[7]

Other initiatives undertaken included the following: (a) technical and on-the-job training under the supervision of the Ministry of Labour and Social Affairs (between 1987 and 1990, some 22,081 women were thus trained); (b) increasing the leave entitlement of women workers from 12 days to one month; (c) establishing centres 'for the employment of needy and guardianless women'; (d) selection, since 1989, of the best woman worker of the year, on Labour Day; (e) training courses for rural women in carpet-weaving, sewing, hygiene, midwifery and dairy production (Islamic Republic of Iran, 1994: 15). A bill was passed in 1992 to guarantee equal payment of New Year bonuses for women and men. Women were encouraged to participate in medicine, pharmacology, midwifery, and laboratory work – 'which is more suitable to their physiological make-up' – and quotas of 25 per cent female in the fields of neurology, brain surgery, cardiology, and similar specializations.

Thus we see that in the first half of the 1990s, political and social liberalization resulted in a more relaxed atmosphere and increased opportunities for women. Parliamentarian Maryam Behruzi was quoted as saying: 'We don't believe that every social change is harmful. Cultural refinement of some traditions, such as patriarchy [*mardsalari*], anti-woman attitudes [*zan-setizi*], and humiliation of women [*tahghir-e zanan*] must disappear. These have been fed to our people in the name of Islam' (quoted in *Zan-e Ruz*, 30 Mehr 1373 [Nov. 1994], p. 4). During the 1995 parliamentary elections, nine women – up from four in previous years – were elected to the Majles. A Women's Bureau was set up in the Office of the President with the express purpose of examining and enhancing the status of women. Women's affairs offices were established in each ministry and government agency, and these offices provided input into the government's planning and policy efforts. In May 1993, a Gender Analysis Workshop was sponsored by UNICEF-Tehran and the Women's Bureau of the President's Office. It sought to encourage planners and programme implementers 'to be more gender sensitive and to involve women as active participants in all levels of programme planning, execution, and evaluation.'[8] According to one of the workshop organizers, 'In our country a change has occurred in looking at the issue of women.' She continued: 'In the 1st National Plan, the role of women was mentioned in passing. In the 2nd National Plan, which is being prepared at present, we note that this role is more conspicuous but it has not reached our ideal level yet.'[9]

Several non-governmental women's organizations were formed during the 1990s. And the women's press became especially active in criticizing gender discrimination and calling for improvements in the status of women.[10] Shahla Habibi, then special advisor to the president on women's affairs, said in her statement to the Fourth World Conference on Women (Beijing, September 1995) that 'the establishment of national machinery for the advancement of women, the increase in the number of women parliamentarians and the enhancement of their participation in various levels of decision-making is indicative of the current pace of progress.'

Observations and Findings in 1994

In 1994, during research travel in Iran, I interviewed Ms Habibi. She described her mandate as helping to change patriarchal cultural attitudes towards women in the work force, strengthening women's position in the family in part through conducive social policies and legal reforms, carrying out social-welfare and legal services for poor women, and coordinating WID activities with other government offices and ministries, as well as with the parliamentary Women's Commission.[11] The Office of Women's Affairs, I was informed, was working with the Central Statistical Office, the World Bank and Iranian WID specialists on a project to improve statistics on women and to ensure that all social indicators be gender-disaggregated. In discussions with a group of WID specialists in Iran, I found that a debate revolved around the definition and enumeration of non-paid voluntary activities, and whether such non-paid activities should be encouraged, or whether a more appropriate strategy would be the generation of gainful employment for women.

During my research I also conducted interviews with managers and women employees at two factories (the state-owned Darupakhsh Pharmaceutical firm in Karaj and the privately-owned Moghaddam Textiles factory in Qazvin), and two hotels (Hotel Laleh in Tehran and Hotel Abbassi in Isfahan). Further, I undertook observations at Tehran's Mehrabad Airport, three travel agencies in Tehran, three UN offices, and shops in Tehran, Isfahan, and Shiraz, in order to discern the gender composition of the work force and interactions between men and women employees. My observations and interviews suggested that women were now engaged in a wider variety of occupations and professions than before, and that there was less gender-segregation at workplaces. For example, flight attendants and travel agency personnel were male and female; men and women workers and professionals worked together at the pharmaceutical firm (less so at the textiles factory, where the gender division of labour is more traditional and clearly defined); women were employed as shop-keepers at airports and large hotels; and both radio and television had women news announcers. On the other hand, there were no women waiting on tables in restaurants or running shops in the bazaars – these remain strictly male occupations. The pay gap was greater in the private sector than in the public sector, where pay scales are established for each post and educational credential, and where highly-educated and qualified women can obtain mana-gerial positions. The female proportion of civil servants was 30–31 per cent.[12] In Tehran in 1994 I was told by a midwife who worked at a large hospital that in the light of the low figures for women in medicine revealed by the 1986 census, the field of gynaecology now favoured women. The occupation of midwife was also promoted.

Nearly half of all employed women were in community, social, and personal services, mainly in professional capacities, according to the 1991 census, and primarily in teaching and health care. But women remained grossly under-represented in administrative and managerial positions, even in those ministries with higher shares of women employees (i.e., Education, Health, Higher Education, Labour and Social Affairs). This may have been to do with the lower educational qualifications of women at upper levels. Data from the Ministry of Culture and Higher Education show that in 1992/93, male enrolments in PhD programmes were far higher than women's in all reported disciplines (medical sciences, humanities sciences, basic sciences, technical engineering, agriculture and veterinary sciences, and fine arts and architecture). In the master's degree programmes, the male-female enrolment gap was the smallest in the humanities, the only discipline where in fact women exceeded men (996 women enrolled compared with 903 men).[13]

These gender gaps in higher education may explain why women's participation in decision-making positions is almost insignificant in today's Iran. In 1995 not only were there no female cabinet ministers, but out of 182 sub-ministerial level positions, women occupied only 0.5 per cent in 1994 (UN, 1995: 174). In the Ministry of Labour and Social Affairs, there were seven deputy ministers, all men. There were, however, women heads of departments and one woman general-director (compared with 24 males).[14] Similarly, at the state-owned Darupakhsh (pharmaceutical) Company in Karaj, out of 26 professional staff with medical degrees in 1994, five were women; and of the five with master's degrees, two were women.[15]

In my research, I found that the problems facing working-class women included depreciating real incomes in a situation of spiralling inflation and insufficient access to paid employment. The 1991 census reported a total of 302,876 women in the manufacturing sector (92,548 urban and 209,296 rural) out of a total of 1.7 million manufacturing workers. It should be noted that fully 1.2 million men are involved in *urban* manufacturing. These imbalances in male and female manufacturing employment suggest discriminatory barriers to women's access to paid industrial jobs. A 1993 manufacturing survey of establishments with 10 and more employees conducted by the Statistical Centre found 605,577 male wage and salaried employees and only 35,868 female wage and salaried employees. In Iran, the 'traditionally female sector of textiles, clothing, and leather' is actually dominated by men, as least as far as employment in the large manufacturing establishments is concerned – 145,813 men compared with 11,174 women. Similarly, in the food, beverage, and tobacco branch, the survey reported 83,094 men and only 5,420 women.[16]

Another problem I found pertained to women's ability to balance work and family life, especially in the private sector. The public sector was far more likely than were private-sector establishments to provide social insurance for their employees and to implement the provisions in the Labour Code for maternity leaves and job-back guarantees, child care facilities, and nursing breaks. For example, an interview with a woman salesperson in a privately-owned shop in the state-owned Laleh Hotel (formerly the Intercontinental) revealed that, unlike the women employees of the Laleh Hotel, she worked 6 days rather than 5 and was not part of a social insurance scheme. At the Abbasi (formerly Shah Abbas) Hotel in Isfahan, I discovered that the 20 women employees (out of a total of 270 hotel employees) were provided with insurance (as well as transportation to and from work, which was especially appreciated by the women on night shift), but there was no child care facility or subsidy. Two important issues for women workers at the hotel were child care and career development. In the goverment sector, some ministries and agencies provided free or extremely inexpensive child care, while others directed parents to privately-owned child care centres, sometimes subsidized.

At the government-owned Darupakhsh pharmaceutical firm in Karaj (which employed 947 men and 360 women) and the large and established privately-owned Moghaddam textile factory in Qazvin (with 795 men and 235 women), I learned that the women enjoy benefits in accordance with labour legislation. At Darupakhsh in 1994 there were 350 children in the child care centre; the women employees, as well as the men, had access to a sports facility, as well as to a restaurant, clinic, and transportation to and from work. Most of the women at the Moghaddam textile factory were long-term employees, and for their children there was a well-staffed and well-equipped nursery and kindergarten, and weekly visits by a doctor. Women workers were entitled to maternity leave and nursing breaks, and all workers received six weeks paid holiday.[17]

The question of the dress code is pertinent to women's employment. The Islamic Republic of Iran mandates an Islamic dress code, mainly for women, which is enforced in all public places. The dress code varies across government agencies and workplaces. The minimum requirement for all women at work and in public is a headscarf and manteau (*rupush/rusari*). Islamically-oriented women will wear a *maghna'eh* (a religiously-derived skirt-like covering of all the hair, neck and shoulders, invariably in black) and a *chador* (the floor-length veil held in place under the chin by one hand, also in black). Women factory workers, however, cannot wear the chador because of its impracticality, but they do wear either a firmly-secured headscarf or a *maghna'eh*, along with the factory uniform. As I observed in 1994, the dress code is strictly adhered to in government agencies and ministries, as well as at airports, but less so at hotels and large private-sector establishments. It was usually not observed inside the non-Iranian international establishments, where the women employees removed their headscarves and manteaux and dressed quite stylishly.

The dress code for men is much more relaxed, or is non-existent. On the streets, in hotels, and in offices men dress fashionably in the Western style. Although there used to be an Islamic dress code for men (beards, collarless shirts worn with a jacket, or regular shirts worn without a tie, no rolled-up sleeves, no jeans), it appears to be no longer enforced. The imposition of a dress code for women and not for men is clearly discriminatory.[18]

Women's Employment at the End of the Century

The Islamic Republic's second ten-year census was completed in November 1996. It shows some continuity and some changes with the patterns and trends in women's socio-economic participation discussed above. In summary: women's share of the total economically active population is 12.7 per cent; of the urban economically active population, 11.7 per cent; of the urban employed population, 11.2 per cent; of total public sector wage earners, 16.4 per cent (a slight increase over 1986). Thus women's labour force shares are still under 20 per cent and therefore still low by international standards, but they are higher than in 1986 and 1991. Women's unemployment rate is 12.5 – considerably lower than in 1986 and 1991, but still higher than men's (8.3 per cent in 1996).[19]

Who are the unemployed women? Of the 271,565 unemployed women, 53 per cent are urban and 47 per cent are rural. Some 38 per cent of the rural unemployed women have completed primary education; 51 per cent of urban unemployed women have a high school education and 12 per cent have higher education. Again, we see the growth of rural women's unemployment, along with barriers to the gainful employment of urban educated women. The figures also show that a higher proportion of educated women find themselves without employment compared with educated men; 27 per cent of urban unemployed men have a high school degree, and only 4.7 per cent have higher education.

The 1996 labour force data also shows that women continue to prefer to work in the public sector, and that the private sector remains underdeveloped, traditional, and rural, at least as far as women's involvement is concerned. Women's manufacturing activity, therefore, remains overwhelmingly rural and traditional, whereas men's manufacturing is urban and more modern. Furthermore, public and private sector employees in Iran remain highly divided by educational attainment; women (and men) tend to have at least a high school education or more in the public sector, whereas the majority in the private sector have completed only primary or intermediate school. Outside agriculture (where their involvement continues to be undercounted) and manufacturing (where women's work is largely rural), women remain over-represented in urban professional jobs (primarily in education and health) and under-represented in all other occupational categories (such as sales and services). Figures 1–3 illustrate these patterns not only for 1996, but also over time.

Figure 1: Female Share of Economically Active and Non-active Population (10 years and above), Iran, 1956–96

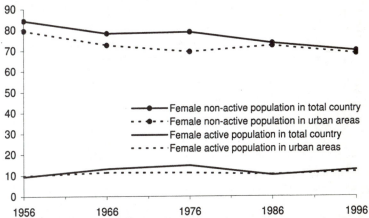

Source: *Statistical Yearbook of Iran*, Statistical Centre of Iran, Plan and Budget Organization, Islamic Republic of Iran, 1997, Table 3–1, p. 70.

Figure 2: Female Employees, (10 years and above), Share of Major Occupations, Iran, November 1996

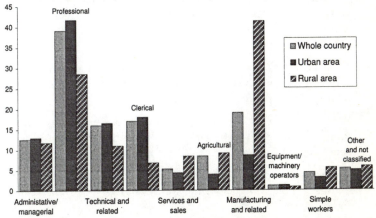

Source: *Statistical Yearbook of Iran*, Statistical Centre of Iran, Plan and Budget Organization, Islamic Republic of Iran, 1997, Table 3–8, p. 80.

Figure 3: Share of Employed Population (10 years and above) by Gender, Iran, 1956–96

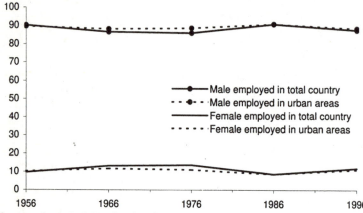

Source: *Statistical Yearbook of Iran*, Statistical Centre of Iran, Plan and Budget Organization, Islamic Republic of Iran, 1997, Table 3–1, p. 70.

The salient characteristics of Iranian women's employment at the dawn of the 21st century may be delineated as follows:

- Although most of the female labour force (55 per cent) is engaged in the private sector (compared with 39.5 per cent in the public sector), the vast majority of women private-sector workers (86.4 per cent) are in the rural areas. By contrast, the majority of women public sector workers (63.3 per cent) are urban.

- Most economically active women (28 per cent) are working in professional fields; in the urban areas, 46 per cent of employed women are in professional fields.

- Women's share of the field of education is 44 per cent for the total country, but it is much higher in the urban areas (48.6 per cent) than in the rural areas (22 per cent).

- Women's share of health services is 39.3 per cent for the total country, though higher in urban areas (40.4 per cent) than in the rural areas (33 per cent).

- Some 21.6 per cent of working women are in manufacturing – higher than in 1986, but mostly in the rural areas where they are non-wage earners.[20] Their share of manufacturing is 22.8 per cent for the total country – but fully 45.2 per cent for rural areas.

• Women are still under-represented in such occupations as administration and management, technical and related jobs, clerical work, service and sales work and agriculture.[21] They are also under-represented in agriculture, urban manufacturing, wholesale and retail trade, finance, and real estate/business services.

• The female share of total private sector employment is 10 per cent (mainly rural) and the share of private sector wage earners is 7.6 per cent. By contrast, women's share of public sector wage earners is 16.4 per cent.[22]

• Women's civil service employment has increased since 1991, and in 1996 women were 38.6 per cent of all civil service employees covered by social security. (Their share of total public sector employment is lower, however, because of their marginal involvement in state-owned industries, hotels, etc.) Women are concentrated in the ministries of Education (44 per cent female) and Health (43 per cent female). In the Ministry of Justice, women make up about 27 per cent of employees.

• Ministries with relatively low female involvement, given their mandates, include Culture and Higher Education (20 per cent), Labour and Social Security (11.3 per cent), Agriculture (7.2 per cent), Development and Housing (13.7 per cent), Commerce (12 per cent female) and Culture and Islamic Guidance (17.8 per cent).

The above analysis suggests the slow rate of progress for women's socio-economic participation. Can the situation be improved? Hopes were high in the wake of the presidential elections of May 1997. After newly-elected President Khatami named Massoumeh Ebtekar, a US-educated lecturer and editor of a women's studies journal, as a vice-president in charge of environmental affairs, Culture Minister Mohajerani appointed Azam Nouri as deputy culture minister for legal and parliamentary affairs. Interior Minister Abdollah Nouri followed by naming Zahra Shoja'i, a professor at al-Zahra University in Tehran and a member of the Interior Ministry's Women's Commission, as Iran's first director-general for women's affairs.[23] In her new position, Ms Shoja'i would be in charge of issues such as social policies pertaining to women and violence against women. These were the first women to serve in top government posts and decision-making positions since the 1979 Revolution, and they signalled a new era for women. However, their work for women seems has been stymied by a conservative parliament.[24]

Challenges of the Future

In attempting to address social and economic problems and in adapting to the imperatives of globalization, the Islamic Republic faces many challenges, including tensions between reformers and conservatives, and the economic sanctions imposed by the United States. But if Iran is to meet the challenges of a globalized world economy, it must implement a long-term strategy for human resource development that includes investment in women. In today's Islamic Republic, women are not yet seen as breadwinners or as contributors to economic growth, with the result that their pursuit of employment is not taken as seriously as that of men, and employment-generation for women is not an official objective. What will be necessary is integration of gender issues, including women's employment, in policies and programmes at all levels and in all sectors, and moving through the various ministries. In this connection, there is a role for the women's advocates, such as reform-minded women parliamentarians, other senior level women, the women-in-development (WID) specialists working in various state agencies, as well as those women elected as municipal officials in the February 1999 local elections.

The Second Five-Year Plan differed from the first in that it placed a priority on mobilizing domestic capital, reducing the role of oil earnings, developing human resources and confronting social problems. According to one analysis, because the First Five-Year Plan was unsuccessful in attracting foreign investment, it was subsequently deemed necessary 'to create a competitive labour force, in line with international trends towards prioritizing human resources' (Amirahmadi, 1995: 11; Amirahmadi, 1996: 142). The growing demand for jobs and services, as well as the population age-structure, pushed the policy-makers to focus on education and employment in the Second Plan. In January 1996 President Rafsanjani called for worker training 'as a decisive factor in bolstering the economy and independence of the country.' As we have seen above, some steps were taken with respect to women's education, training, and employment.[25] However, much more needs to be done, and in a systematic and coordinated fashion.

Investing in the education and employability of women could contribute to one of the Islamic Republic's current goals, as reflected in the Second Five-Year Plan: greater domestic resource mobilization through enhanced taxation of its working population (as well as other forms of taxation). As Karshenas has pointed out, central government tax revenue in Iran has fluctuated at around 5 per cent of the GDP since the end of the Iran–Iraq War. 'This compares with tax/GDP ratios ranging between 15 to 25 per cent for middle income countries and 10 to 20 per cent in low income countries, making Iran one of the lowest taxed economies in the world' (Karshenas, 1995: 19). By encouraging more women to enter the labour force and by introducing fiscal reform to make the system of taxation more efficient, the government can mobilize increased domestic resources to finance investments in infrastructural development, improvements in the quality of education and future structural reforms, industrial restructuring, and adjustment.

In 1999 the Khatami government was faced with growing income inequalities, rising prices, and deteriorating household budgets – as well as growing societal dissatisfaction with the slow pace of his promised social and political reforms. Government publications claim that there are policies to improve women's self-employment opportunities by providing them with training, credits and loans to set up small- and medium-sized businesses, and to provide them with booths to display and market their products. Certainly the extension of credit and training for low-income women would contribute both to poverty alleviation of households and to an enhanced status for poor women. Women's self-employment could surely be encouraged by removing the legal obstacles that exist in family law – such as the unequal inheritance rights of women (which give women a lesser share of family wealth), and the husband's right to prevent his wife 'from engaging in a profession or trade unfit to the family's welfare or prestige.'

What effects might privatization and encouragement of the private sector have on women's employment? Since women are an insignificant part of state-owned industries, any effects of privatization would be far more deleterious for male workers. The government sector (civil service) will probably see an ever-growing proportion of women workers, even as recruitment is stabilized, due to the demand for women in health and education, due to the growth of an educated job-seeking female population, and due to the gravitation of men to more lucrative private-sector jobs.

One positive outcome of privatization and liberalization could be the promotion of a cultural climate and a financial environment conducive to women-owned or managed businesses. There are many kinds of community, social and personal services that would benefit from women's enhanced participation. Some of these are already recognized by the authorities (e.g., medicine and teaching) but others remain untapped. Women should be encouraged – perhaps through the equivalent of a Small Business Bureau and a special fund for women entrepreneurs – to start such businesses as shops, restaurants, cleaning services, catering services, health clubs, child care centres, dental clinics, urban transport services, bookstores etc. Not only would this expand women's participation as owners and managers of such businesses and provide additional job opportunities for women, but it would also expand the range of women-friendly and child-friendly services available in Iran.

A related area for research and policy is the status of women in rural carpet production, given its importance in Iranian manufacturing, and given the large numbers of women workers in this sector. In Iran the carpet industry earns huge amounts of foreign currency that rival those of the oil industry and exceed those of (non-oil) industrial exports. It would be worthwhile to investigate women's employment status, work conditions and income received for this culturally important and financially lucrative product. How the income is controlled and spent within the rural household is also important from the perspective of both policy and social justice.

Policymakers need to address some of the pressing concerns facing women: barriers to paid employment, the absence of women in decision-making positions, the high rates of female unemployment, the need for social supports for working mothers, the dearth of employment services and programmes for women, and the need for more accurate labour force information. All the above, however, depend on the ability of the Islamic government to overcome outdated ideological concerns and implement a long-term strategy for economic growth and human development.

Notes

1 I discuss the patriarchal gender contract in my book, *Women, Work, and Economic Reform in the Middle East and North Africa* (Moghadam, 1998). Some of the material in this chapter is derived from the chapter on Iran in that book.

2 The figures vary; a labour force of 1.3 million women and 11.5 million men has also been reported. The percentages, however, remain roughly the same.

3 See Islamic Republic of Iran (1991), Table 3.8, p. 73.

4 These reasons were offered by Ms Mehrangiz Changizi, Statistical Centre of Iran, Tehran, in an interview with the author on 16 May 1994.

5 In the Islamic Republic, there have always been women employees holding supervisory positions, whether in factories (as in the case of some women engineers) or in government agencies (as with some highly-trained statisticians, as well as physicians). However, women's roles in managerial and administrative positions are extremely limited in Iran, as they are in all MENA countries.

6 Observations during the author's research travel.

7 Bureau of Women's Affairs, National Report, p. 37. Regarding the under-enumeration of the female rural population, an interview with Ms Mehrangiz Changizi, statistician at the Statistical Centre of Iran, confirmed my suspicion that there had been a lack of coordination between the Ministry of Agriculture and the Statistical Centre, leading to different definitions of work and different statistics. According to Ms Changizi, this situation is being corrected. Personal interview, Tehran, 16 May 1994.

8 Remarks by Nilufar Purzand of UNICEF-Tehran, Gender Analysis Workshop: Proceedings (Tehran: UNICEF-Tehran and Women's Bureau of the President's Office, 1993), p. 12.

9 Remarks by Engineer Marzieh Sedighi, ibid., p. 7.

10 The best known is the magazine Zanan, which espoused a feminist re-reading of the Koran and a revision of Islamic family laws based on patriarchal interpretations.

11 Author's interview with Shahla Habibi and members of her staff, Tehran, 14 May 1994.

12 Information from Ms Changizi, Statistical Centre of Iran. See also Statistical Yearbook 1370 [1991], p. 79, which shows that out of 1.6 million civil servants, there were 511,818 females.

13 Figures kindly provided by UNIDO, WID Office, 1995.

14 Information kindly provided by UNIDO, WID Office, 1995.

15 Interviews with A. A. Najari and I. Razzaghi, production managers, Darupakhsh, Karaj, 17 May 1994.
16 Figures kindly provided by UNIDO, WID Office, 1995.
17 Observations and interviews at Moghaddam Textile Factory, Qazvin, Iran, 17 May 1994.
18 The authorities in the Islamic Republic, and the Islamic women in government or quasi-government NGOs, are keen to respond to criticisms of compulsory veiling and to show that veiling does not hamper women's public activities, including education, employment, sports, art, music, and voting. In a glossy publication prepared for the Beijing conference, *Hijab: Immunity, Not Limitation* (published in Tehran by the Centre for Mosques' Affairs, Women Section), colour photographs show women in all kinds of activities, including horse-back riding, *hejab* strictly observed.
19 Data from Iran Statistical Yearbook 1375/1996 (IRI, 1997), Table 3–1, p. 70.
20 Ibid., Table 3–4, p. 74.
21 Ibid., Table 3–8, p. 80.
22 Ibid., Table 3–9, p. 81.
23 Associated Press, 'Woman Named Iran Culture Deputy', 31 August 1997, via Internet; 'Women's Activist Gets Iranian Post', 2 Sept 1997, via Internet; Agence France Presse, 'Iranian President Names Woman as Advisor', 18 October, 1997, via Internet.
24 Parliamentary elections scheduled for February 2000 will be significant, given the current tensions between reformers and conservatives.
25 That a group of women's NGOs recommended that the government sign and ratify the United Nations's Convention on the Elimination of All Forms of Discrimination Against Women – and circulated a leaflet to that effect at the FWCW in Beijing – was one sign that issues of discrimination could be receiving more attention.

8

The State and the Social Position of Women: Female Employment in Post-Revolutionary Iran

Parvin Alizadeh

1. Introduction

This paper is concerned with the changing pattern of female employment in Iran since the Islamic Revolution in 1979. The tentative proposition raised here is that the control of women's social position is central to the nation-building process. The state is essentially implicated in gender relations, which are defined here as socially constructed power relationships between men and women. Hence each state embodies a specific gender regime. Women on the one hand bear the burden of being 'mothers of the nation', a duty that is ideologically defined, reflecting the ideological orientation of the state. On the other hand, women as mothers and educators transmit culture and tradition and subsequently reproduce the boundaries of ethnic/national groupings. The role and social position of women, therefore, has specific importance during the process of either nation building or redefinition of nationhood.

It is in the above framework that the establishment and consolidation of the Islamic Republic has played a decisive role in shaping the form and the extent of women's social participation.

The structure of the paper is as follows: Part 2 examines the Iranian data and shows that economic development in Iran since

Parvin Alizadeh

the revolution has been accompanied by a decline in the share of female employment and increased occupational sex segregation. Part 3 provides a brief review of the empirical evidence and theoretical issues on female employment. The next part provides a summary of the current debate on female employment in Iran. Part 5 focuses on the relationship between women's social position in Iran and the process of nation building. Discussions in this part provide an explanation for the changing pattern of female employment in Iran in the 1980s and 1990s. The conclusion is in part 6.

2. The Trend in Female Employment in Iran

The trend in female employment in Iran over the last four decades is presented in Tables 1–3. These data are based on the population census that takes place every ten years. The years covering 1956 to 1996 can be divided into two distinct periods (see Table 1). The first period extends from 1956 to 1976 and the second from 1976 to 1996. The dividing line between the two periods is the popular revolution of 1979 which was followed by a radical change in state ideology.

Table 1: Gender Composition of Employment in Iran (1956–96)

| | Percentage Share | | |
	Females	Males	Total
Feminization period			
1956	9.7	90.3	100
1966	13.27	87.73	100
1976	19.46	80.54	100
De-feminization period			
1986	8.94	91.06	100
1996	12.1	87.9	100

Sources: Statistical Centre of Iran, *National Census of Population and Housing* 1976, 1986,1996, Islamic Republic of Iran, Plan and Budget Organization 1985, 1988, 1997; International Labour Office, *Yearbook of Labour Statistics*, Retrospective edition 1945–1989, Geneva 1991.

The State and the Social Position of Women

Table 2: Gender Composition of Employment

	Males	Females	Total
Shares 1956			
Professional	80.77	19.23	100.00
Administrative	97.42	2.58	100.00
Clerical	95.58	4.42	100.00
Sales	98.50	1.50	100.00
Services	76.08	23.92	100.00
Agricultural	95.21	4.79	100.00
Production	80.32	19.68	100.00
Miscellaneous	99.57	0.43	100.00
Total Employment	90.30	9.70	100.00
Total Employment (000)	5334.30	573.30	5907.60
Shares 1966			
Professional	74.29	25.71	100.00
Administrative	96.74	3.26	100.00
Clerical	93.18	6.82	100.00
Sales	98.90	1.10	100.00
Services	78.02	21.98	100.00
Agricultural	93.60	6.40	100.00
Production	74.96	25.04	100.00
Miscellaneous	93.61	6.30	100.00
Total Employment	86.73	13.27	100.00
Total Employment (000)	5948.40	909.90	6858.30
Shares 1976			
Professional	66.22	33.78	100.00
Administrative	96.66	3.34	100.00
Clerical	85.52	14.48	100.00
Sales	98.60	1.40	100.00
Services	84.27	15.73	100.00
Agricultural	77.19	22.81	100.00
Production	80.24	19.76	100.00
Miscellaneous	92.43	7.57	100.00
Total Employment	80.54	19.46	100.00
Total Employment (000)	7649.70	1848.30	9498.00

Source: See Table 1.

Parvin Alizadeh

Table 1 is a summary table that is accompanied by more detailed data given in tables 2 and 3. The salient feature of the first period (1956–1976) is a continuous rise in the share of female employment from 9.7 per cent of total employment in 1956 to nearly 20 per cent in 1976 (see Table 1). The first period can be considered as the period of feminization, which is defined here as the rise in the share of female employment. The second period (1976–1996), however, witnessed a sharp decline in the share of female employment from nearly 20 per cent in 1976 to around 12 per cent in 1996. The latter period, hence, is a period of de-feminization. De-feminization is defined here as the decline in the share of female employment.

Table 3: Gender Composition of Employment

	Males	Females	Total
Shares 1986			
Professional	67.43	32.57	100.00
Administrative	96.55	3.45	100.00
Clerical	87.27	12.73	100.00
Sales	98.51	1.49	100.00
Services	92.96	7.04	100.00
Agricultural	91.93	8.07	100.00
Production	93.67	6.33	100.00
Miscellaneous	95.97	4.03	100.00
Total Employment	91.06	8.94	100.00
Total Employment (000)	10054.3	987.1	11041.4
Shares 1996			
Professional	67.10	32.90	100.00
Administrative	87.20	12.80	100.00
Clerical	83.00	17.00	100.00
Sales and services*	94.90	5.10	100.00
Agricultural	91.10	8.90	100.00
Production	89.00	11.00	100.00
Miscellaneous	94.70	5.30	100.00
Total Employment	87.90	12.10	100.00
Total Employment (000)	12808.40	1763.10	14571.50

* Classification of occupations has changed slightly since the latest census in 1996. Sales and Services are combined according to new classification.
Source: See Table 1.

The main decline in the share of female employment occurred over the period 1976 to 1986, although since then it has increased slightly, from 9.7 per cent of total employment in 1986 to 12.1 per cent in 1996 (Table 3). Nevertheless, the share of female employment has still not recovered its pre-revolutionary level.

2.1 A Comparative Perspective

Let us see how Iran compares with other countries. Tables 4–5 provide data on the female employment and activity rate in four Muslim countries, namely Turkey, Egypt, Pakistan and Malaysia. Iran, Turkey and Egypt have a comparable level of population: around 65, 60, and 57 millions respectively in the mid-1990s (World Development Report 1995). The population of Pakistan was 123 million while that of Malaysia was only 19 million. Iran and Turkey are classified by the World Bank as lower middle income countries, while Egypt and Pakistan are low income countries and Malaysia, with a higher level of income, is an upper middle income country (World Bank Development Report 1997).

Table 4: Middle Income Countries

Iran Activity rate(6+)	Lower middle income			
	1966	1976	1986	1996
Women	8.3	16.9	8.2	9.1
Men	50.7	69.3	68.7	60.7
Total	30.2	42.5	39.2	35.3
Women in total employment	13.3	19.5	8.7	12.1
Women in non-agricultural sector	19.1	17.4	9	13

Turkey Activity rate(12+)	Lower middle income			
	1965	1975	1985	1990
Women	33.4	33	30.6	31.1
Men	53	51.7	54.3	56.2
Total	43.4	42.5	42.6	43.8
Women in total employment	40.2	35.6	36.4	31.8
Women in non-agricultural sector	7.1	12.6	11.6	14.4

Parvin Alizadeh

Table 4: Middle Income Countries (continued)

Malaysia(Peninsular) Activity rate(10+)	Upper middle income			
	1957	1970	1980	1991
Women	17.4	20.9	25.3	22.6
Men	50.5	44.2	49.6	47.3
Total	34.5	32.6	37.5	35.1
Women in total employment	24.6	31.3	33.3	34.2*
Women in non-agricultural sector	13.8	25.6	30.6	35.1*

* Data is for 1993.

Source: *Year Book of Labour Statistics*, various years, International Labour Organization, Geneva.

The data in Table 4 indicate that female employment in Turkey, as well as in Malaysia, has been always much greater than that in Iran. Nevertheless, the gap in women's share of employment between Iran and these two countries has widened since 1976. The share of female employment in Turkey in the 1990s was two-and-a-half times greater than that of Iran: female employment accounted for 31.8 per cent of total employment in Turkey in contrast to only 12.1 per cent in Iran (Table 4). Similarly, the share of female employment in Malaysia is nearly three times greater than that in Iran. In fact, the share of female employment in Iran is similar to that of a low income country like Pakistan and even below that of Egypt.

A similar comparative picture emerges where the female activity rate (FAR) is concerned. The activity rate refers to the working age population that is seeking employment. The definition of working age population differs between countries. In Iran the working age population is defined as the population above six years of age. Needless to say, the activity rate is not only influenced by the general level of economic activity and business cycles, but above all by the presence of opportunities for employment. The level of female activity rate in Iran has been below that of Turkey and Malaysia throughout the whole period. Furthermore, the gap in the female activity rate between Iran and these countries has been widened since 1976. The data in Table 4 indicate that the FAR declined sharply for Iran from 16.9 per cent in 1976 to 8.2

per cent in 1986. This implies that by 1986 only 8.2 per cent of the working age female population were seeking employment. The low level of FAR in Iran is similar to that of Pakistan and Egypt although FAR for Egypt has recently increased.

Let us now turn to how the composition of female employment in these countries differs. Table 4 indicates that the high level of female employment and female activity rate in Turkey is due to the high level of female activity and employment in agriculture. A large share of female employment in Turkey is concentrated in agriculture where female employment accounted for more than 30 per cent of total employment in 1990. However, if agricultural employment is excluded from this data, women's employment declines to only 14.4 per cent of total non-agricultural employment. Similarly, as the data in Table 5 indicate, women's employment in Egypt is highly concentrated in agriculture.

Table 5: Low Income Countries

Egypt Activity rate(6+)	1966	1976	1986	1992
Women	4.2	5.5	8.9	14.2
Men	51.2	54.1	46.7	43.5
Total	27.9	30.2	28.2	29.2
Women in total employment	6.4	6.6	not available	21.2
Women in non-agricultural sector	3.5	1.2	not available	15.4

Pakistan Activity rate(10+)	1961	1972	1981	1993
Women	not available	9.8	2.1	8.6
Men	not available	61.6	50.6	45.9
Total	not available	39.3	27.6	27.9
Women in total employment	8.9	4.9	3.5	14
Women in non-agricultural sector	6.1	4.1	4.5	8.1

Source: *Year Book of Labour Statistics*, various years, International Labour Organization, Geneva.

In fact, a comparison of Iran and Turkey indicates that the share of female employment in non-agricultural activities was actually much higher for Iran than for Turkey before 1976. However, since then the female share in non-agricultural employment in Iran has moderately lagged behind that in Turkey.

The structure of female employment in Malaysia differs from that in the Middle East. Although women's employment was initially concentrated in agriculture during the 1950s, it has evolved to spread across the sectors. In fact female employment in Malaysia, as well as in several other East Asian countries, is concentrated in manufacturing industries (Karshenas 1996). Table 4 shows that female employment in Malaysia accounts for around 35 per cent of total non-agricultural employment.

In a comparative study of female non-agricultural employment in developing countries, Karshenas (1996) shows that the level of female non-agricultural employment in the Middle East countries is on average considerably below that of East Asian countries. A significant portion of female employment in the latter countries is concentrated in the manufacturing sector, while female employment in the manufacturing sector is very limited in the former countries.

To sum up: The data in Tables 1–5 highlight three important trends. Firstly, the overall share of activity rate and female employment in Iran is considerably lower than that in Turkey and Malaysia and is similar to low income countries. Furthermore, the gap in female employment between Iran and the above-mentioned countries has widened since 1976. Lastly, there are structural differences between a high level of female employment in Malaysia, a South-East Asian country, and a high level of employment in a Middle Eastern country like Turkey. In the latter the agricultural sector accounts for a significant share of female employment, while in the former female employment is spread across the sectors.

2.2 The Changing Structure of Occupations in Iran

The sharp decline in female employment has also been accompanied by changes in its composition. A closer look at data over the period 1976 to 1986, the period of sharp decline, reveals that the fall in female employment by more than 860,000 is highly concentrated in agriculture and production (Table 6). The latter consists of industrial and manufacturing activities. The data also point to the growth of female employment in professional and technical occupations, which in absolute terms increased by 155,109 between 1976 to 1986. In other words, the composition of female employment over this period altered. A substantial decline of female employment in agriculture and manufacturing activities was concurrent with an increased share of female employment in professional and technical occupations. In 1986 nearly 35 per cent of female employment was concentrated in professional and technical jobs compared with 10 per cent in 1976. This trend has prevailed since 1986 although the share of women's employment in manufacturing (production) has moderately increased over the period 1986–1996.

Table 6: Distribution of Female Employment

	1976	%	1986	Change in Female Employment
Professional	188164	10.2	343273	155109
Administrative	1356	0.1	1534	178
Clerical	63538	3.4	46787	-1675
Sales	8391	0.5	11329	2938
Services	68286	3.7	32052	-36234
Agricultural	822771	44.5	263175	-559596
Production	658945	35.7	230823	-428122
Miscellaneous	36840	2.0	58130	21290
Total Employment	1848291	100.0	987103	-861188

Source: See Table 1.

In this respect the composition of female employment in Iran differs from both comparable countries in the Middle East region like Turkey and Egypt, as well as South East Asian countries. The former have a high level of female employment in agriculture while the latter have a high level of employment in manufacturing industries.

2.3 Occupational Sex Segregation

A number of indices have been developed to measure the extent to which particular social groups are concentrated in specific sectors or occupations in the labour market (Watts and Rich 1993, Jacobson 1994). The most commonly used index to measure sex and race segregation is the Duncan index of dissimilarity. The index ranges from zero to 100. The former represents complete integration and the latter complete segregation. The index is based on the implicit definition of integration as a situation in which the proportional representation of each sex is the same in all occupations as in total employment. Zero segregation is defined where each occupation has the same gender proportion as the employed labour force in aggregate. For instance, if 20 per cent of total employment consists of women, then the index will be zero only if 20 per cent of employment in each occupation consists of women.

The index measures the proportion of total employment that must relocate, with full replacement by the opposite sex, to achieve zero segregation. An interpretation of the index is that it shows what percentage of men or women would have to switch occupations in order to achieve zero segregation. If the index equals 20, for instance, either 20 per cent of men would have to switch into relatively female-dominated occupations or 20 per cent of women would have to switch into male-dominated occupations in order to achieve zero segregation. In other words, the ID index points to those occupations in which male/female employment is concentrated as well as the extent of concentration.

Alizadeh and Harper have measured the index of dissimilarity (ID) for occupational segregation in Iran between 1976 and 1996.[1] This is presented in Table 7. The overall ID has increased from 14 per cent in 1976 to 29 per cent in 1986 and 31 per cent in 1996. This is a substantial rise in occupational segregation. Most occupations are now considered as male dominated because the share of female employment in these occupations has declined considerably since 1976. In fact, with the exception of professional and technical as well as clerical occupations, all occupations are now male dominated. These data also indicate that currently female employment is heavily concentrated in professional and technical work. The ID index of female employment for professional and technical work, which was 5 in 1976, increased to 30 by 1996.

Table 7: Employment Adjustment Required for Zero Segregation in Female/Male Dominated Occupations, Iran, 1956–1991

1956	Female Dominated	Male Dominated
Professional and technical	2	
Administrative and managerial		
Clerical and related		2
Sales		5
Service	12	
Agricultural and related		31
Production	27	
Miscellaneous		3
Total Employment	41	41

1966	Female Dominated	Male Dominated
Professional and technical	3	
Administrative and managerial		
Clerical and related		2
Sales		8
Service	6	
Agricultural and related		27
Production	30	
Miscellaneous		2
Total Employment	39	39

1976	Female Dominated	Male Dominated
Professional and technical	5	
Administrative and managerial		(below one)
Clerical and related		1
Sales		7
Service		1
Agricultural and related	8	
Production	(below one)	
Miscellaneous		4
Total Employment	14	14

Table 7: Employment Adjustment Required for Zero Segregation in Female/Male Dominated Occupations, Iran, 1956–1991 (continued)

1986	Female Dominated	Male Dominated
Professional and technical	28	
Administrative and managerial		(below one)
Clerical and related	1	
Sales		6
Service		(below one)
Agricultural and related		3
Production		11
Miscellaneous		8
Total Employment	29	29

1996	Female Dominated	Male Dominated
Professional and technical	30	
Administrative and managerial		(below one)
Clerical and related	1	
Sales		7
Service		2
Agricultural and related		10
Production		10
Miscellaneous		1
Total Employment	31	31

Source: Calculated from the same source as Table 1.

To sum up: The trend in female employment in Iran since the late 1970s points to two distinct developments. Firstly, there has been a sharp rise in the de-feminization of employment since 1976, and particularly over the period 1976 to 1986. Secondly, there has been a continuous increase in occupational sex segregation since the revolution.

3. Women's Employment: A Survey of the Literature

What factors affect the female employment and activity rate? Is there a positive relationship between the process of economic development and female employment? Does the level of female employment alter with the level of economic activities?

Studies by Boserup (1970, 1990), Tilly and Scott (1987) and Cagatay and Ozler (1995) indicate that the relationship between the long-term process of capitalist development and women's labour force participation is U-shaped. Accordingly, the women's labour force participation rate during the initial stages of commercialization and capitalist development decreases and then increases with increased urbanization and with further economic development.

In a pioneering study, concerned with female employment in a historical perspective, Boserup (1970, 1990) argued that in the early phase of capitalism and economic development women's share in the labour force declines. This is because of men's monopoly control over technology and education inherited from the previous mode of subsistence economies. In subsistence agricultural economies the use of improved techniques is usually monopolized by the men. The skill gap between women and men widens during the transition to capitalist development; 'boys get systematic training as apprentices in family enterprises, while girls continue to be taught only simple household and agricultural operations by their mothers' (Boserup 1990:19). Hence the skill gap between the sexes widens at the early stage of capitalist development and industrialization. Furthermore, education systems have started everywhere with the schooling of boys, particularly from the upper classes. Thus the early stages of urbanization and economic development are associated with the downward portion of the U curve. However, beyond the early stage of capitalist development women's share in the labour force increases. The expansion of industry is concurrent with increased urbanization, increased female education, falling fertility rates and the commodification of domestic labour. Hence women's share of employment expands. This more mature phase of capitalist development coincides with the upward portion of the U shape.

This relationship between the process of economic development and female employment is known as 'feminization U'. Feminization in this context refers to an increase in the share of female labour force. De-feminization has the opposite meaning.

Historical studies concerned with development of capitalist production organizations in France and England support the feminization U hypothesis (Tilly and Scott, 1987). The fact that female employment increases with the growth of urbanization, a decline in the fertility rate and increased female education has been reflected in a noticeable growth of female employment in OECD countries since the 1950s (Howes and Singh, 1995). For instance, in the advanced industrialized countries of the northern hemisphere the ratio of women's to men's labour force participation, on average, increased from 36.8 per cent in the 1950s to 55.6 per cent in the 1980s (Blau and Ferber 1992: 300–4, Table 10.1).[2]

Furthermore, it has been shown that the countries of East Asia, the Caribbean and Latin America, as well as most East European countries, experienced a significant increase in female employment over the period from the 1950s to the 1980s (Blau and Ferber, 1992: 300–4, Table 10.1). In East Asia the ratio of women's to men's labour force participation increased from 45.8 per cent in the 1950s to 56.6 per cent in the 1980s. For Caribbean countries, on average, this ratio increased from 53.6 to 63.7 per cent over the same period, although for individual countries like Jamaica the increase in female employment was much faster – from 54.2 per cent in the 1950s to 82.8 per cent in the 1980s (Blau and Ferber, 1992: 300–4, Table 10.1). The share of female employment in Latin America is below that of East Asia and the Caribbean. However, female employment in Latin America has increased moderately from 21.5 to 33.1 per cent over the same period.

The other group of countries with a high level of female participation are the East European. For these countries the ratio of women's to men's labour force participation increased from 56.7 per cent in the 1950s to 75.1 per cent in the 1980s (Blau and Ferber, 1992: 300–4, Table 10.1).

The Middle East and North Africa are known to have a relatively low level of female labour force participation (Moghadam 1993). Nevertheless, even in this group of countries female employment, on average, experienced a modest increase from 15 per cent in the 1950s to 19.2 per cent in the 1980s (Blau and Ferber 1992: 300–4, Table 10.1).

In other words the empirical evidence indicates a global upward increase in female employment since the 1950s.[3]

3.1 Other Factors Affecting Female Employment

Cagatay and Ozler (1995) have highlighted other factors, including changes in industrial policy and ideological factors, that have also influenced the growth of female employment. For example, a change of trade and industrial policies from import substitution to an export-oriented strategy, has been often cited as an important factor for the rise in the share of female labour in several developing countries (Wood, 1991; Jokes, 1987; Pearson, 1992). The growth of labour-intensive manufactured exports from developing countries in several instances, although not universally, has increased the demand for female labour. In this respect increased female employment has arisen from the intensity of global competition and employers' search for lower wages (Standing, 1989). Women are usually 'cheap' and 'flexible' workers who are substituted for men.

Ideological factors have been also important in influencing the extent of feminization. This is reflected, for instance, in the high level of female employment in ex-socialist countries which placed high priority on female social participation. Similarly, the potency of the 'male bread-winner' ideology is often discussed as an impediment to the feminization process in Muslim and Catholic countries (Cagatay and Ozler, 1995).

4. The Debate on Female Employment in Iran

Iran in terms of per capita income is comparable with Turkey and several middle income countries of Asia, the Caribbean and Latin America. In this respect it is plausible to expect that Iran, like these countries, would be in the upward portion of the feminization U process. Nevertheless, as discussed earlier, the level of female employment and activity rate for Iran is not only rather low by international standards, but has also declined through time.

If Feminization U reflects the 'normal' pattern of female employment, then how can deviation from the normal path be explained? Karshenas (1996) has offered an explanation that is not exclusively focused on Iran but concerns the relatively low level of non-agricultural female employment in several Middle Eastern countries. His proposition is that a favourable land–labour ratio as well as oil and other mineral exports in the Middle East region have allowed persistently high wages in the countries of the region. High wages, in his interpretation, mean wages that are above the stock and the level of education, skill and technological development of the country or the region in question. The presence of high wages in the countries of the region has allowed the one-bread-winner patriarchal family structure to linger. By contrast, in the countries of East Asia, where population pressure on land has been extreme, per capita wages have been historically low. Consequently, the one-bread-winner family in the modern non-agricultural sector is not affordable. Hence low wages necessitate a high level of female labour force participation in the non-agricultural sector. His proposition is based on econometric analysis of panel data for 51 developing countries of Asia, Africa, the Middle East and Latin America.

Karshenas's proposition is, however, concerned with non-agricultural employment and does not explain why female employment in Iran has, through time, been below that of Turkey. Karshenas maintains that data for agricultural employment in developing countries are unreliable and non-comparable between countries. Different countries employ different statistical procedures so far as census data on agricultural sector is concerned. From this perspective only non-agricultural employment is comparable between developing countries.[4]

4.1 Other Explanations for the Decline in Female Employment

A number of studies with varying emphasis have paid attention to the changing pattern of female employment in Iran (see for instance Afshar, 1985; Moghadam, 1989, 1991; Fatemeh Moghadam, 1994 and Alizadeh and Harper, 1995). These studies have identified a number of factors as the explanatory variables. These include a decline in economic activity, methodological bias, demographic trends and ideology. Here we shall briefly refer to these debates before offering an alternative explanation.

A number of adverse external shocks in the aftermath of the Iranian revolution influenced the level of economic activity including investment and employment (Karshenas 1995a). A sharp decline in the demand for oil and the subsequent fall in the price of oil reduced the foreign exchange earnings from the oil exports upon which the economy is highly dependent. The shrinkage of oil revenue was combined with the protracted and costly war with Iraq, economic sanctions from the West, political uncertainty, a rapid increase in the working age population and an increasing flood of refugees from Afghanistan (Amirahmadi, 1990; Karshenas, 1995a).

The decline in investment and the rise of unemployment in the post revolutionary period is in sharp contrast with the rapid growth of the economy during the 1960s and 1970s. Unemployment in 1986 in fact increased sharply to 14.1 per cent from only 3 per cent in 1976 (Alizadeh and Harper 1995).

The rapid growth of the economy in the pre-revolutionary period was accompanied by the implementation of a vigorous policy of import substitution which was financed and fuelled by increasing income from oil exports as well as the easy availability of foreign aid and loans (Alizadeh 1985).

Moghadam (1989, 1991) and Alizadeh and Harper (1995) have acknowledged the importance of economic conditions. Why, however, should a deterioration in the economic situation lead to a decline in female employment? A deterioration in the economic situation in many developing countries has, in fact, been accompanied by the replacement of male workers with 'cheap' female workers. The literature on feminization points exactly to this. It is well known that with a poorer economic situation more family members, particularly among the low income groups, are forced to seek paid employment to compensate for declining family income (Cagatay and Ozler, 1995). A deterioration in economic conditions can, however, affect female employment when the ideology of the 'male bread winner' is very potent.

It has been suggested that the sharp decline in female employment in the post-revolutionary period might be largely due to the prevalence of 'methodological bias' in census data (Moghadam, 1991), where a large number of women, particularly in agriculture, may not be counted and are consequently underestimated in employment data. While this possibility cannot be totally ruled out, there is no indication that the methodological procedure used in the 1986 census differed in any way from the earlier period. Furthermore, the decline in female employment in production and agriculture was not, on the whole, incompatible with the pattern of output in these sectors (Alizadeh and Harper, 1995).

Another explanation given for the changing pattern of female employment after the revolution is government demographic policies (Afshar, 1985; Moghadam, 1991; Alizadeh and Harper 1995). The rapid increase in the fertility rate and the subsequent population explosion was induced in response not only to the state's increased ideological emphasis on 'motherhood' but also to the opposition of government to family planning up until the late 1980s (Moghadam, 1991). There was a sharp decline in the activity rate of women of child-bearing age over the period 1976–86. Nevertheless, it is difficult to identify the direction of causation and to assess to what extent the lack/reduction of employment opportunities for women has contributed to increased population growth. In the absence of employment opportunities women depend on motherhood for status and on child labour as a strategy for survival (Ward, 1984; Moghadam, 1991).

5. The Role of Ideology in the Process of Nation Building

The role of Islamic ideology in shaping the pattern of female employment in Iran has been acknowledged by Afshar (1985), Moghadam (1989, 1991), Fatemeh Moghadam (1994), Alizadeh and Harper (1995). In particular Fatemeh Moghadam (1994) focuses her analysis on the role of Islamic ideology. She argues that in Islam female sexuality is treated as a tradable object. 'In a Muslim marriage the buyer (the man) and the seller (the woman or her guardian) should agree voluntarily on the terms of the contact and on the price for female sexuality, *mehr*... Once the transaction is completed, the owner has complete and monogamous right to the object' (Fatemeh Moghadam, 1994: 84). She argues that the process of modernization in the pre-revolutionary period was an important step towards the deregulation of female sexuality and that it had a positive impact on female employment and female social participation. The modernization process overshadowed a long tradition of sex segregation and the seclusion of women. With the Islamic revolution and the imposition of forced veiling in 1980 the state regulated female sexuality and undermined the earlier trends directed towards its deregulation. In her analysis female employment is closely related to the treatment of female sexuality in Iran.

The approach to the issue of ideology in this paper does not contradict the above approach but has a different emphasis. The potency of the Islamic ideology will be discussed here in the process of nation building and the period in which nationhood is redefined.

Let us first clarify the relationship between the role of women and Islamic ideology in the aftermath of the Iranian revolution. It is important to examine which aspect of women's position was highlighted in the context of the Constitution of the Islamic Republic that came into being after the revolution. The role of women in the Islamic Republic was specified in the constitution, although the constitution itself does not provide an interpretation of Islamic law (Paidar 1995: 256–67). The constitution considered the family as the main element in the identity of the Islamic nation and emphasized that the family is the fundamental unit of Islamic society. Hence all laws and regulations should facilitate the foundation of a family and protect its stability and sanctity. In this context, as Paidar has pointed out, 'women as citizens and political beings were subjugated to women as mothers. Since the women's role within the family was a special one, motherhood was not considered equal in status with other dimensions of womanhood. Motherhood was the essence of a woman's being and as a result all other dimensions of womanhood were conditional upon it.' (Paidar, 1995: 259). Furthermore, the role of the state, as specified in the constitution, is the creation of an Islamic society that, among other things, ensures the conformity of women's position with Islamic law. However, since the constitution did not define Islamic law, women's constitutional rights were left to be determined by the state and outside the boundaries of the constitution (Paidar, 1995:261).

In this paper we borrow the views of Kandiyoti (1991), Najmabadi (1991) and Paidar (1995) that the social position of women, and the form and extent of their social participation, have all been shaped by the process of nation building and the ideological orientation of nation state. We further contribute to this debate by proposing that the importance of the 'women's question' diminishes with the relative developmental maturity of the nation state.

In the process of nation building women are likened to the mother of the nation. They are the transmitters of tradition, culture and the educators of children. Thus their social role is intimately linked to the ideological orientation of the state. However, the emphasis on the 'motherhood' aspect of the social position of women diminishes as the process of nation building proceeds and the ideological orientation of the state is well established.

5.1 The Modern Nation State and the Changing Social Position of Women in Iran 1900–1941

In Iran women for centuries worked at home as seamstresses, spinners and weavers, and worked in other people's homes as maids, nannies, midwives, healers, educators, matchmakers, weavers, etc. (Paidar, 1995: Chapters 3 and 4). However, the social participation of women in education and employment, and indeed their presence in a desegregated public space, is closely intertwined with the process of modernization which swept through the Middle East in the late nineteenth and early twentieth centuries (Jayawardena, 1986; Najmabadi 1991; Paidar 1995). In the late nineteenth/early twentieth centuries, the era of progress and modernization, the 'women's question' was central to the emerging climate of political ideas and concerns (Najmabadi, 1991; Kandiyoti, 1991).

The first drive towards modernization in Iran found its manifestation in the Constitutional Revolution during the period 1905–1911.[5] The Constitutional Revolution, which was driven by urban elements from diverse social groups, challenged the operation of an incapacitated pre-capitalist state ruled by the Qajar monarchs.[6] Constitutionalists called for a wide range of economic and social reforms which encompassed a general move towards secularism, including women's emancipation. Just as they did elsewhere in the Middle East, reformers of women's condition emerged from the ranks of an educated, nationalist male elite (Kandiyoti 1991). Upper class women followed their men folk in founding and joining secret societies and writing and delivering speeches on constitutionalism and women's emancipation. One of the principal activities of these women's groups was propaganda regarding the need for education for girls and the opening of girls' schools (Jayawardena, 1985; Paidar, 1995).

Although the Constitutional Revolution succeeded in creating a system of parliamentary government, this was not accompanied by the implementation of social and economic reforms. The operation of the parliament (Majles), as legislator, was seriously crippled by the absence of a strong executive power (Paidar, 1995). The number of girls' schools, however, increased, reflecting the concern with female education.

The second step towards modernization and women's emancipation came to the fore during the 1920s to the early 1940s, when the state acted as an instrument of social reform. Reza Khan, a military man, who came to power in 1921 through a bloodless coup, deposed the Qajar dynasty in 1925 and a year later made himself king. He crushed all opposition and created a monolithic power structure to control the population.

Reza Shah, who ruled until 1941, established the first modern centralized state in Iran, which provided a context for capitalist development. He embarked on a series of programmes of reform aimed at modernizing the economy. These reforms included the establishment of a strong central government, the establishment of a basic infrastructural network, legal and administrative reforms including the secularization of education and of the judiciary, which were the monopoly of the clergy during the Qajar period, and the compulsory unveiling of women.

Compulsory unveiling, which was made state official policy in 1936, was intended to integrate women into the society and to strengthen the image of modern nationhood. (Paidar, 1995). Compulsory unveiling was accompanied by the implementation of a series of measures to increase women's education and employment opportunities. The number of girl's schools increased considerably after the 1930s. Female employment, however, was primarily concentrated in teaching and midwifery (Paidar, 1995). No reform was introduced in the electoral law and the state did not grant suffrage to women. The extent of reform in family and marriage codes also remained limited during Reza Shah's reign. Nevertheless, the state policy of opening the public space to women was rooted in the ideology of modernization. Ironically, the Shah's policy of crushing all opposition was pursued simultaneously with his effort to 'emancipate' women.

However, the centrality of the 'women's question' during Reza Shah's period, as well as in the earlier period of the Constitutional Revolution, coincided with the process of nation building in Iran (Najmabadi, 1991; Paidar, 1995). The language of nationhood revolved around the notion of national progress and women's position was defined in terms of national interest. Women were linked to the nation in a distinctively different way from men. Paidar has elaborated this point clearly: 'Women were likened to the nation in a way different from men. Nation was automatically taken to include men and the interest of the two merged inseparably. The link between women and nation, however, had to be specified' (Paidar,1995: 101). The role of women as the main pillar and the firm foundation of ethnicity, religion, language, culture and national heritage implied that they could exert enormous influence on the education of the new generation.

In other words, during the process of nation building the role of women as biological reproducers of the nation, educators of children and transmitters of culture is central to the definition of any society.

5.2 *Women's Social Position, 1941–1979*

With the forced abdication of Reza Shah in 1941, the power of the central state weakened and with it the discipline imposed on women's dress code broke down (Afkhami, 1994). Some women, who were forced to unveil previously, reverted to the veil. However, during the 1940s and 1950s a number of women's groups and associations were established which had the support of the growing number of urban educated middle class women.

Nevertheless the 'strong state' re-emerged in 1954, following a coup which ousted the democratically elected government of Mosaddeq (Katouzian, 1981; Abrahamian, 1982). Women were given the right to vote in 1963, although women's dress code remained flexible. Reforms in the marriage and family codes during the 1960s and 1970s benefited urban middle class women, although their 'trickle down' effect on the majority of rural and urban women has remained controversial to this day (Afkhami, 1994).

Female employment increased rapidly in the 1960s and 1970s. This was a period of rapid economic growth that was accompanied by the implementation of a policy of import substitution and increasing availability of oil revenue. However, what distinguishes this period is that, despite the implementation of various reforms to increase women's social participation, the issue of 'women' was not as central as it was during the reign of Reza Shah. This is because the modern state had been already formed and with it the social position of women had been already defined. Furthermore, reforms of the family code and marriage code in the 1960s and 1970s strengthened the position of women as individual citizens rather than the 'mother of the nation'.

5.3 *The Popular Revolution of 1979 and the Redefinition of Nationhood*

The most significant and lasting impact of the popular revolution of 1979 and its aftermath was the redefinition of nationhood that was simultaneously accompanied by the Islamization of gender relations. The decline in female employment opportunities in Iran in the post revolutionary period is a clear reflection of this change.

The change in state ideology was accompanied by the redefinition of the role and the position of women within the society. The Constitution of the Islamic Republic, which was ratified in 1980, articulated the concept of women's rights within an Islamic context. Article 20 of the constitution specified that men and women enjoy equal protection under the law in keeping with Islamic principles (Esfandiari, 1994). The terminology 'in keeping with Islamic principles', as mentioned earlier, was not defined. However, it was interpreted at the time to indicate that Islam bars women from serving in certain professions, including as judges, and from leadership positions. The theological reasoning behind this interpretation is that there are 'natural' differences between the sexes, which should be taken into consideration. That is, the conformity of Islamic law with the purpose of divine or natural creation requires the acknowledgement of 'natural' differences between the sexes (Afkhami, 1994).

One of the most significant changes after the revolution was the enforcement of Islamic dress code for women in offices and public places. Veiling has remained in force to this day. The Islamic Republic, once firmly established, showed enormous concern with the Islamization of women and the reinforcement of various aspects of Islamic gender relations, including safeguarding the Islamic family and legitimizing gender-based discrimination in employment and education (Paidar, 1995). The total exclusion of women from employment was not politically feasible. This was partly because of their active role during the revolution, partly because their social support was essential for the preservation of the Islamic state during the protracted war with Iraq (which ended in 1988) and partly because of the skill requirements of a modern Islamic state (see below). Furthermore, the acute skill shortage which has prevailed since the revolution, following a substantial flight of the skilled and educated population, made female employment in white-collar occupations indispensable for narrowing the skill shortage gap.

Nevertheless, women were excluded from certain fields of employment and education. A large number of university fields of study were closed to women. Also women working in factories were dismissed or were encouraged to quit their job after the revolution (Moghadam, 1992). Women in the civil service who had a senior decision-making position were soon purged or given early retirement after the revolution (Esfandiari, 1994). The new labour law in 1982 also made female employment conditional on the consent of the husband unless a woman was in employment prior to marriage and the prospective husband had agreed with the continuation of her employment.

The attempt at the segregation of public space and the enforced veiling of women in the Islamic Republic was reminiscent of the desegregation of the public sphere and the enforced unveiling of women during Reza Shah's reign. In both instances, a change in the social position of women has been central to the redefinition of nationhood and the nation state.

5.4 Islamic Ideology and Occupational Sex Segregation

How can the heavy concentration of women in professional and technical work be explained? Why has the decline of female employment been concentrated in agriculture and manufacturing? The lack of desegregated data does not allow us to study the structure of occupations within each major category. Casual empiricism, however, indicates that female employment within professional and technical occupations has been increasingly redirected at certain professions and away from others. There are numerous examples of female engineers, architects, agronomists and judges who have been unable to find employment in their field and have turned to the teaching profession (Paidar, 1995). Nevertheless, the complete physical segregation of occupations has not been feasible due to skill shortages.

Indeed 'selective discrimination' has been an important factor in shaping the pattern of female employment after the revolution. Selective discrimination has also been vigorously applied to female education. Women were, until recent years, barred from studying in most fields of engineering and agronomy, which were considered incompatible with women's role as wives and mothers. These are occupations that require substantial direct contact with men. Women are still considered unsuitable (i.e. too emotional) to take up occupations in the judiciary, although more recently women can become assistant judges. In contrast, women's education and employment in certain fields such as teaching, nursing midwifery, medical practice and social work has been encouraged.

The most likely reason for the deliberate encouragement of these occupations amongst women is that they are indispensable for the reproduction of physical sex segregation in the context of a modern economy (Alizadeh and Harper, 1995; Paidar, 1995). Training women to train other women is indispensable for preserving sex segregation. For segregation to be operational there is an acute need to train women teachers, doctors, nurses, midwives, social workers, etc. to serve other women. These are also occupations in which sexual segregation does not impose a heavy cost on employers. For example, female teachers are destined for girl's schools. In manufacturing and agriculture the segregation of male and female workers is costly at plant/farm level since it entails duplication of machinery and equipment, workshops, and supervisors. Therefore women are either discouraged from taking up employment in these fields, or are pressurized to quit their jobs, or are provided with financial incentives to retire early.

6. Conclusion and Recent Trends

This study indicates that the process of feminization/de-feminization in Iran has been closely intertwined with the process of nation building/redefinition of nationhood. It has been shown that a sharp rise in the de-feminization of employment, which has been concurrent with a continuous increase in occupational sex segregation, has altered the structure of employment and occupations since 1976. However, more recent trends point to a modest increase in female employment.

What about the future? There is general consensus that the question of 'women' and their social position is still central to the Islamic Republic. However, recent trends indicate that selective discrimination against women's employment and education is on the decline. In fact, a large number of university fields which were closed to women after the revolution have been opened recently. Also recent enthusiasm concerning women's participation in sports in the Islamic Republic indicates that the image of women as individual citizens rather than mother and wife alone has started to emerge. It is likely that women's social participation, including their engagement in formal employment, will increase in the future. However, it remains to be seen whether increased feminization will reduce occupational segregation or not. Recent legislation concerning gynaecological problems aims at the medical segregation of women. Women should be treated by female gynaecologists except under very special circumstances (Zanan, 40, 41). This trend, if it prevails, is surely in the direction of further sex segregation.

Parvin Alizadeh

Notes

1 A version of this paper, co-authored by Barry Harper, has been published under the title 'The Feminization of the Labour Force in Iran', in A. Mohammadi (ed.) (2000), *Iran Encountering Globalization: Problems and Prospects*, Book Extra, 2000.

2 For certain individual countries like Sweden and the USA this ratio increased much faster than the average and for certain countries like Greece the growth of female employment lagged behind. For Sweden and the USA, over the period 1950 to 1980, the ratio of women's to men's labour force participation increased from 35.9% to 76.5% and 39.1% to 67.7% respectively. For Greece this ratio increased from 27.7% to 34% over the same period. See Blau and Ferber (1992, pp. 300–4, Table 10.1).

3 Feminization is not a universal phenomenon. See for instance Cagatay and Berik (1991), Elson (1996). However, it can be considered as an 'expected' pattern of female employment.

4 However, agricultural employment accounts for the most significant share of female employment in several developing countries. The exclusion of agricultural employment data reduces the share of female employment in many developing countries to a negligible level. Moreover, the intensity of women's activity in peasant farming, that is the dominant form of agricultural activities in many developing countries, differs substantially across countries. Anecdotal evidence suggests that intensive female involvement in agriculture might not be as widespread in Iran as in Turkey. This is not to deny the intense activity of women in rice and tea cultivation in the northern provinces of Iran, but there is not much evidence to support the existence of widespread female employment in Iranian agriculture as a whole.

5. During the age of imperialist expansion in the nineteenth century, Iran was not a formal colony. However, the expansionist ambitions of the Russian imperial power in Central Asia and the determination of the British to protect their interests in India (which then shared a border with Iran) turned Iran into a sphere of influence and domination by these foreign powers. The Constitutional Revolution stemmed from the twin roots of Iran's relationship with the West, which on the one hand resulted in the domination and manipulation of the Iranian economy and policy, and on the other hand the enthusiasm generated for Western institutions and technical progress. See Paidar (1995) and Abrahamian (1968, 1982).

6 The Qajar monarchs, who ruled Iran from 1796 until 1925, faced several military defeats which undermined their sovereignty and

independence. Consequently they granted increasing concessions to European traders which undermined the interests of Persian merchants and handicraft producers. The Qajar monarchs were incapable of preserving national sovereignty, safeguarding the interests of Persian merchants against European traders, shielding home industry from foreign competition, catering for the basic infrastructural needs of the economy, or providing an institutional framework for economic progress. See Abrahamian (1968, 1982).

Bibliography

Abrahamian, E. (1968), 'The Crowd in Iranian Politics 1905–1953', *Past and Present*, 4, 1, December.

— (1982), *Iran Between Two Revolutions*, Princeton: Princeton University Press.

— (1985), 'The Crowd in Iranian Politics, 1905–53', in Haleh Afshar (ed.) *Iran: A Revolution in Turmoil*, Basingstoke: Macmillan Press.

— (1993), *Khomeinsim: Essays on the Islamic Republic*, Berkeley: University of California Press.

Adelman, Irma and Cynthia Taft Morris (1984), *Economic Growth and Social Equity in Developing Countries*, Stanford: Stanford University Press.

Afghah, Seyed Morteza (1995), 'The Effect of Non-economic Factors in the Economic Development of Third World Countries: a Case Study of Iran', PhD Thesis, University of Birmingham.

Afkhami, M. (1984), 'A Future in the Past: The Pre-Revolutionary Women's Movement', in B. Morgan (ed.), *Sisterhood is Global*, Harmondsworth: Penguin.

— and E. Friedl (eds), (1994), *In the Eye of the Storm*, London: I.B.Tauris.

— (1994), 'Women in Post-Revolutionary Iran: A Feminist Perspective', in Afkhami and Friedl (eds), *In the Eye of the Storm*.

Afshar, Haleh (1985), 'Women State and Ideology in Iran', *Third World Quarterly*, vol. 7, no. 2.

Aghajanian, A. (1989), 'Population Policy, Fertility and Family Planning in Iran', in K. Mahadevan (ed.), *Fertility Policies of Asian Countries*, New Delhi: Sage.

— (1991), 'Population Change in Iran, 1976–86: A Stalled Demographic Transition?' *Population and Development Review*, vol. 17, no. 4, December.

Aghayan and Associates (1980), 'Constitution of The Islamic Republic of Iran', Tehran: *Official Gazette of the Islamic Republic of Iran*, no. 10, 170, January.

Ahmad, Khurshid (1994), *Economic Development in an Islamic Framework*, Leicester: The Islamic Foundation.

Akhtar, M. Ramazan (1993), 'Modelling the Economic Growth of Islamic Economy', *The American Journal of Islamic Social Science*, vol. 10, no. 4.

Alizadeh, Parvin (1985), 'The Process of Import Substitution Industrialization in Iran', Ph.D. thesis, Sussex University.

— (1992), 'Industrial Development in Iran', Middle East Study Series, Institute of Development Economics, 31 (Tokyo, Japan).

— and B. Harper (1995), 'Occupational Sex Segregation in Iran 1976–1986', *Journal of International Development*, vol. 7, no. 4.

Amirahmadi, H. (1990), *Revolution and Economic Transition: The Iranian Experience*, Albany: State University of New York Press.

— (1992), 'Economic Costs of the War and the Reconstruction in Iran', in Bina and Zanganeh (eds), *Modern Capitalism and Islamic Ideology in Iran*.

— (1995), 'Iran's Second Development Plan', *Middle East Executive Reports*, January, February.

— (1995b), 'Bunyad', in John L. Esposito (ed.) *Encyclopedia of the Modern Islamic World*, 1995, vol. 1.

— (1995c), 'An Evaluation of Iran's First Development Plan and Challenges Facing the Second Plan', *Proceedings of a One-Day Conference: Economic Development in Post-Revolutionary Iran*, The Department of Economics and Finance, School of Business Administration, 3 March.

— (1996), 'Iran's Development: Evaluation and Challenges', *Third World Quarterly*, vol. 17, no. 1.

Amsden, Alice H. (1989), *Asia's Next Giant: South Korea and Late Industrialization*, New York: Oxford University Press.

Amuzegar, Jahangir (1997), *Iran's Economy under the Islamic Republic*, London: I.B.Tauris.

— (1998), 'Khatami's Iran, One Year Later', *Middle East Policy*, vol. VI, no. 2.

Ansari, Mohammad I. (1994), 'Islamic Perspectives on Sustainable Development', *The American Journal of Islamic Social Science*, vol. 11, no. 3, Spring.

Ashraf, A. (1970), 'Historical Obstacles to the Development of Bourgeoisie in Iran', in M. A. Cook (ed.), *Studies in the Economic History of the Middle East from the Rise of Islam to Present Day*, Oxford: Oxford University Press.

— (1980), *Mavane-ye Tarikhi-ye Roshd-e Sarma'i-dari dar Iran: Dowreh-e Qajarieh*, Tehran: Zamineh.

Balassa, B. (1981), *The Newly Industrializing Countries in the World Economy*, New York: Pergamon Press.

— (1981), 'Adjustment to External Shocks in Developing Economies', *World Bank Staff Working Paper* No. 472.

— et al. (1971), *The Structure of Protection in Developing Countries*, Baltimore: Johns Hopkins University Press.

Bakhash, Shaul (1986), *The Reign of the Ayatollahs: Iran and the Islamic Revolution*, New York: Basic Books.

Bank-e Markazi Iran (1984), *Barresi-ye Tahavvolat Eqtesadi Ba'd az Enqelab*, Tehran: Bank-e Markazi.

— (1993), *Natayej-e Barresi-ye Kargaha-ye Bozorg-e Sana'ti-ye Keshvar, 1370*, Tehran: Bank-e Markazi.

— (1997/8), *Natayej-e Barresi-ye Kargaha-ye Bozorg-e San'ati-ye Keshvar, 1375*, Tehran: Bank-e Markazi.

— *National Income of Iran, 1952–1977*.

— *Annual Report and Balance Sheet*, various issues: Tehran.

Bauer, J. (1991), 'A Long Way Home: Islam in the Adaptation of Iranian Women Refugees in Turkey and West Germany', in A. Fathi (ed.), *Iranian Refugees and Exiles*.

Bayat, Assef (1987), *Workers and Revolution in Iran*, London: Zed Press, 1987.

Behdad, Sohrab (1988), 'Foreign Exchange Gap, Structural Constraints, and the Political Economy of Exchange Rate Determination in Iran', *International Journal of Middle East Studies*, 20.

— (1994), 'Disputed Utopia: Islamic Economics in Revolutionary Iran', *Comparative Studies in Society and History*, 36/4.

— (1994b), 'Production and Employment in Iran: Involution and de-Industrialization Theses', in Colville (ed.), *The Economy of Islamic Iran*.

— (1996), 'The Post-Revolutionary Economic Crisis', in Rahnema and Behdad (eds), *Iran After the Revolution*.

— (1997), 'Islam, Revivalism and Public Policy', in S. Behdad and F. Nomani (eds), *Islam and Public Policy*, Greenwich: JAI Press.

Behnam, M. Reza (1986), *Cultural Foundations of Iranian Politics*, Salt Lake City: University of Utah Press.

Bibliography

Bhagwati, J. (1978), *Foreign Trade Regimes and Economic Development: Anatomy and Consequences of Exchange Control Regimes*, Lexington, MA: Ballinger.

Bina, Cyrus and Hamid Zanganeh (eds), (1992), *Modern Capitalism and Islamic Ideology in Iran*, London: Macmillan.

Blau, F. D. and M. A. Ferber (1992), *The Economics of Women, Men, and Work*, Princeton, NJ: Prentice-Hall.

Boserup, E. (1990), 'Economic Change and the Roles of Women', in I. Tinker (ed.), *Persistent Inequalities: Women and World Development*, New York: Oxford University Press.

— *Women's Role in Economic Development*, New York: St Martin's Press.

Brass, W. (1996), 'Demographic Data Analysis in Less Developed Countries: 1946–1996', *Population Studies*, vol. 50.

Bulatao, R. A. and Gail Richardson (1994), 'Fertility and Family Planning in Iran', *Middle East and North Africa Discussion Paper Series*, no. 13, Washington: The World Bank, November.

Cagatay, N. and S. Ozler (1995), 'Feminization of the Labour Force: The Effects of Long-Term Development and Structural Adjustment', *World Development*, vol. 23, no. 11, November.

— and G. Berik (1991), 'Transition to Export-led Growth in Turkey: Is There a Feminisation of Employment?' *Capital and Class*, no. 43, Spring.

Charlton, R. and D. Donald (1992), 'Bringing the Economy Back In: Reconsidering the Autonomy of the Developmental State', paper presented at Political Studies Association Conference, Panel on Contemporary State Theory, Belfast, 7–9 April.

Colville, Thierry (ed.), (1994), *The Economy of Islamic Iran: Between State and Market*, Louvain: Peeters for Institut Français de Recherche en Iran.

Corsetti, G., P. Pesenti, and N. Roubini (1998), 'Paper Tigers? A Preliminary Assessment of the Asian Crisis', a paper presented at *NBER-Bank of Portugal International Seminar on Macroeconomics*, Lisbon, June 14–15.

Dadkhah, Kamran (1996), 'Iran and Global Financial Markets: Foreign Investment vs. Borrowing', *Middle East Executive Reports*, August.

Denoeux, Guilan (1993), *Urban Unrest in the Middle East: A Comparative Study of Informal Networks in Egypt, Iran, and Lebanon*, Albany: State University of New York Press.

Edwards, S. (ed.), (1991), *The Macroeconomics of Populism in Latin America*, Chicago: University of Chicago Press.

Eggertson, T. (1997), 'The Old Theory of Economic Policy and the New Institutionalism', *World Development*, vol. 25, no. 8.

Ehteshami, Anoushirvan (1995), *After Khomeini: The Iranian Second Republic*, London: Routledge.

Elson, D. (1996), 'Appraising Recent Developments in the World Markets for Nimble Fingers', in A. Chhachhi and R. Pittin (eds), *Confronting State, Capital and Patriarchy: Women Organizing in the Process of Industrialization*, Basingstoke: Macmillan.

Esfandiari, Haleh (1994), 'The Majles and Women's Issues in the Islamic Republic of Iran', in Afkhami and Friedl (eds), *In the Eye of the Storm*.

Evans, P. B. (1985), 'Transnational Linkages and the Economic Role of the State: An Analysis of Developing and Industrialized Nations in the Post-World War 11 Period', in P. B. Evans et al. (eds), *Bringing the State Back In*, New York: Cambridge University Press.

Bibliography

— (1989), 'Predatory, Developmental and Other Apparatuses: A Comparative Political Economy Perspective on the Third World State', *Sociological Forum*, vol. 4, no. 2.

Farhi, Farideh (1990), *States and Urban-Based Revolutions: Iran and Nicaragua*, Urbana: University of Illinois Press.

Farzin, Y. H. (1995), 'Foreign Exchange Reform in Iran: Badly Designed, Badly Managed', *World Development*, vol. 23, no. 6.

— (1996), 'The Political Economy of Foreign Exchange Reform', in Rahnema and Behdad (eds), *Iran After the Revolution*.

Fathi, A. (ed.), (1991), *Iranian Refugees and Exiles Since Khomeini*, Costa Mesa, California: Mazda Publishers.

Fischer, B. (1989), 'Iran', in *The Middle East and North Africa 1990*, 36th edn.

Fischer, S. (1993), 'Factors in Growth', paper presented at the conference *How Do National Policies Affect Long Term Growth?* Washington: World Bank.

Ghasimi, M. R. (1992), 'The Iranian Economy After the Revolution: An Economic Appraisal of the Five-Year Plan', *International Journal of Middle East Studies*, vol. 24, no. 4.

Ghoreishi, Ahmad and Dariush Zahedi (1997), 'Prospects for Regime Change in Iran', *Middle East Policy*, vol. V, no. 1, January.

Gros, D. and A. Steinherr (1995), *Winds of Change: Economic Transition in Central and Eastern Europe*, London and New York: Longman.

Halliday, Fred (1979), *Iran: Dictatorship and Development*, London: Penguin.

Handoussa, H. (ed.), (1997), *Economic Transition in the Middle East – Global Challenges and Adjustment Strategies*, Cairo: American University Press.

Harik, Iliya (1992), 'Privatization: The Issue, the Prospects, and the Fears', in Iliya Harik and Denis J. Sullivan (eds), *Privatization and Liberalization in the Middle East*, Bloomington: Indiana University Press.

Hiro, Dilip (1985), *Iran Under the Ayatollahs*, New York: Routledge.

Hoselitz, Bert F. (1952–53), 'Non-Economic Barriers to Economic Development', *Economic Development and Cultural Change*, vol. 1.

Howes, A. and A. Singh (1995), 'Long-term Trends in the World Economy: The Gender Dimension', *World Development*, vol. 23, no. 11, November.

Huntington, Samuel (1968), *Political Order in Changing Societies*, New Haven: Yale University Press.

International Labour Office (1972), *Employment, Income and Equality: A Strategy for Increasing Productive Employment in Kenya*, Geneva: ILO.

— (1985), *Yearbook of Labour Statistics*, Geneva: ILO.

— (1991), *Labour Statistics, Retrospective Yearbook Edition on Population Censuses 1945–1989*, Geneva: ILO.

— (1994), *Yearbook of Labour Statistics, 1994*, Geneva: ILO.

— (1997), *Labour Statistics 1996 Yearbook*, Geneva: ILO.

Iran Research Group (1989), *Iran Yearbook 1989–1990*, Bonn: MB Medien & Bucher Verlagsgesellschaft mbH.

Islamic Republic of Iran (1994), *Women and Development: A Report on Important Measures Taken for Women Since the Victory of the Islamic Revolution*, Tehran: Showra-ye Hamahangi-ye Tablighat-e Islami.

— (1995a), *National Report on Women in the Islamic Republic of Iran: Prepared for the Fourth World Conference on Women*, Tehran: Bureau of Women's Affairs.

Bibliography

— (1995b), *Hijab: Immunity, Not Limitation*, Tehran: Centre for Mosques' Affairs, Women Section.

Jayawardena, K. (1986), *Feminism and Nationalism in the Third World*, London: Zed Books.

Joekes, S. with R. Moayedi (1987), 'Women and Export Manufacturing: A Review of the Issues and AID Policy', International Centre for Research on Women, Washington DC.

Johnson, C. (1981), 'Introduction: The Taiwan Model', in J. S. Hsiung (ed.), *Contemporary Republic of China: The Taiwan Experience, 1950–1980*, New York: Praeger.

— (1982), *MITI and the Japanese Miracle*, Stanford, CA: Stanford University Press.

Kandiyoti, Deniz (ed.), (1991), *Women, Islam and the State*, London: Macmillan.

— (1993), 'Identity and its Discontents: Women and the Nation', in P. Williams and L. Chrisman (eds), *Colonial Discourse and Post-Colonial Theory*, New York, London: Harvester, Wheatsheaf.

Karshenas, Massoud (1990), *Oil, State and Industrialization in Iran*, Cambridge: Cambridge University Press.

— (1994), *Macroeconomic Policies, Structural Change and Employment in the Middle East and North Africa*, Geneva: ILO, May.

— (1995a), 'Structural Adjustment and the Prospects of the Iranian Economy', Working Paper Series no. 57, Department of Economics, School of Oriental and African Studies, University of London.

— (1995b), 'Economic Liberalization, Competitiveness and Women's Employment in the Middle East and North Africa', Paper prepared for the seminar on Economic Liberalization and Women's Employment in the Middle East and North Africa, Nicosia, 10 November.

— (1998), 'Structural Adjustment and the Iranian Economy', in N. Shafik (ed.), *Economic Challenges Facing Middle Eastern and North African Countries – Alternative Futures*, Basingstoke and London: Macmillan Press.

— (1999), 'Purchasing Power Parity Exchange Rates and World Agriculture', mimeo, Department of Economics, SOAS, University of London.

— and Adnan Mazarei Jr (1991), 'Medium-Term Prospects of the Iranian Economy', *Iran and the Arabian Peninsula: Economic Structure and Analysis*, London: The Economist Intelligence Unit.

— Adnan Mazarei Jr and M. Hashem Pesaran (1994), 'Exchange Rate Unification: The Role of Markets and Planning in the Iranian Economic Reconstruction', in Colville (ed.), *The Economy of Islamic Iran*.

— (1995), 'Economic Reform and Reconstruction of the Iranian Economy', *Middle East Journal*, vol. 49, no. 1, Winter.

Katouzian, M. A. Homa (1981), *The Political Economy of Modern Iran: Despotism and Pseudo-Modernism 1926–1979*, London: Macmillan.

— (1997), 'Arbitrary Rule: A Comparative Theory of the State, Politics and Society in Iran', *British Journal of Middle Eastern Studies*, 24.

Katzman, Kenneth (1993), *The Warriors of Islam: Iran's Revolutionary Guard*, Boulder CO: Westview Press.

Kavoussi, Rostam M. (1985/86), 'Trade Policy and Industrialization in an Oil-Exporting Country: The Case of Iran', *The Journal of Developing Areas*, vol. 20.

Kazemi, Farhad (1996), 'Civil Society and Iranian Politics', in Augustus Richard Norton, *Civil Society in the Middle East*, vol. 2, New York: E. J. Brill.

Bibliography

Keddie, Nikki R. (1995), 'Can Revolutions Be Predicted?', in Nikki R. Keddie (ed.), *Debating Revolutions*, New York: New York University Press.

Khalatbari, Firouzeh (1994), 'The Tehran Stock Exchange and Privatization of Public Sector Enterprises in Iran: A Study of Obstacles to Private Sector Development', in Colville (ed.), *The Economy of Islamic Iran*.

Khomeini, Ayatollah Ruhollah (1981), *Hokumat-e Islami* (Islamic Government) as translated in Hamid Algar, *Islam and Revolution: Writings and Declarations of Imam Khomeini*, Berkeley: Mizan Press.

Krueger, A. O. (1978), *Foreign Trade Regimes and Economic Development: Liberalization Attempts and Consequences*, Lexington, MA: Ballinger.

Lautenschlager, W. (1986), 'The Effects of an Over-Valued Exchange Rate on the Iranian Economy, 1979–1989', *International Journal of Middle East Studies*, 18.

Lawyers' Committee for Human Rights (1993), *The Justice System of the Islamic Republic of Iran*, New York: Lawyers' Committee for Human Rights.

Leftwich, A. (1995), 'Bringing the Politics Back In: Towards a Model of the Developmental State', *The Journal of Developmental Studies*, 31, February.

Levine, R. (1997), 'Financial Development and Economic Growth: Views and Agenda', *Journal of Economic Literature*, 35.

Little, I., T. Scitovsky and M. Scott (1970), *Industry and Trade in Developing Countries*, London: Oxford University Press.

Loescher, L. and A. D. Loescher (1994), *The Global Refugee Crisis – A Reference Handbook*, Santa Barbara, California: ABC–CLIO.

Looney, Robert E. (1977), *A Development Strategy for Iran Through the 1980s*, London: Praeger Publishers.

— (1982), *Economic Origins of the Iranian Revolution*, New York.

Mackey, Sandra (1996), *The Iranians: Persia, Islam and the Soul of a Nation*, New York: E. P. Dutton.

Mahdavi, H. (1970), 'Patterns and Problems of Economic Development in Rentier States: The Case of Iran', in M. A. Cook, (ed.), *Studies in the Economic History of the Middle East*, Oxford: Oxford University Press.

Mazarei, A. (1995), 'The Parallel Market for Foreign Exchange in an Oil Exporting Economy: The Case of Iran, 1978–90', IMF, *Working Paper*, WP/95/69.

— (1995b), 'Imports under a Foreign Exchange Constraint: The Case of the Islamic Republic of Iran', Middle Eastern Department, IMF, *Working Paper*, WP/95/97, October.

— (1996), 'The Iranian Economy Under the Islamic Republic: Institutional Change and Macroeconomic Performance (1979–1990)', *Cambridge Journal of Economics*, vol. 20.

McDaniel, Tim (1991), *Autocracy, Modernization, and Revolution in Russia and Iran*, Princeton: Princeton University Press.

McKinnon, R. (1973), *Money and Capital in Economic Development*, Brooking Institutions, Washington.

Mehryar, A. H. (1995), 'Repression and Revival of Family Planning in Post-Revolutionary Iran, 1979–1994', Tehran: Institute for Research on Planning and Development, Research Group on Population and Social Policy, Working Paper, no. 2.

— and M. Tabibian (1997), 'Correlates of Fertility Decline in Iran, 1986–1996', Tehran: Institute for Research on Planning and Development.

— and M. Malekpour (n.d.), 'Changing Pattern of Mortality in Iran: A Review of

Bibliography

Available Evidence', Tehran: Institute for Research on Planning and Development, Research Group on Population and Social Policy, Working Paper, no. 9.

Meier, Gerald M. and Robert E. Baldwin (1963), *Economic Development: Theory, History, Policy*, New York: John Wiley & Son.

Menashri, David (1997), *Revolution at a Crossroads: Iran's Domestic Politics and Regional Ambitions*, Washington: The Washington Institute for Near East Policy.

Moaddel, Mansour (1993), *Class, Politics, and Ideology in the Iranian Revolution*, New York: Columbia University Press.

Mofid, Kamran (1987), *Development Planning in Iran: from Monarchy to Islamic Republic*, Middle East & Northern African Studies Press.

Moghadam, Fatemeh (1990), 'Property Rights and Islamic Revolution in Iran', in H. Esfandiari and A. L. Udovitch (eds), *The Economic Dimensions of Middle Eastern History*, Princeton: The Darwin Press, 1990.

— (1994), 'Commoditization of Sexuality and Female Labour Participation in Islam: Implications for Iran, 1960–1990', in Afkhami and Friedl (eds), *In the Eye of the Storm*.

— (1996), 'Property Relations in Iran 1800–1979', in Rahnema and Behdad (eds), *Iran After the Revolution*.

Moghadam, Valentine M. (1988), 'Women, Work, and Ideology in the Islamic Republic', *International Journal of Middle East Studies*, vol. 20, no. 2.

— (1989), 'Zan, Kar va Ideologi', *Nimeh-ye Digar*, no. 10.

— (1991), 'The Reproduction of Gender Inequality in Muslim Societies: A Case Study of Iran in the 1980s', *World Development*, vol. 19, no. 10.

— (1992), *The Political Economy of Female Employment in the Middle East*, Helsinki: World Institute for Development Economics Research (WIDER).

— (1993), *Modernizing Women: Gender and Social Change in the Middle East*, Boulder, CO: Lynne Rienner Publishers.

— (1995a), 'Gender Aspects of Employment and Unemployment in a Global Perspective', in Mihaly Simai (ed.), *Global Employment: An Investigation into the Future of Work*, London: Zed Books and Tokyo: UNU Press.

Naghash, Davood (1991), *Work and Production in Islam*, Tehran: Sazeman-e Tablighat-e Islami.

Najmabadi, A. (1987), 'Depoliticization of a Rentier State: The Case of Pahlavi Iran', in H. Beblawi and G. Luciani (eds), *The Rentier State*, New York.

— (1991), 'Hazards of Modernity and Morality: Women, State and Ideology in Contemporary Iran', in Kandiyoti, (ed.), *Women, Islam and the State*.

Nassehy, Guity (1993), 'Women: A Situation Analysis', Tehran: UNDP.

Nassehy-Behnam, Vida (1991), 'Iranian Immigrants in France', in A. Fathi (ed.), *Iranian Refugees and Exiles*.

Nili, Massoud (1997), 'Tahlil-e Amal Kard-e Siasatha-ye Ta'dil-e Eqtesadi', in M. Nili (ed.), *Eqtesad-e Iran*, Tehran: Institute for Research in Planning and Development.

Nomani, Farhad and Ali Rahnema (1990), *The Secular Miracle*, Zed Press.

— (1994), *Islamic Economic Systems*, London: Zed Books.

North, D. C. (1981), *Structure and Change in Economic History*, New York: Norton.

— (1990), *Institutions, Institutional Change and Economic Performance*, Cambridge: Cambridge University Press.

Nowshirvani, Vahid (1995), 'Sarnevesht-e Barnameh-ye Ta'dil-e Eqtesadi', *Iran Nameh*, XIII/1–2, 1995.

Bibliography

— and Patrick Clawson (1994), 'The State and Social Equity in Post-Revolutionary Iran', in M. Weiner and A. Banuazizi (eds), *The Politics of Social Transformation in Afghanistan, Iran, and Pakistan*, Syracuse: Syracuse University Press.

Omid, Homa (1994), *Islam and the Post-Revolutionary State in Iran*, New York: St. Martin's Press.

Pack, H. and L. Westphal (1986), 'Industrial Strategy and Technological Change: Theory versus Reality, *Journal of Development Economics*, 22.

Page, J. and L. Van Gelder (1988), 'Missing Links: Institutional Capability, Policy Reform and Growth in the Middle East and North Africa'. Paper presented to the conference on *The Changing Role of the State in the Middle East and North Africa*, at the School of Oriental and African Studies, London, May 6.

Paidar, Parvin (1995), *Women in the Political Process of Twentieth Century Iran*, Cambridge: Cambridge University Press.

Pakdaman, Nasser (1987), 'Iran's Population: Present, Past and Future', *Cheshmandaz*, no. 2, (in Persian), Spring.

Parsa, Mizagh (1994), 'Mosque of Last Resort: State Reform and Social Conflict in the Early 1960s', in John Foran (ed.), *A Century of Revolution: Social Movements in Iran*, Minneapolis: University of Minnesota Press.

PDS (1998), 'Pre-Processing Data System – Economic Time Series Database of Iran', Tehran: Institute for Research in Planning and Development.

Pearson, R. (1992), 'Gender Issues in Industrialization', in T. Hewitt, J. Hazel, and D. Wield (eds), *Industrialization and Development*, Oxford: Oxford University Press.

Pesaran, M. Hashem (1982), 'The System of Dependent Capitalism in Pre- and Post-Revolutionary Iran', *International Journal of Middle East Studies*, 14.

— (1985), 'Economic Development and Revolutionary Upheavals in Iran', in H. Afshar (ed.), *Iran: A Revolution in Turmoil*, London: Macmillan.

— (1992), 'The Iranian Foreign Exchange Policy and the Black Market for Dollars', *International Journal of Middle East Studies*.

— and B. Pesaran (1997), *Working with Microfit: Interactive Econometric Analysis*, Oxford: Oxford University Press.

— B. Pesaran and Y. Shin (1998), 'An Auto-Regressive Distributed Lag Modelling Approach to Co-integration Analysis', in S. Strom, A. Holly and P. Diamond (eds), *Centennial Volume of Rangar Frisch, Econometric Society Monograph*, Cambridge: Cambridge University Press.

Plan and Budget Organization (1988), *Peyvast: Qanun-e Barnameh-ye Avval Towse'eh-ye Eqtesadi, Ejtema'i va Farhangi-ye Jomhuri-ye Eslami-ye Iran, (1368–72)*, Tehran: Plan and Budget Organization.

— *A Summary Report on the Performance of the First Five-Year Economic, Social and Cultural Development of the Islamic Republic of Iran (1989–1993)*, Tehran: Plan and Budget Organization.

— (1996), *General Policies, Strategies and Goals of the Second Five-Year Economic, Social and Cultural Development Plan of the Islamic Republic of Iran (1995–1999)*, Tehran: Plan and Budget Organization.

Pourian, H. (1995), 'The Experience of Iran's Islamic Financial System and Its Prospects for Development', in *Development of Financial Markets in the Arab Countries, Iran and Turkey*, Economic Research Forum for Arab Countries, Iran & Turkey, Cairo.

Rahnema, S. (1996), 'Continuity and Change in Industrial Policy', in Rahnema and

Bibliography

Behdad (eds), *Iran after the Revolution*.

Rahnema, Said and Sohrab Behdad (eds), (1996), *Iran after the Revolution: Crisis of an Islamic State*, I.B. Tauris: London.

Rashidi, Ali (1994), 'De-Privatization Process and the Iranian Economy after the Revolution of 1979', in Colville (ed.), *The Economy of Islamic Iran*.

Riordan E. M. et al., (1998), 'The World Economy and Implications for the Middle East and North Africa Region, 1995–2010', in Shafik (ed.), *Economic Challenges Facing Middle Eastern and North African Countries*.

Rodrik, D. (1995), 'Trade and Industrial Policy Reform', in Behrman and Srinavasan (eds), *Handbook of Development Economics*, vol. 3.

Roghani-Zanjani M. et al. (1997), 'Tahlil-e Amal Kard-e Budgeh', in M. Nili (ed.), *Eqtesad-e Iran*, Tehran: Institute for Research in Planning and Development.

Safadi, R. (1997), 'Global Challenges and Opportunities Facing MENA Countries at the Dawn of the Twenty-First Century', in Handoussa (ed.), *Economic Transition in the Middle East*.

Salehi-Isfahani, Djavad (1996), 'The Oil Sector after the Revolution', in Rahnema and Behdad (eds), *Iran After the Revolution*.

Sardar, Ziaudin (1977), *Science, Technology and Development in the Muslim World*, London: Croom Helm.

Schirazi, Asghar (1993), *Islamic Development Policy: The Agrarian Question in Iran*, Boulder: Lynne Rienner Publishers.

Seers, Dudley (1972), 'What are We Trying to Measure?', *The Journal of Development Studies*, vol. 8, no. 3, April.

Shadpour, K. (1994), *The PHC Experience in Iran*, English ed., Tehran: UNICEF.

Shafik, Nemat (ed.), (1998), *Economic Challenges Facing Middle Eastern and North African Countries – Alternative Futures*, Basingstoke and London: Macmillan Press.

Shaw, E. S. (1973), *Financial Deepening in Economic Development*, Oxford: Oxford University Press.

Skocpol, Theda (1979), *States and Social Revolutions: A Comparative Analysis of France, Russia, & China*, Cambridge: Cambridge University Press.

— (1982), 'Rentier State and Shi'a Islam in the Iranian Revolution', *Theory and Society*, vol. 11.

Standing. G. (1989), 'Global Feminisation Through Flexible Labour', *World Development*, vol. 17, no. 7.

Statistical Centre of Iran (1978), 'Population Growth Survey of Iran, Final Report, 1973–1976', Tehran: The Statistical Centre of Iran.

— 1363 (1985), *National Census of Population and Housing 1976*, Tehran: Plan and Budget Organization.

— 1366 (1988), National Census of Population and Housing 1986, Tehran: Plan and Budget Organization.

— 1370 (1991), *Iran Statistical Yearbook 1370*, Tehran: Statistical Centre of Iran.

— 1372 (1993), *Amargiri-ye Jari-ye Jami'at 1370, Natayej-e Omumi, Kol-e Keshvar*, Tehran: Statistical Centre of Iran.

— (1997), *Iran Statistical Yearbook 1375* [1996], Tehran: Statistical Centre of Iran.

— 1376 (1998), *National Census of Population and Housing 1996*, Tehran: Plan and Budget Organization.

Tames, Richard (1982), *World Religions in Education: Approaches to Islam*, London: John Murray Ltd.

Thirlwall, A. P. (1999), *Growth and Development*, London: Macmillan Press, 6th edn.

Bibliography

Tilly, L. A. and J. W. Scott (1987), *Women, Work and Family*, 2nd edn, New York: Routledge.

Todaro, Michael P. (1994), *Economic Development*, 5th edn, London: Longman.

United Nations (1992), *Child Mortality Since the 1960s – A Database for Developing Countries*, New York: United Nations, Department of Economic and Social Development.

— (1995a), *World Population 1996*, New York: United Nations, Population Division, Department for Economic and Social Information and Policy Analysis.

— (1995b), *The World's Women 1995: Trends and Statistics*, New York: UN.

UNESCO (1994), *Education for All: Status and Trends 1994*, Paris: UNESCO.

— (1995), *World Education Report 1995*. Paris: UNESCO.

UNFPA (1995), 'Islamic Republic of Iran', *Programme Review and Strategy Development Report*, no. 44, Technical and Evaluation Division, New York.

UNICEF, Tehran (1993), *Gender Analysis Workshop: Proceedings*, Tehran: 1993.

UNIDO (1992), 'Women in Industry Country Information: Iran', Vienna: UNIDO, Tehran: UNICEF-Tehran and Women's Bureau of the President's Office.

Vakili-Zad, Cyrus (1992), 'Continuity and Change: The Structure of Power in Iran', in Bina and Zanganeh (eds), *Modern Capitalism and Islamic Ideology in Iran*.

Vorozheikina, Tatiana (1994), 'Clientelism and the Process of Political Democratization in Russia', in Luis Roniger and Ayse Gunes-Ayata (eds), *Democracy, Clientelism and Civil Society*, Boulder: Lynne Reinner Publishers.

Wade, R. (1990), *Governing the Market: Economic Theory and the Role of Government in East Asian Industrialization*, Princeton, N.J: Princeton University Press.

Ward, K. (1984), *Women in the World System*, New York: Praeger.

Watts, M. J. and J. Rich (1993), 'Occupational Sex Segregation in Britain, 1976–1986: The Persistence of Sexual Stereotyping', *Cambridge Journal of Economics*, vol. 17, no. 2, June.

Weeks, John (1985), *Limits to Capitalist Development: The Industrialization of Peru, 1950–1980*, Boulder, CO: Westview Press.

World Bank (1998), *World Development Indicators*, CD ROM, Washington DC.

White, G. (ed.), (1988), *Developmental States in East Asia*, London: Macmillan.

— and R. Wade (1988), 'Developmental States and Markets in East Asia: An Introduction', in White (ed.), *Developmental States in East Asia*.

Wood, A. (1991), 'North-South Trade and Female Labour in Manufacturing: An Asymmetry', *Journal of Development Studies*, vol. 27, no. 2.

Workman, W. Thom (1994), *The Social Origins of the Iran–Iraq War*, Boulder: Lynne Rienner Publishers.

World Bank (1993), 'Adjustment in Africa: Reform, Results, and the Road Ahead', *Policy Research Department*, The World Bank, Washington: October 1993.

— (1995, 1997), *World Development Reports 1995, 1997*, World Bank: Washington.

— (1997), *World Development Indicators*, CD ROM, Washington.

Yuval-Davis, N. and F. Anthias (eds), (1989), *Women-Nation State*, London: Macmillan.

Zanan, no. 40, 10 & 11, 1376 (January/ February 1998); no. 41, 12, 1376 (February/ March 1998).

Zan-e Ruz. (Tehran) 30 Mehr 1373/1994.

Zubaida, Sami (1988), *Islam, The People and The State*, London: Routledge.

Index

Abbasid dynasty, 136
Abu Dharr, 136
Afghanistan, 185, 191
Africa, 13, 14, 16, 30, 274, 276
agriculture, 104, 109, 224, 241
employment in, 130, 241, 246;
female activity in, 246, 252, 268–9,
277
Akbarabad, 123
Ali b. Abi Talib, Imam, 132, 136
Amsden, Alice, 14, 36
Anthias, F., 2
anti-capitalism, 11, 205–6, 213
Arak, 123
Armenia, 156
Asia, 13, 31, 32, 63, 156, 274, 275
Bangladesh, 156
Bani-Sadr, President Abol-Hassan, 100,
104, 161
Bank Markazi (Central Bank), 78,
79–80, 87, 90, 91, 115, 119, 121,
213, 218
banking system, 207, 213, 218, 221–2,
227
bazaar, 148, 160
Beheshti, Ayatollah, 132
Behruzi, Maryam, 247
birth rate, 181–2
bonyads (foundations), 3, 8–9, 12, 40,
56, 80, 102, 129, 131, 134, 158,
148, 160–1, 165–8; economic
impact, 162–4; history, 149–52;
position in economy, 8–9, 10, 37,
59, 112–13, 148, 152–3; and privatization 127, 165–6
Bonyad-e Mostazafin (BMJ), 9, 37, 80,
102, 112–13, 127, 151, 153–66,
167; accountability, 158; and arms
industry, 159; assets 153–4, 155–6;
as charity, 157; economic activities,
155–7, 164; and economic policy,
166; and bazaar, 160, 161; and
Hezbollah, 159; position in
economy, 155, 159–61, 164–5;

and privatization, 165–6; protests
against and scandals, 162, 164–5;
and clerical hierarchy, 157, 159,
161–2; relationship to state, 154,
157–9, 167; structure of, 155–6
Bonyad-e Astan-e Qods, 149, 164, 167
Bonyad-e Omur Mohajerin-e Tahmili
151, 152
Bonyad-e Panzdah-e Khordad, 102,
149
Bonyad-e Resalat, 152
Bonyad-e Shahid, 151, 158, 166
Bosnia, 156
bourgeoisie, 18, 113, 161
Brazil, 50
Bulgaria, 237
bureaucracy, 131, 146, 215–16, 218,
222, 226,

capital, 218; shortages of, 216–18
capital accumulation, 5, 7, 11, 105,
112, 133, 134, 160
capitalism, 105, 133, 205
Caribbean region, 275
censuses, 178; (1968), 241; (1976), 236;
(1986), 178, 184–7, 192, 233, 236,
277; (1991), 186, 242, 249, 250;
(1996), 177, 178, 179, 188–9, 252
Chaebol (Korea), 14
China, 156
Civil Registration Organization, 179
Clawson, Patrick, 115
clergy, 145, 149, 157, 160, 281;
authority of, 146
Clinton, President Bill, 167
Constitution of the Islamic Republic,
102, 126, 132, 133; role of women
in, 278–9, 282–3
Constitutional Revolution, 160, 280,
281
consumer price index, 121
consumption, 45, 48, 49, 64–5, 79,
112, 122, 125, 129, 132, 207;
private, 68, 69

Index

Bibliography

302